JULIE RAYBURN

Be Still and Know...

365 Devotions for
Abundant Living

Dear Mark,
Thank you for your
faithful encouragement
over the years. May you
"Be Inspired"!

Jim

John 10:10

Scripture taken from the HOLY BIBLE, NEW INTERNATIONAL VERSION®. NIV®. Copyright © 1973, 1978, 1984, 2011 by Biblica, Inc.™ Used by permission. All rights reserved worldwide.

Published by Barbour Books, an imprint of Barbour Publishing, Inc., P.O. Box 719, Uhrichsville, Ohio 44683, www.barbourbooks.com

Our mission is to publish and distribute inspirational products offering exceptional value and biblical encouragement to the masses.

 Member of the
Evangelical Christian
Publishers Association

Printed in China.

JULIE RAYBURN

Be Still
and Know...

365 Devotions for
Abundant Living

BARBOUR BOOKS
An Imprint of Barbour Publishing, Inc.

I dedicate this book to Jerry Ann Murray,
my mother, my mentor, my friend.

"Well done, good and faithful servant."

*Even when I am old and gray,
do not forsake me, my God,
till I declare your power
to the next generation,
your mighty acts to
all who are to come.*

PSALM 71:18

INTRODUCTION

*T*he story behind this book is one worth telling because it has the fingerprints of God all over it. I do not say this proudly, but humbly, knowing that only God could have brought this to pass. In November 1998, my mother was diagnosed with cancer. For Christmas I gave her a daily journal—one with dates and blank pages to write in throughout the new year. I don't know what I expected. Perhaps I thought she would express her feelings as she endured chemotherapy. Or maybe she would pass on some motherly wisdom to me. Little did I know at the time, but 1999 would be the last year of her life.

After her death I discovered the journal and was astonished by what I read. There were no personal entries—nothing about losing her hair, nothing about enduring chemotherapy, nothing about fearing death. Every day, until mid-November, she faithfully penned a scripture verse, a title, and what the Lord had taught her through His Word. It was succinct yet profound. Pondering the treasure I had been given, I began to understand how she was able to walk toward death with such peace and joy in the midst of the greatest challenge she'd ever faced. I had observed that with each passing day, it was as if she had one foot in heaven and the other on earth—with the heel and then toe of her earthly foot slowly leaving the ground. Although she was fighting for her life, she had been preparing to meet the Lord. Being still before Him, she gleaned spiritual insight right up until the day they met face-to-face. That was the secret to abundant living!

Over the years I had planned to meticulously read through her journal, yet I suspect my sorrow had prevented it. But in

December 2012, Jodi, my best friend from college, was battling recurrent cancer. I asked the Lord how I might encourage her in the coming year. He reminded me of Mom's journal and placed the desire within my heart to share her daily entries with Jodi. (Jodi had known my mother and had observed her faith over the years.) Since Mom had no idea that her entries would be read by anyone, I began the process of editing and rewriting her scriptural insights. I tried to stay true to the titles and daily Bible verses she had chosen. Those daily e-mails became the content for this devotional book.

This book is not about death, but about living the abundant Christian life now! My mother possessed clear spiritual focus the last year of her life. It is my greatest desire that the spiritual truths she gleaned from the Lord would be passed on to the next generation. We all desperately yearn for peace in the midst of life's challenges. When we are "still" before the Lord, meditating on scripture, He imparts spiritual truth. We can experience abundant living when we apply those truths to our everyday lives. May you be inspired to follow my mother's example!

My gratitude to the Lord, for inspiring my mother to record the truths You taught her from Your Word; to Scott, my husband of thirty-seven years, for your faithful love, encouragement, support, and input; to Teresa, for being my second pair of eyes; to my readers and friends who have been with me on this journey and encouraged me to persevere.

Day 1

Facing Life's Challenges

"For we have no power to face this vast army that is attacking us.
We do not know what to do, but our eyes are on you."
2 Chronicles 20:12

As we embark on a brand-new year, we are hopeful and optimistic. Yet realistically we know that each year is filled with peaks as well as valleys. There will be challenges in the coming year. How will we face those challenges? What will be our strategy?

As King Jehoshaphat was facing an invasion of Edom's vast army, he said to the Lord, "We do not know what to do, but our eyes are on you." Then God's Spirit spoke through one of the men of Judah, saying, "Do not be afraid or discouraged because of this vast army. For the battle is not yours, but God's" (2 Chronicles 20:15). As the people began to sing and praise, the Lord set ambushes against the invading armies and defeated them.

Whatever challenges we face in life, we have a choice: to either turn to God and bow down before Him or to run away in fear. If we cave in to the emotion of fear, we will be running for the rest of our lives. This is not what God wants for us. The Lord desires to give us victory in the battles we face. We are called to follow Christ for a purpose—to trust Him to do the impossible. He can and will intervene. Our life is in His hands.

Dear Lord, I don't know what challenges I will face this coming year, but You do. Help me keep my eyes on You. Fight my battles, and give me the victory that is found in You. Amen.

Day 2

Priority of Prayer

Pray continually.
1 THESSALONIANS 5:17

━━━━━◈━━━━━

In today's reading, the apostle Paul instructs us to "pray continually." We are to pray without ceasing. What exactly does that mean? We have jobs, families, and responsibilities. Who can sit in church all day or have their eyes closed at work for extended periods of time?

We can live in an attitude of prayer even when we are engaged in everyday activities. To pray without ceasing means to be in constant communication with our heavenly Father. Pray about all things—things trivial or earthshaking. God is listening and ready to help. It does not matter where we are. We can be driving a car or sitting in a church pew because God is with us at all times. When we communicate with Him throughout our day, we experience intimate fellowship that enables us to face whatever life throws our way. Let's make prayer a priority this year.

Dear Lord, help me establish the habit of communicating with You throughout my day regardless of where I am or what I am doing. You desire intimate fellowship with me. May I desire the same with You. Amen.

Day 3

Total Commitment

*Lord, who may dwell in your sacred tent? Who may
live on your holy mountain? The one whose walk
is blameless, who does what is righteous.*
Psalm 15:1–2

Making a total commitment to Christian living involves voluntarily binding oneself to the principles of scripture. It means doing the right thing when you have the opportunity to do wrong. It means doing the right thing even when no one will know or even care. God cares. He knows.

How do we keep from faltering? First, we must read, study, and meditate on God's Word. How can we do what is right if we don't know what God requires of us? We must call on God for help every day. It is impossible to live the Christian life victoriously in our own strength and by our own efforts. We desperately need God's power through the indwelling Holy Spirit. Finally, we must draw on the support of other believers. God never intended for us to walk this journey alone.

Making the commitment is easy. Following through is the challenge.

*Dear Lord, I desire to be totally committed to You,
yet I find it very difficult. Help me feed upon Your Word,
relying upon Your power and the support of other believers. Amen.*

Day 4

Sin

*When the woman saw that the fruit of the tree was good
for food and pleasing to the eye, and also desirable for gaining
wisdom, she took some and ate it. She also gave some to
her husband, who was with her, and he ate it.*

GENESIS 3:6

Many of us are familiar with the fall of Adam and Eve as described in Genesis 3. As we ponder their choice to disobey God, have we ever stopped to examine our own hearts? Do we ever engage in mental conversation with our adversary? Do we add to God's Word? What temptations are satisfying to our flesh, pleasing to our eyes, or will make us feel important?

Sin is a disease, not a weakness. It is rebellion against God—that simple. Our theology of sin needs to be in line with what the Bible teaches. The world tries desperately to ignore, suppress, or erase the concept of sin. To admit "I have sinned" is very difficult. And yet this is exactly what we must confess if we are to have a right relationship with God.

We are not unlike Adam and Eve. We all have sinned and fallen short. God is ready to forgive and restore. Let's be quick to confess our rebellion.

Dear Lord, help me see my rebellion as sin. Help me admit and confess that sin. Restore me to a right relationship with You. Amen.

Day 5

Getting Your Life Back on Course

He [Elijah] replied, "I have been very zealous for the Lord
God Almighty. The Israelites have rejected your covenant,
torn down your altars, and put your prophets to death with the
sword. I am the only one left, and now they are trying to kill me too."
1 Kings 19:10

At times life can feel overwhelming, and we can easily become discouraged. We may scale a spiritual mountain one moment, only to find ourselves trudging through a dark valley the next. Feelings of loneliness and despair can characterize the valleys of life. The prophet Elijah could relate.

When Elijah had a showdown with the prophets of Baal, God intervened in a miraculous way and gave Elijah victory. Ahab then reported this defeat to Queen Jezebel. Elijah should have been praising God, but because he was afraid of Jezebel, he was running for his life instead.

After a spiritual victory, be prepared for a time of serious testing. This is when our personal relationship with our Lord becomes the apex of our direction. Be prepared. Testing will come. Will we be fearful like Elijah running from Jezebel, or will we stand firm? We should not flee in fear. Instead, we need to face the obstacles by drawing on God's strength and presence in our lives. The Lord is walking with us—even in the valleys. We are never alone!

Dear Lord, prepare me to face the times of testing in my life. Take
away my fear. Help me run to You so that I can stand firm. Amen.

Day 6

Success

Blessed is the one who does not walk in step with the wicked or
stand in the way that sinners take or sit in the company of mockers,
but whose delight is in the law of the Lord, and who meditates
on his law day and night. That person is like a tree planted by
streams of water, which yields its fruit in season and whose
leaf does not wither—whatever they do prospers.

Psalm 1:1–3

Most of us could easily identify a vibrant, healthy fruit tree. The branches would be teeming with fruit and the leaves would not be withered. This verse credits the water source for the tree's success and prosperity.

What is your definition of success? The world paints a picture of success based on one's material possessions, worldly accomplishments or power. God's view is quite different. Success in God's eyes is a matter of godly attitude and perspective. It is not based on what we own but rather on whom we serve and what we do with our service.

The focus of our heart needs to be fixed on Jesus in order to attain true success. God's pathway to success is achieved by obeying His Word throughout a lifetime. How are you doing? Are the things of this world preventing you from achieving true success? We have a water source: Jesus Christ—the Living Water. Are we tapping into Him daily?

Dear Lord, it is so easy to get caught up in worldly pursuits.
Help me to desire success from Your point of view. Amen.

Day 7

The Idol of Success

"You shall have no other gods before me."
DEUTERONOMY 5:7

———— ❧ ————

God desires for us to be successful in whatever we undertake. However, the Bible warns us not to let success "go to our head." We are not to have a haughty attitude toward success so that our principal focus is our own achievements. When that happens, we have allowed success to become an idol in our lives.

The first commandment warns us not to have any other gods before the Lord. "I am the LORD your God, who brought you out of Egypt, out of the land of slavery. You shall have no other gods before me (Deuteronomy 5:6–7)." An idol is anything that takes God's rightful place as number one in our lives. Our principal focus must always be on Jesus Christ.

What idols have subtly found their way into your life—success, family, children, spouse, work, materialism, physical beauty, Facebook, exercise, or food? These things have their proper place. However, the Lord desires preeminence. When we allow the Lord His rightful place, we will live successful lives. Rather than shining the spotlight on ourselves, let's shine it on the Lord so that He receives the glory for the success He has granted us.

Dear Lord, help me to live successfully by keeping my focus on You, not self. Show me anything that I have allowed to become an idol in my life. Amen.

DAY 8

Attitude

Whatever you do, work at it with all your heart, as working for the Lord, not for human masters, since you know that you will receive an inheritance from the Lord as a reward. It is the Lord Christ you are serving.

COLOSSIANS 3:23–24

This may be our attitude when volunteering at church, but what about when we're at work or doing household chores? It's easy to cop a bad attitude with an unreasonable boss or laundry that never seems to end. We may need an "attitude adjustment," but how can we experience that?

We may not be able to change our workload or boss, but the Lord can give us a new perspective. Realize that ultimately we are working for the Lord, not man. Our Boss is kind and encouraging. He rewards our efforts. As our perspective changes, so does our attitude.

As Christians, regardless of where we are or what we are doing, we are to serve Christ. Our attitude speaks volumes about who we are and in whom we believe. We should serve Jesus at home, in church, and in our secular life—there should be no differentiation. When we acknowledge who our true Boss is, we find pleasure in serving Him!

Dear Lord, help me serve You wherever I am. When that is my desire, my attitude will not only be pleasing to You but also to those around me. Amen.

DAY 9

The Lord's Prayer

"Our Father in heaven, hallowed by your name, your kingdom come, your will be done, on earth as it is in heaven."
MATTHEW 6:9–10

❧

In Luke's account, the disciples asked Jesus to teach them how to pray. Jesus responded by reciting what we recognize as the Lord's Prayer or "Our Father." Perhaps we have uttered these words so often by rote that they have lost their meaning.

Jesus purposely begins this prayer with "Our Father." This name for God demonstrates His paternal love. Not only is God majestic and holy, but He is also personal and loving. As believers, we are privileged to be able to call God our Father! God is a Father who loves and cares for each of His children. His love is extreme! Our heavenly Father will search us out and rescue us from the pit. His love is everlasting! There is nothing we could ever do to make Him stop loving us. This nurturing, paternal love is one of security and encouragement. What a source of hope!

Because of God's great love for us, we look to Him with awe and wonder. We hold Him in highest esteem and revere His name. We desire that His will be done because we truly believe that it is best.

Dear Lord, thank You for being my heavenly Father. May I ponder the extent of Your love for me and bask in that love today. Amen.

Day 10

Wicked vs. Righteous

Be still before the Lord and wait patiently for him;
do not fret when men succeed in their ways,
when they carry out their wicked schemes.
Psalm 37:7

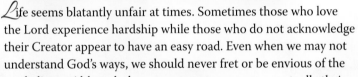

*L*ife seems blatantly unfair at times. Sometimes those who love the Lord experience hardship while those who do not acknowledge their Creator appear to have an easy road. Even when we may not understand God's ways, we should never fret or be envious of the nonbeliever. Although they may seem to prosper, eventually their ways will be exposed. Nothing is lasting for the evil man or woman.

How should we then live? Our lives should reflect a heart that trusts the Lord and delights in Him. We should do good works and be faithful. We should trustfully commit our way to the Lord. We should be still before Him and wait patiently for Him to act on our behalf. Anger should have no place in our lives. The results will be the following: "The salvation of the righteous comes from the Lord; he is their stronghold in time of trouble. The Lord helps them and delivers them; he delivers them from the wicked and saves them, because they take refuge in him" (Psalm 37:39–40).

Dear Lord, may I not be envious of others, but live
my life according to Your Word. Help me to be still
and wait for You to intervene on my behalf. Amen.

Day 11

Stages of Our Christian Life

*Consider it pure joy, my brothers and sisters, whenever you face
trials of many kinds, because you know that the testing of your
faith produces perseverance. Let perseverance finish its work so
that you may be mature and complete, not lacking anything.*

James 1:2–4

*L*ife is full of many trials and heartaches as well as joyful and
happy times. Let's face it, it's much easier to embrace sunny days
than gloomy ones! As we bask in the good times, do we tend to
leave God out of the equation? James 1:17 says, "Every. . .perfect
gift is from above, coming down from the Father of the heavenly
lights." When experiencing smooth sailing, give thanks to God and
acknowledge that your blessings have come from Him.

But what happens when trials and suffering come unexpectedly
into our life and rock our world? Our trials are not random. They
have divine purpose. Are we able to experience the peace that God
promises us, even in the midst of suffering? Do we live each day as
if it were our last? When our attention is focused on God rather
than our circumstances, we can have confidence that He is maturing our faith. We will have peace. Is this not *my* choice?

*Dear Lord, trials and suffering are never what we would choose, yet
You promised to give us peace during our darkest moments. May I
feel Your presence today. Thank You for walking beside me. Amen.*

Day 12

Sufficient Grace

*To keep me from becoming conceited, I was given a thorn in my
flesh, a messenger of Satan, to torment me. Three times I pleaded
with the Lord to take it away from me. But he said to me, "My grace
is sufficient for you, for my power is made perfect in weakness."*

2 Corinthians 12:7–9

*W*as Paul's thorn in the flesh physical or emotional? It doesn't
really matter. What is important to realize is that the Lord allowed
Paul to suffer. Why? Paul acknowledges that it was to keep him
from becoming proud. The Lord wanted Paul to continue to rely
on His power and not Paul's own. God's grace was sufficient for
Paul. God gave Paul power amid his weakness.

This spiritual principle wasn't just meant for Paul; it is applicable for all of us. A total commitment to God will cover *any* thorn
in the flesh that we may have. There is such joy when we *accept*
God's will for our life! Then, like Paul, we will be able to say, "When
I am weak, then I am strong" (2 Corinthians 12:10). As we lean on
God's power, He is glorified, because in our weak state, He is made
known.

*Dear Lord, help me in my weakness. May I depend totally
on You to give me the strength that I need every day. Amen.*

Day 13

Barometer for Spiritual Growth

*"Be still, and know that I am God; I will be exalted
among the nations, I will be exalted in the earth."*

Psalm 46:10

Today's society is fast paced. Productivity is esteemed. "Go-getters" rule the world. This may be true in the corporate world, but what about in our spiritual lives? We may feel as though we are stagnant, standing still spiritually. We are not making progress fast enough. We may wonder what God is doing and become depressed.

Rest assured. Times of spiritual rest are necessary. Do not fret. We may feel like we are standing still, but God is at work behind the scenes! There are times when we need to be still and be refreshed by God's Spirit. During those times we can be quiet and meditate on His Word. When we are still, we are better able to hear God's voice. Then we will be prepared for the Lord to move us along to do His will.

So, if you are in a season of rest—embrace it! God is preparing you now for a season of activity later. Listen and learn so that you will be adequately equipped for what the Lord has planned for you next.

*Dear Lord, may I not become discouraged when I feel like
nothing is happening in my spiritual life. Allow me to be
still before You. Prepare me to do Your will. Amen.*

Day 14

Church Fellowship

And let us consider how we may spur one another on
toward love and good deeds, not giving up meeting together,
as some are in the habit of doing, but encouraging one
another—and all the more as you see the Day approaching.
Hebrews 10:24–25

———————⬥———————

Why is it necessary to go to church? Can't I worship God in my own way? Let's consider that Jesus Christ established the Church. He is the head and we are the body. A headless body is lifeless. That's a sobering thought to ponder.

There are also practical reasons for meeting together as a church body. As we corporately worship and pray together, we give glory to God and acknowledge His Lordship in our lives. Fellowship with other believers is designed to encourage and spur us on to love and good works. Jesus started the Church because its benefits are not only vital to the believer's life but also to the advancement of His eternal kingdom.

So, resolve today to be in church this Sunday. You will never regret that decision, because it is God's will for you.

Dear Lord, may I commit to becoming more involved
in my church this year. Thank You for establishing the
Church to help me live out the Christian life so that
others may come to know You as Lord and Savior. Amen.

Day 15

Heaven

*"Do not let your hearts be troubled. You believe in God; believe
also in me. My Father's house has many rooms; if that were not so,
would I have told you that I am going there to prepare a place for
you? And if I go and prepare a place for you, I will come back and
take you to be with me that you also may be where I am."*

John 14:1–3

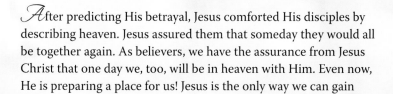

After predicting His betrayal, Jesus comforted His disciples by
describing heaven. Jesus assured them that someday they would all
be together again. As believers, we have the assurance from Jesus
Christ that one day we, too, will be in heaven with Him. Even now,
He is preparing a place for us! Jesus is the only way we can gain
access to this heavenly home.

This is His promise to us, and we can count on His truthful-
ness. Being in the Lord's presence for *all* eternity is the ultimate.
The very thought of Christ returning to take us to heaven should
have a purifying effect on us today. What a future! What a hope!
Thank You, Lord!

*Dear Lord, thank You that Jesus paid the penalty for my sins when
He died on the cross. By accepting this gift for myself, You have
assured me a heavenly home with You forever. Thank You! Amen.*

Day 16

God's Way

*Jesus replied, "Anyone who loves me will obey my
teaching. My Father will love them, and we will
come to them and make our home with them."*
JOHN 14:23

*J*esus plainly stated that if we love Him, we will obey Him. It's
easy to confess our love to the Lord yet much harder to obey Him.
However, obedience to God is the key to living a victorious Christian life. God knows all the twists and turns that our lives will take.
He will guide us through whatever comes our way. The question
we face is this: How much control are we going to let God have?

We may seek to control our lives, yet our efforts prove futile
over and over again. The older we get, the more we learn that there
is little we really have control over. Therefore, why not relinquish
all control to the Lord? When we trust and obey Him completely,
He will bring beauty from the ash heaps of our lives. Since God
created each one of us, doesn't it stand to reason that He alone
knows what's best for us? Trust and obey—it's the only way!

*Dear Lord, why is it so hard for me to give up control?
May I realize that You have my life in Your hands
so that I can trust You completely. Amen.*

Day 17

The Local Church

Shout for joy to the LORD, all the earth. Worship the
LORD with gladness; come before him with joyful songs.
PSALM 100:1–2

When seeking a church home, we may consider many things. How far is the church from our home? How convenient are the worship times? Is the music contemporary or traditional? Do people wear jeans or their Sunday best? Are donuts served in the narthex after service?

These considerations may seem important, but Jesus did not establish the Church with any of them in mind. The "Church" refers to the body of believers, not a physical structure. The real issue should be whether or not the church strikes a balance between worshipping the Lord, equipping the saints, and spreading the Gospel.

Worship and praise are to come first. The body of Christ should come together to bring honor and glory to the Lord corporately each week. The Church also has a ministry to believers—to teach, equip, and disciple. Finally, the Church is charged to spread the Gospel and to have a concern for lost souls. If any one of these components is missing, continue your search. Seek a church home that embraces these priorities.

Dear Lord, I realize no church is perfect, but lead me to a
church that puts You first. Help me find a place where I can
be equipped to share the Good News with others. Amen.

Day 18

Praise

Praise the Lᴏʀᴅ, my soul, and forget not all his benefits—
who forgives all your sins and heals all your diseases,
who redeems your life from the pit and crowns you with
love and compassion, who satisfies your desires with good
things so that your youth is renewed like the eagle's.

Psᴀʟᴍ 103:2–5

There are times in our lives when it is difficult to praise God. When circumstances overcome us and sorrow clouds our eyes, spiritual blindness seems to take over. Beware! This is the very time when Satan goes on the offensive. He tries to convince us that God does not care—that He has abandoned us. Satan lies. First Peter 5:8 sends this warning: "Be alert and of sober mind. Your enemy the devil prowls around like a roaring lion looking for someone to devour."

We must *always* be on guard. Satan seeks to discourage and rob us of our joy. The secret to spiritual victory is to praise the Lord during our most difficult moments. Praise demonstrates our belief that God loves us and will never leave us. Faith is exercised through praise. Satan must flee because praise ushers in God's presence. Nothing can separate us from His love!

Dear Lord, help me praise You in my most difficult moments.
Trials are never my desire, yet I can still offer You praise because
I know You are with me and will see me through. Amen.

DAY 19

True Praise

Lift up your heads, you gates; be lifted up, you ancient doors,
that the King of glory may come in. Who is this King of glory?
The LORD strong and mighty, the LORD mighty in battle.

PSALM 24:7–8

*P*raising God takes on many forms. It is not just singing worship songs in church, acknowledging an answered prayer to a friend, or thanking God for our blessings. True praise is an attitude of the heart. It is present in good times as well as bad. It is present even when feelings are not. It is present because God is worthy! He is the King of glory, strong and mighty!

Consider the following actions as steps needed in order to truly praise God:

1. Submit to God regardless of the circumstances.
2. Repent of any known sin so your walk with Him is not hindered.
3. Love God with your whole heart.
4. Remove a critical spirit that implies that you are right and others are wrong.
5. Remove any evidence of fear so you are not paralyzed or isolated.
6. Focus on Christ and not the circumstances.
7. Share Christ in your relationships with others.

Dear Lord, search my heart and reveal any obstacles in
my life that are preventing me from truly praising You.
You and You alone are worthy of my utmost praise! Amen.

DAY 20

The Door of Praise

"Here I am! I stand at the door and knock. If anyone hears my voice and opens the door, I will come in and eat with that person, and they with me."

REVELATION 3:20

The Lord is patiently standing at our heart's door knocking. He will not barge in uninvited. He desires that we open the door and welcome His fellowship. He desires to be a part of our daily lives—moment by moment, in good times or bad.

Praise opens the door of our hearts to His knocking and ushers in His presence. When we praise God during our most difficult trials and sufferings, it demonstrates our total dependency on Him. It communicates our trust in our heavenly Father no matter what. The Lord is well pleased when we rely solely on Him.

God is fully aware of our circumstances. Since He is always standing at the door of our hearts knocking, why would we hesitate to open the door and let Him in? Why do we sometimes abandon Him when we need Him the most? Our focus should *always* be on praising Him for who He is. We will see Him interceding on our behalf. Open the door. Let Him in.

Dear Lord, may I open the door of my heart to You. May I praise You today and always as we walk through life together. Amen.

Day 21

The Word of God

And beginning with Moses and all the Prophets,
he [Jesus] explained to them what was said
in all the Scriptures concerning himself.

Luke 24:27

After Jesus' death and resurrection, He encountered two of his followers on the road to Emmaus. Although they were prevented from recognizing Him until supper later that day, Jesus conveyed truth as they journeyed together.

During Jesus' earthly ministry, He referred to the Old Testament scriptures frequently. He did so to validate that His teachings were indeed God's truth. Imparting truth was central to Jesus' ministry. Jesus himself stated in John 14:6, "I am the way and *the truth* and the life. No one comes to the Father except through me"(emphasis added). Just as Jesus imparted truth to the men on the road to Emmaus, He desires to convey spiritual truth to us today.

It is essential that we *daily* study and meditate on the truth that is found in the Bible. We are privileged to have access to God's Word. The Old Testament truths are essential if we desire to get a complete picture of our loving Messiah. Neglecting the Bible is neglecting our spiritual growth.

Dear Lord, may I never take having access to Your Word
for granted. Help me set aside time daily to read and
meditate on your Truth that is found in the Bible. Amen.

Day 22

Goals

And we know that in all things God
works for the good of those who love him,
who have been called according to his purpose.
Romans 8:28

Business goals. Financial goals. Personal goals. Setting goals is part of our culture. Research has shown that if goals are identified and written down, the success rate for achieving those goals is much higher.

Since God has a plan for our lives, wouldn't it be wise to consult Him when setting goals? As we do, He will direct our path and show us the way we should go. Proverbs 3:5–6 encourages us to do the following: "Trust in the Lord with all your heart and lean not on your own understanding; in all your ways submit to him, and he will make your paths straight." This is the secret to remaining in the center of His will.

Prayer is a vital component of goal setting. Pray that the Lord makes you sensitive to His desires for your future. Never lose hope. Be encouraged that God our Father is beside you—leading you in the right direction. You will receive blessing upon blessing. So, go ahead and write down the goals the Lord lays on your heart. Refer to them often. God's plans for your life will unfold as you achieve one goal after another.

Dear Lord, help me set goals that are consistent with
Your will for my life. May I trust You with my future. Amen.

DAY 23

Be Alert and Self-Controlled

*For the Lord himself will come down from heaven, with a loud
command, with the voice of the archangel and with the trumpet call
of God, and the dead in Christ will rise first. After that, we who are
still alive and are left will be caught up together with them in
the clouds to meet the Lord in the air. And so we will be
with the Lord forever.*

1 THESSALONIANS 4:16–17

The Day of the Lord will come like a thief in the night. Jesus said
in Matthew 24:36, "But about that day or hour no one knows, not
even the angels in heaven, nor the Son, but only the Father." What
does this mean? We must be ready! We do not know when we will
stand before our Maker, so we must prepare ourselves today.

Our lives should be disciplined so that we are ready for whatever comes. There will always be spiritual warfare that we must
recognize and meet head-on. The Lord has not left us defenseless.
When we put on His full armor, we will be equipped for any battle
we face. Our belief about the future should impact our lives today.
Let's not be caught off guard.

*Dear Lord, may I live my life today with eternity in mind.
May I put on the spiritual armor that You have provided
so that I will be victorious in life's battles. Amen.*

DAY 24

God's Word

How can a young person stay on the path of purity?
By living according to your word. I seek you with all my
heart; do not let me stray from your commands. I have
hidden your word in my heart that I might not sin against you.

PSALM 119:9–11

The Bible is God's instruction book for believers. Most of us have access to a Bible, yet how often do we open it? Instead, we may choose to spend hours watching TV or surfing the net. Perhaps our jobs or children take all of our time. However, when we neglect the reading of His Word, we are flying blind through life. We are unable to discern God's will and easily fall prey to sin.

If we believe that the Bible is *really* God's Word, how could we ignore it? Peace with God only comes when we have a close relationship with Him. Relationships are built by spending time together. God already knows all about us. We come to know Him through spending time in His Word. Choose to grow in your relationship with the Lord by reading the Bible. Open the road map to life so you do not get lost. Hide God's truth in your heart so that it is always with you!

Dear Lord, thank You for giving me Your instruction book for life.
May I spend time in Your Word so that I may know You. Amen.

DAY 25

Our Understanding Savior

For we do not have a high priest who is unable to empathize with our weaknesses, but we have one who has been tempted in every way, just as we are—yet he did not sin.

HEBREWS 4:15

*H*ave you ever felt all alone—like there is no one who can relate to what you are going through? Take heart. There is good news! There is nothing we have or will experience that Jesus did not encounter while here on earth. He felt pain, rejection, loneliness, betrayal, and temptation. Jesus also knew love, joy, hope, and peace. He *knows* what we're going through firsthand. He can relate, even if no one else can.

Jesus also knows what it takes to rise *above* the circumstances. He was triumphant even over death. Because of this ultimate victory, He can help guide us through the trials we face. He intercedes on our behalf as our High Priest. When we trust Him, we, too, can experience victory!

So, do not lose heart. Turn to Jesus. Pour out your emotions. When He was betrayed, He forgave. When He was anxious, He prayed. Learn from Jesus. Your weakness will be turned to strength. You will experience victory rather than defeat.

Dear Lord, You can give me peace regardless of what I am experiencing. Help me turn to You so I can rise above my circumstances. Amen.

DAY 26

God's Attributes

You have searched me, LORD, and you know me. . . . Where can I go
from your Spirit? Where can I flee from your presence? . . .
For you created my inmost being; you knit me
together in my mother's womb.

PSALM 139:1, 7, 13

Infinite God is incomprehensible to finite man. It is impossible to wrap our heads around all that God is and all that God does. He is God. We are not. His ways and thoughts are higher than our own. In an attempt to understand Him, we can ponder some of His attributes.

God is omniscient. He is the all-knowing Creator. God laid the earth's foundation and set the constellations in their places. Yet, at the same time, He knows the very number of hairs on our heads. Science only discovers what Creator God knew from the beginning. God knows every detail of our existence.

God is omnipresent. He is everywhere at the same time. He sees all. We cannot flee from His presence. This is comforting when we feel alone yet sobering when we attempt to run away from Him. There is no escape.

God is omnipotent. He is all powerful. He spoke creation into existence! The sun rises and sets at His command. He is sovereign over life and death. God's power raised Jesus from the dead.

As we ponder God's attributes, we are compelled to place our trust in Him! He alone is worthy! What a comfort to our heart and soul.

Dear Lord, help me grasp just how almighty You are!
In this moment, may I trust You completely. Amen.

DAY 27

Good Things in Life

*Taste and see that the LORD is good; blessed is the one who
takes refuge in him. Fear the LORD, you his holy people,
for those who fear him lack nothing. The lions may grow weak
and hungry, but those who seek the LORD lack no good thing.*

PSALM 34:8–10

God's idea of "good things" is much different than our own. Our
perspective is physical; His is spiritual. In God's eyes even suffering, trials, and heartache can be "good" if they fit within His
purpose and plan for our lives.

Consider the Old Testament hero Joseph. In spite of betrayal,
slavery, and imprisonment, Joseph trusted in God's good plan.
Somehow he was able to put his present sufferings within the
context of God's sovereignty. Years later, Joseph was reunited with
his brothers and testified to the following in Genesis 50:20: "You
intended to harm me, but God intended it for good to accomplish
what is now being done, the saving of many lives."

When we seek the Lord, we shall not lack any good thing. His
Holy Spirit confirms this truth: the more we seek Him, the more
we are satisfied with the good things in life.

*Dear Lord, help me gain Your perspective. When the storms
of life head my way, may I seek You. Help me know that You
have a "good" plan for me—even in painful times. Amen.*

Day 28

Measuring Spiritual Growth

Therefore, rid yourselves of all malice and all deceit, hypocrisy,
envy, and slander of every kind. Like newborn babies,
crave pure spiritual milk, so that by it you may grow up in your
salvation, now that you have tasted that the Lord is good.

1 Peter 2:1-3

*H*ow can we assess if we are maturing spiritually? The following are some characteristics that indicate spiritual growth:

1. We have a hunger to know God.
2. We have increasing awareness of sin.
3. We have a sincere repentance and desire to be more Christlike.
4. We view spiritual battles as avenues of growth.
5. We have a desire to be used by God in the lives of others.
6. We have a desire for godly obedience.
7. We have an increasing faith.
8. We have a hunger for private devotion.
9. We have a desire to please God.
10. We have a vibrant love for God.

How are you doing? The good news is that there is no limit! We can continue growing spiritually until we meet Jesus face-to-face. Continue to step closer to Him each day. In a year you will be able to look back and see signs of spiritual growth!

Dear Lord, You know how inadequate I feel many times
in my spiritual walk. May I not become discouraged.
Help me take daily steps in Your direction. Amen.

DAY 29

Seeking God

You, God, are my God, earnestly I seek you;
I thirst for you, my whole being longs for you,
in a dry and parched land where there is no water.

PSALM 63:1

Is your soul thirsty, or are you completely satisfied? We were created to know our Creator. We were made to be in a love relationship with our heavenly Father. There is a restlessness in our soul—a search that compels us to seek Him. We are not satisfied until we find Him.

Our search begins with an act of the will. We must earnestly seek the Lord by setting our minds to do so. This involves humility, sincerity, and purpose of heart. We must admit our spiritual thirst and hunger and seek the One who can satisfy our yearning.

Begin by reading the Bible. If you don't know where to start, turn to the Gospel of John. Get involved in a Bible study or Sunday school class, or read a daily devotional. Allow the Holy Spirit to teach you and open your mind to spiritual truth. Communicate to the Lord through prayer. Allow Him to speak to you by being still and listening. When we earnestly seek Him, we will be richly rewarded!

Dear Lord, I want to know You more. Help me take the necessary
steps needed to grow in my relationship with You. Amen.

Day 30

Setting Goals

*Trust in the LORD with all your heart and lean not
on your own understanding; in all your ways submit
to him, and he will make your paths straight.*

PROVERBS 3:5–6

Life can be confusing, perplexing, or downright scary at times. Although we may try to make the best decisions possible, we still falter. Experience is a great teacher, but we may occasionally fall flat on our faces. How can we navigate successfully through life? How can we make wise decisions? How can we live without regrets?

God did not intend for us to wander aimlessly through life. Humbly acknowledge that the Lord possesses the understanding you lack. Defer to Him in your decision-making process. Trust in Him with all your heart. He will show you the way to go. He will make your paths straight. Periodically set goals for yourself, and trust God to bring them to fulfillment. In order to practically accomplish this:

1. Set aside time to be alone with God every day.
2. Align your heart with God by confessing sin.
3. Identify areas in your life that need attention.
4. Purpose to glorify God and not yourself.
5. Be patient and diligent. God's timetable may not be yours.

*Dear Lord, help me take inventory of my life and
set goals that are in keeping with Your will. Amen.*

Day 31

The Truth

Dear friends, do not believe every spirit,
but test the spirits to see whether they are from God,
because many false prophets have gone out into the world.

1 John 4:1

Theology matters because it seeks the truth about God—the source of all truth. We must be alert to the fact that Satan is actively undermining truth in today's world. In John 8:44, Jesus rebukes those who did not believe in Him by saying, "You belong to your father, the devil, and you want to carry out your father's desire. He was a murderer from the beginning, not holding to the truth, for there is no truth in him. When he lies, he speaks his native language, for he is a liar and the father of lies." Beware! Deception is his strategy. The ultimate test of truth is found in our belief about Jesus; who He is and why He came to earth.

Spiritual truth involves more than just having head knowledge. Belief must move from the head to the heart. The results are life changing! We forsake sin and submit to the Lord Jesus Christ. We desire to serve Him. We trust the Lord and put Him *first*. We depend on Him for every little thing. We love Him with our whole heart.

Dear Lord, I desire to know truth, not just in my head but in my heart. Help me seek spiritual truth by seeking You. Amen.

DAY 32

God Speaks to Us

*That you may love the LORD your God,
listen to his voice, and hold fast to him.*
DEUTERONOMY 30:20

*D*o you believe that God speaks to us today? Joan of Arc was once asked why God spoke only to her. She replied, "Sir, you are wrong. God speaks to everyone. I just listen." When God speaks, He desires that we listen. We must always be attuned to His voice. He wants to communicate His love and impart truth. He longs to have a personal relationship with us.

God is constantly trying to get our attention. Yet sometimes we are so distracted that we miss it. Busyness can be used as an excuse for not hearing His voice. Most often we must be still in order to hear God speak.

God communicates to us in many ways. He clearly speaks through His Word, the Bible. The Holy Spirit whispers in a still, small voice to our hearts. Other believers might impart God's wisdom. Nature boldly proclaims His praises and reveals His attributes. God may also speak loudly through our circumstances that He providentially arranges. God is speaking. Are we being still enough to listen?

*Dear Lord, help me be attuned to Your voice throughout
the day. Help me set aside the busyness. Give me a
heart that truly wants to hear from You. Amen.*

Day 33

A Sense of Urgency

"Don't you have a saying, 'It's still four months until harvest'? I tell you, open your eyes and look at the fields! They are ripe for harvest."

John 4:35

*M*any times the disciples were so focused on physical priorities that they missed the spiritual truth that Jesus was trying to teach them. What about us? It is easy to become so consumed with work, deadlines, children's schedules, and our homes that we miss spiritual reality.

There is *nothing* more important than the redemption of a person's soul. How can I play a part in this? Does my life exemplify one that is serving the Lord? The question has been asked: If you were on trial for being a Christian, would there be enough evidence to convict you? That is a sobering question.

What influence do I have to lead others to Christ? How much emphasis do I put on this? Is my life consumed with temporal interests, or do I see things from an eternal perspective? Jesus calls us "the light of the world" in Matthew 5:14. He then exhorts us in verse 16 to "let your light shine before others, that they may see your good deeds and glorify your Father in heaven." Is your light helping others see Christ more clearly?

Dear Lord, help me reach out to others who do not know You. Teach me Your ways. Amen.

How God Gets Our Attention

That night the king could not sleep; so he ordered the book of the chronicles, the record of his reign, to be brought in and read to him.
ESTHER 6:1

———— ❊ ————

When King Xerxes woke up in the middle of the night, he decided to read. God used the king's restlessness to ultimately carry out His will. In an unexpected turn of events, Mordecai was honored for exposing an assassination attempt on the king's life while Haman was hung on the gallows he had prepared for Mordecai. (Read this fascinating story in Esther, chapters 6 and 7.)

God works in extraordinary ways. His plan for us will prevail. How does God get our attention? He may give us a restless spirit. Things just might not seem "right." Or perhaps we experience a sleepless night. A recurrent thought or idea might continue to come to mind despite our efforts to suppress it.

Do not ignore these occurrences. Seek the Lord. Now that He has your attention, ask Him to speak. Listen. Wait for a word from Him. Many times once we agree that His direction will be ours, He speaks loud and clear. The Lord gets our attention in order to communicate His will so that we can follow Him—it's that simple.

Dear Lord, You have ways of getting my attention.
May I take heed and follow wherever You are
leading me. May Your will be done. Amen.

DAY 35

Speak, Lord

*The LORD came and stood there, calling as at the
other times, "Samuel! Samuel!" Then Samuel said,
"Speak, for your servant is listening."*

1 SAMUEL 3:10

*L*ittle Samuel was ministering before the Lord under Eli, the priest. One night, as Samuel was lying down in the temple, God called to him. Thinking it was Eli, Samuel responded by running to Eli. After this occurred a second time, Eli realized that God must be calling Samuel. So Eli told Samuel what to say if he heard his name a third time. When God spoke once again, Samuel responded by saying, "Speak, for your servant is listening."

God has numerous ways of getting our attention. It has been said that God whispers in our pleasure and shouts in our pain. Have you found that God has your undivided attention more during times of tragedy, unanswered prayer, disappointment, or financial difficulty?

When enduring the storms of life, we have a choice. We can either turn toward God or away from Him—becoming either better or bitter. Purpose to run toward God. Respond by examining every facet of your life. Ask the Lord to clarify what He is trying to show you and how He wants you to proceed. May we respond as Samuel did by saying, "Speak, for your servant is listening."

*Dear Lord, may I turn to You and learn to
listen when life knocks me to my knees. Amen.*

DAY 36

Identifying the Voice of God

"My sheep listen to my voice;
I know them, and they follow me."
JOHN 10:27

$\mathcal{A}$ shepherd knows each of his sheep by name. When he calls, they respond because they know his distinct voice. A good shepherd protects his sheep against predators. He also provides food, water, and shelter. So, when the sheep hear his voice, why wouldn't they follow their shepherd?

Jesus is the Good Shepherd and we are His sheep. Jesus asserts that His sheep can discern His voice. So, how do we know when God is speaking to us? When trying to make a decision, we may be pulled in several directions. How can we be *sure* of God's will? How can we identify His voice?

The Bible is the standard of truth. If you need to hear God speak audibly, read the Bible out loud! We come to know the heart of God by spending time in His Word. Because bankers handle real money day in and day out, they can quickly spot a counterfeit. Are we regularly soaking in God's truth so that we are able to discern truth from lies? Jesus always leads us in the right direction! Let's listen to our Good Shepherd and follow Him.

Dear Lord, help me spend time in Your Word so
that I can discern Your voice and follow You. Amen.

Day 37

Waiting on the Lord

Truly my soul finds rest in God; my salvation comes from him.
Truly he is my rock and my salvation; he is my
fortress, I will never be shaken.
PSALM 62:1–2

Waiting requires patience. For most of us patience is not an attribute that comes easily. Have you ever prayed for patience and then found yourself standing in the longest line at the checkout counter? Patience must be learned. Waiting also requires humility. Rather than barging ahead with our own solution, we defer to someone else instead.

Waiting on the Lord is always the right choice. We must never forget the anchor of our souls. God promises to never leave us nor forsake us. Waiting on the Lord requires faith and *patience*, as well as constant prayer and discipline. We can wait with an expectancy that God will answer as He has promised.

Seeking our own answers is not the solution. Throw all your trust on God to handle *every* situation in His perfect way. His timing is best. He is faithful and will never disappoint us! If you have not received clear direction from the Lord about something, wait until you have clarity and peace before making a move. You will be glad you did!

Dear Lord, it is so hard to wait on You in a
world that seeks instant solutions. Help me
to be as trusting as You are faithful! Amen.

DAY 38

Children

Jesus said, "Let the little children come to me, and do not hinder them, for the kingdom of heaven belongs to such as these."
MATTHEW 19:14

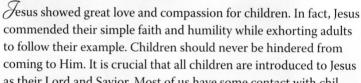

𝒥esus showed great love and compassion for children. In fact, Jesus commended their simple faith and humility while exhorting adults to follow their example. Children should never be hindered from coming to Him. It is crucial that all children are introduced to Jesus as their Lord and Savior. Most of us have some contact with children: our own children, grandchildren, nieces, nephews, neighbors. Do we look for opportunities to pass God's truth on to them? Do we take them to church, Sunday school, and Vacation Bible School? Is our behavior consistent with what we profess to believe?

Children can understand the simple message of the Gospel found in John 3:16, "For God so loved the world that he gave his one and only Son, that whoever believes in him shall not perish but have eternal life." We must examine our own hearts. Are we approaching Jesus with childlike humility and faith? These are prerequisites for salvation. Let's set a godly example in word and deed to the children in our spheres of influence.

Dear Lord, help me to be a good example to the children in my life. May they see humility in me and place their faith in You. Amen.

DAY 39

Hearing from God

"Though he slay me, yet will I hope in him;
I will surely defend my ways to his face."
JOB 13:15

God had permitted Satan to test Job. Job lost it all—his children, his livestock, his health. Even his wife and friends turned against him. Yet Job never lost his faith and never sinned against God. In his despair, Job was honest with God and said, "Though he slay me, yet will I hope in him." Job made a conscious decision to continue to trust God even though he was an emotional wreck. God eventually restored Job by blessing the latter part of his life more than the first.

Our attitude has a lot to do with how God answers our concerns. Honest emotions should be conveyed, but not with an egotistical, self-sufficient, rebellious attitude. What pleases God is being submissive to His will. We need to trust with genuine faith that God will never lead us in the wrong direction. We can have a grateful heart, knowing that regardless of the circumstances, God has our best interest at heart. He will never leave or forsake us. Let's follow Job's example by purposing to trust God even when our emotions are volatile.

Dear Lord, thank You that I can be honest before You.
Help me to have an attitude like Job's. May I put my
hope in You regardless of my circumstances. Amen.

Day 40

Who Is This God I Worship?

God is faithful, who has called you into
fellowship with his Son, Jesus Christ our Lord.

1 Corinthians 1:9

———— ❧ ————

How do you view God?

Father: Do you view Him as loving or demanding? Many times God is compared to our earthly fathers, and wrong conclusions are formed. Your perfect heavenly Father loves you unconditionally.

Friend: Is God an intimate or distant friend of yours? God is a true friend. He will never forsake nor abandon you. He will stick with you through thick and thin.

Teacher: Is God's teaching style patient or intolerant and critical? God is the perfect teacher because He knows everything! He is patient with you. He does not discourage or criticize.

Guide: Does God guide you gently or strictly? God does not force Himself on you. He is a gentle Shepherd who desires to lead you on paths of righteousness.

Counselor: Is God understanding or insensitive? God made you so He understands you better than you understand yourself. Trust Him.

Provider: Do you view God as generous or stingy? God lavishes you with His love and blessings every day. He provides the very air you breathe!

Supporter: Is God faithful or inconsistent? You can trust Him explicitly. He is always faithful and true, even when you are not.

Dear Lord, may I come to know You for who You really are.
Reveal Yourself to me today. Amen.

Day 41

Quiet Time

*"Be still, and know that I am God; I will be exalted
among the nations, I will be exalted in the earth."*

PSALM 46:10

In our hustle-bustle world, it's difficult to find time to be still. It seems nearly impossible to have "quiet time." Yet that is exactly what our soul yearns for. In fact, the busier our lives, the more quiet time is needed.

When we do make time for prayer, are we more apt to be listening or talking? Prayer is a two-way conversation. It has been said that perhaps God gave us two ears and one mouth for a reason—we should listen twice as much as we talk! When we take time to be quiet, we are able to listen to, meditate on, and digest His words found in the Bible. Quiet time also allows the Holy Spirit to speak to our hearts in a still, small voice. Not only do these spiritual truths guide us in that moment, but the Holy Spirit is able to bring them to mind even years later!

Prayer time also involves praising God for who He is. With humble hearts we petition God for our own needs and intercede on behalf of others. May our prayer time incorporate both speaking *and* listening. Let's make time for the Lord today. We need it!

*Dear Lord, it seems like I come before You with so many needs and
requests. Help me to be still so that I can hear from You. Amen.*

Day 42

Our Real Needs

*Because of the LORD's great love we are not consumed,
for his compassions never fail. They are new
every morning; great is your faithfulness.*

LAMENTATIONS 3:22–23

❈

As Steve battled cancer, he felt as if his whole world was falling apart. During his quiet time in the early morning hours, he couldn't even pray. Instead, he just stared out the window, fixing his eyes on the horizon where he knew the sun would rise. Steve was filled with renewed hope, as each sunrise was a reminder of God's faithfulness to him.

God provides for our physical needs: food, clothing, shelter. But because we live in a fallen world, we are not exempt from experiencing illness. Although our health may be threatened, God will remain faithful. Take heart. Even when we do not know how to pray, the Holy Spirit is interceding on our behalf in accordance with God's will. (See Romans 8:26–27.)

Because of God's great love for us, we know His compassions will never fail. His mercy is new with every sunrise! He is good to those whose hope is in Him. Great is His faithfulness! Rely on God's faithfulness to uphold you. His love will never fail.

*Dear Lord, I praise You for Your faithfulness and mercy
in my life, especially when illness strikes. Help me to
keep my eyes on You during difficult times. Amen.*

DAY 43

Dealing with Unmet Needs

And God said, "I will be with you."

EXODUS 3:12

God had an assignment for Moses and called to him from a burning bush. Moses had been chosen by God to lead the Israelites out of Egypt to the Promised Land. However, Moses did not immediately embrace God's plan. He came up with excuse after excuse why he couldn't obey.

Moses was hesitant to approach Pharaoh and ask for the Israelites' freedom. The Lord responded to Moses by assuring him that He would be with him. The Lord wanted Moses to depend on Him rather than himself.

The same is true for us today. When the Lord gives us a divine assignment, He will be with us. He will meet our needs and enable us to accomplish His will. God wants us to totally depend on Him. Take the following steps when you want God to meet your needs:

1. Acknowledge your need by going to the Lord in prayer with a humble heart.
2. Seek God's direction, trusting that He will provide the answer.
3. Claim God's promises found in His Word, asking the Holy Spirit to open your heart and mind to truth.
4. Be willing to wait patiently for God's best.
5. Thank God in advance for meeting your needs.

Dear Lord, thank You that You are with me. Help me trust
You and wait patiently for You to meet my needs. Amen.

DAY 44

Waiting

*Wait for the LORD; be strong and
take heart and wait for the LORD.*
PSALM 27:14

❦

God has three possible answers for our prayers: yes, no, and not yet. The definitive answers are easier to handle. Waiting is difficult! Have you ever wondered why God doesn't answer all of our prayers instantaneously? Waiting for God's answer does not necessarily mean the answer will be no.

Sometimes waiting allows God to work on our hearts. One of the biggest hindrances to unanswered prayer is unconfessed sin. It blocks the flow of God's grace in our lives. Ask the Lord to reveal any hidden sin in your heart. Confession will restore your relationship. An unforgiving spirit is another roadblock. How can we expect God to forgive us when we harbor ill will toward others?

Many times our free will gets in the way. Becoming impatient for the Lord to act, we may take matters into our own hands and jump ahead of His perfect plan. A lack of trust may be the culprit. The Lord may allow us to wait on Him in order to build our trust and grow our faith. He can then demonstrate His faithfulness. Let's submit to His plan completely and be willing to wait on Him for answered prayer. Then we will be ready for whatever answer He gives us.

*Dear Lord, waiting is so hard! Give me the grace to place my trust
solely in You and not take matters into my own hands. Amen.*

Day 45

God's Great Love for Us

But God demonstrates his own love for us in this:
While we were still sinners, Christ died for us.
ROMANS 5:8

There are times when all of us feel unlovable. We may look unkempt or have a lousy attitude. Perhaps we have sinned and are riddled with guilt. Regardless of our feelings, God's love for us never changes. Remember how God proved His love to us: when we were alienated from God, God reached down to us by sending Jesus to die in our place. We can do nothing to earn His love. We can do nothing to take away His love. His love never changes.

God has adopted us into His family through His Son, Jesus. He has chosen us before the foundation of the world. He has redeemed us. He has forgiven all our sins—past, present, and future. He has prepared a place for us. He has sealed us for the day of redemption. His love is unconditional.

So, if you are feeling unlovable, look at the outstretched arms of Jesus. Be reminded of His love for you. He could not love you any more or any less than He always does! Receive His love today!

Dear Lord, there is no greater love than the love that
You have for me. May I not only receive Your love
but walk confidently in that love today. Amen.

Day 46

Humility

"God opposes the proud but shows favor to the humble."
James 4:6

---

*H*umility goes against our human nature. We naturally think of ourselves first. Yet, to experience the life of Christ, we need the inner discipline of humility—being humble before God and our fellow man.

Although humility is difficult to teach, Jesus perfectly modeled it for us. In Philippians 2:5–8, the apostle Paul describes Christ's humble attitude: "Have the same mindset as Christ Jesus: Who, being in very nature God, did not consider equality with God something to be used to his own advantage; rather, he made himself nothing by taking the very nature of a servant, being made in human likeness. And being found in appearance as a man, he humbled himself by becoming obedient to death—even death on a cross!" Even though Jesus was fully God, He humbly died on the cross for us!

Humility looks to the interests of others, not just our own. Humility is an inner discipline to which we aspire and enter into by degrees. It is a process by which we displace self by enthroning God. God saves the humble, guides the humble, sustains the humble, and crowns the humble. We can always find someone to serve. The humble life produces joy and profound daily appreciation.

Dear Lord, You modeled true humility for me. Help me learn by Your example. May humility, not pride, characterize my life. Amen.

Day 47

Build on the Rock

"Therefore everyone who hears these words of mine and puts them into practice is like a wise man who built his house on the rock."

MATTHEW 7:24

❖

Many of us are familiar with the children's song based on Jesus' words in Matthew 7:24–27. As a child we may have enjoyed clapping our hands when the house on the sand went "smash." However, as an adult, the reality of being buffeted by the storms of life is very sobering.

Our only true source of identity is Jesus Christ. Yet how often do we seek our identity in other ways? We may become wrapped up in material pleasures, powerful people, or perfect families. When we build our lives on any foundation other than Jesus Christ, the Rock, it is only a matter of time before our sandy foundation begins to sink.

When hearts are not fully committed to Christ, attitudes such as pride, selfishness, greed, and materialism creep in. We are not to seek gratification in temporal pleasures. Our identity is secure in Christ alone. Let's build our house on the Rock—Jesus Christ. Only then will we be able to stand, regardless of our circumstances. Our security depends on it!

Dear Lord, may I seek my identity in You alone. You are my Rock. When I build my life on You, I have a firm foundation. Amen.

Day 48

Overcoming Doubt

*Let us hold unswervingly to the hope
we profess, for he who promised is faithful.*

Hebrews 10:23

Doubt is a common human emotion. Many times it is rooted in the belief that what we want will not come to pass. Have we ever doubted that God is going to provide for our needs? In that example, doubt is failing to trust God. Doubt can lead to fear and hinder our walk with Him.

Jesus tells a story in Mark 9:14–27 about healing a boy with an evil spirit. When Jesus asked the boy's father if he believed that Jesus could heal his son, the father exclaimed, "I do believe; help me overcome my unbelief!" The father honestly admitted that he struggled with doubt. Yet Jesus still answered the father's prayer and healed his son.

Jesus understands that we all have doubts and unbelief. So let's be honest. Let's follow this father's example by asking the Lord to infuse us with faith to believe. God will be faithful. He is there to meet our needs. He can even help us overcome our unbelief. Let us hold unswervingly to the hope we profess and trust Him to help in our areas of weakness. He who promised is faithful!

*Dear Lord, You know that many times I fail to trust
You as I should. Help me overcome my unbelief! Amen.*

DAY 49

God Comes to Us

Jesus said to her, "Mary." She turned toward
him and cried out in Aramaic, "Rabboni!"
JOHN 20:16

On the first day of the week after Jesus' crucifixion, Mary Magdalene went to the tomb. When she saw that the stone had been removed from the entrance, she ran to tell the disciples Peter and John. They entered the tomb and discovered strips of linen lying there, but Jesus' body was gone.

Mary Magdalene was so distraught! Who had taken her beloved Jesus? Peter and John eventually left the tomb and went back to their homes. But all Mary could do was stand there and cry. Her world had fallen apart. Her hope had been shattered. That is precisely the moment when Jesus came to her and spoke her name, "Mary." Immediately she recognized His voice and instinctively tried to grab on to Him.

Jesus came to earth to save the lost from eternal death, not to judge mankind. He died and rose again. He is alive and is totally interested in the lives of each one of us. What is your greatest need? The Lord will fulfill it when you cry out to Him. He is there, ready to respond. In your darkest hour, He will come to you and call your name.

Dear Lord, You are always there, even though I may not
"see" You. I am crying out to You. Meet me in this very hour.
Speak my name. Meet my needs. Amen.

DAY 50

God Meets Our Needs

"Those who find me find life and receive favor from
the LORD. But those who fail to find me harm
themselves; all who hate me love death."

PROVERBS 8:35–36

As is the case with all of us, Lisa yearned to be loved. Unfortunately she looked for love in all the wrong places. She tried to earn the love she so desperately craved. Perfectionism and materialism failed to satisfy her. Poor choices in relationships only led to heartache and pain. There had to be a better way!

God sent His Son, Jesus, to meet our need for love. First John 4:10 states, "This is love: not that we loved God, but that he loved us and sent his Son as an atoning sacrifice for our sins." God is love. When we find Him, we find life as we are embraced by His unconditional love.

Blessings come as we allow the Lord to meet our needs. Attempting to strike out on our own will only lead to costly defeat. God's truth can be suppressed for only so long. Eventually it will prevail.

God yearns to bless us, show us favor, and meet our needs. But we must listen to Him; watch and wait for Him to answer. When we place our trust in Him, we will never be disappointed. Let's find life by finding the Lord and allowing *Him* to be in control.

Dear Lord, I want the kind of life You have designed for me.
Help me trust You to meet my needs. Amen.

Day 51

Servant Leadership

*"For even the Son of Man did not come to be served,
but to serve, and to give his life as a ransom for many."*
MARK 10:45

Although Jesus was God in the flesh, He never flaunted His authority or lorded it over others. Instead, Jesus came into this world to serve and to give His life as a ransom for many. Servant leadership requires that the leader voluntarily become the "slave of all." The focus is on serving others rather than on being served.

During the Last Supper, Jesus modeled servant leadership by washing his disciples' feet. In John 13:14–17, Jesus said, "Now that I, your Lord and Teacher, have washed your feet, you also should wash one another's feet. I have set you an example that you should do as I have done for you. Very truly I tell you, no servant is greater than his master, nor is a messenger greater than the one who sent him. Now that you know these things, you will be blessed if you do them."

If we are Christ's followers, we, too, are called to emulate His example. Let's be a servant leader to those around us. We will be blessed indeed.

*Dear Lord, I must admit, I think more about how others
should meet my needs than about how I can meet theirs.
Give me opportunities to serve others in Your name. Amen.*

Day 52

Our Life's Goal

*For we must all appear before the judgment seat of Christ,
so that each of us may receive what is due us for the
things done while in the body, whether good or bad.*

2 Corinthians 5:10

$\mathcal{D}$eath is a taboo subject in our society. We act as if we are immortal. Yet it has been said that our lives are but a dash—as depicted by the dash between the dates of our birth and death on our tombstones. No one escapes physical death.

If we have accepted Jesus as our personal Lord and Savior, we have been given spiritual life and need not fear condemnation. However, we will still stand before Christ one day to have our lives evaluated—not to determine our salvation, but to receive our rewards. No one knows when that time will come. That should not scare us, but motivate us.

Will we be exposed? Have our lives counted for anything? Have we shown the love of Christ to those around us? The Gospel is urgent business. Our life's goal should be to please and serve the Lord.

Let's live for the One who gave us life! May His love compel us! Someday, when we meet face-to-face, may He be able to say, "Well done, my good servant!" (Luke 19:17).

*Dear Lord, may I be about Your business.
May I be found faithful and live for You. Amen.*

DAY 53

Be Holy

As obedient children, do not conform to the evil desires you had
when you lived in ignorance. But just as he who called you is holy,
so be holy in all you do; for it is written: "Be holy, because I am holy."
1 PETER 1:14–16

*W*hy do we tend to shrink back from this command? Perhaps we
are intimidated, thinking we could never be perfect like God. Or
maybe we think that being holy would rob us of enjoyment and
fun. What exactly is God asking of us? To be holy means to be "set
apart." Christians are to be "set apart" for His use.

God is challenging us to make a choice. James 4:4 states that
"friendship with the world means enmity against God." We are
asked to embrace the Lord rather than the world; to have eternal
priorities as opposed to earthly ones. We are to be in the world,
but not of this world. Our citizenship is in heaven. When our
priorities are temporal, our lives are full of greed, lust, idolatry,
or wrongful attitudes. Our spiritual insight becomes cloudy. God
desires the best for us. When we seek holiness, we begin to see
things as God sees them. Not only are we blessed, but we can then
be used to bless the lives of others.

Dear Lord, please forgive me for compromising my
faith by chasing worldly passions. May I desire
to be holy and seek Your heart. Amen.

DAY 54

Conformation vs. Transformation

Do not conform to the pattern of this world, but be transformed
by the renewing of your mind. Then you will be able to test and
approve what God's will is—his good, pleasing and perfect will.

ROMANS 12:2

*L*iving a godly life is impossible without God. He is the One who has given us a new nature. When we accept Jesus as our Lord and Savior, we are born spiritually. The Holy Spirit comes to reside within us. He is our Counselor and Comforter. It is through the Holy Spirit that transformation takes place. We grow spiritually and become more and more Christlike.

Although physically we live in this world, our eternal place of residence is heaven. While on earth, we are being shaped and molded into the image of Christ. Through the power of the Holy Spirit, God is purifying us and enabling us to live a godly life. We must participate in this process by allowing Him to change us. Transformation cannot occur in our own strength.

Dear Lord, I cannot live the Christian life without Your help.
Thank You for giving me the power and strength to follow
You and to be changed into Your image. Amen.

DAY 55

Forgiveness

Be kind and compassionate to one another,
forgiving each other, just as in Christ God forgave you.
EPHESIANS 4:32

*A*lthough we are commanded to forgive others, sometimes it is nearly impossible to do. If you struggle in this area, you are not alone. Begin with acknowledging how much God has forgiven you. Forgiveness is the cornerstone of the salvation message. Jesus did for us what we could not do for ourselves: He forgave *all* our sin—past, present, and future.

Do we realize the significance of this? Romans 5:8 states, "But God demonstrates his own love for us in this: While we were still sinners, Christ died for us." God proclaimed His faithful, eternal love by forgiving our sins. There is nothing we can do that is beyond His ability to forgive. He restores our lives and brings hope to every area.

So what should our response be? First, we must accept His love and forgiveness. Then and only then can we truly extend it to others. The Lord changes our hearts and gives us the ability to forgive. What right do we have to withhold forgiveness from others when we have been forgiven so much? Be kind and compassionate. Ask the Lord to help you forgive someone today.

Dear Lord, may I grasp the extent of Your forgiveness
so I can readily extend it to others. Amen.

Refusing to Forgive

Bear with each other and forgive one another if any of you has a grievance against someone. Forgive as the Lord forgave you.

COLOSSIANS 3:13

❖

God has set the example. Because He has forgiven us, we are called to forgive others. When we refuse to extend forgiveness to those who have offended us, the following negative consequences can ensue:

1. We can become consumed with bitterness, anger, resentment, and deep frustration.
2. We have difficulty loving others and being loved. Our life is filled with hardness.
3. An unforgiving spirit blocks our relationship with God. Our prayers are not heard.
4. Physical problems can actually emerge when we carry grudges and hatred in our hearts.

Extending forgiveness not only benefits the person being forgiven, but it releases the burden we are carrying. Many times an unforgiving spirit only hurts the one bearing the grudge.

When someone has committed an offense against you, acknowledge your hurt to the Lord. Do not deny the pain you may be experiencing. Then lay it at the foot of the cross. Give up your right to retaliate or hold on to the pain. Forgiving others brings peace. Let's not delay, but forgive today!

Dear Lord, sometimes it is nearly impossible to forgive others, yet I know it is Your will. Enable me to forgive as You have forgiven me so that peace, not bitterness, will rule my heart. Amen.

DAY 57

God's Blessings

Praise be to the God and Father of our Lord Jesus Christ,
who has blessed us in the heavenly realms with
every spiritual blessing in Christ.
EPHESIANS 1:3

Why is it that we tend to think of God's blessings in the material sense? When things go our way and God answers our prayers, we thank God for our blessings. The "prosperity gospel" touts that God promises material blessings to His followers. However, God's truth asserts that the greatest blessings have nothing to do with material things or social position. God's blessings are spiritual. Therefore they have everything to do with the closeness of His presence.

God hath not promised skies always blue,
Flower-strewn pathways all our lives through,
God hath not promised sun without rain,
Joy without sorrow, peace without pain.

But God hath promised strength for the day,
Rest for the labor, light for the way.
Grace for the trials, help from above,
Unfailing sympathy, undying love.
UNKNOWN

Dear Lord, thank You for the true blessing of You.
You will never leave me nor forsake me, and
that is the greatest blessing of all! Amen.

DAY 58

The Power of the Holy Spirit

But we have this treasure in jars of clay to show that this
all-surpassing power is from God and not from us.

2 CORINTHIANS 4:7

When trying to reach the lost for Christ, we must not become
discouraged or distressed when our efforts seem to be in vain. It
is the power of the Holy Spirit that draws people to God. Only the
infinite power of God can overcome spiritual blindness—removing
the spiritual blinders of sin.

So, what is our role? We are to be living testimonies of His
truth. When hardship strikes, we are to cling to the Lord and allow
the Holy Spirit to give us strength and power to endure. Non-
believers will take notice. Then the light of Christ will shine forth
brightly and reveal the power of the Holy Spirit that is at work
in our lives. Like the apostle Paul, we will be able to say: "We are
hard pressed on every side, but not crushed; perplexed, but not
in despair, persecuted, but not abandoned; struck down, but not
destroyed" (2 Corinthians 4:8–9). Pray that our witness is directed
and empowered by the Holy Spirit.

Dear Lord, may my life be a testimony of the
power of the Holy Spirit. May others see You at
work and be drawn to You as a result. Amen.

DAY 59

Pride

All of you, clothe yourselves with humility toward one another, because, "God opposes the proud but shows favor to the humble." Humble yourselves, therefore, under God's mighty hand, that he may lift you up in due time.

1 PETER 5:5–6

Man is prideful—plain and simple. Pride convinces us that we know best. Pride compels us to do things our way, when we want and how we want. Pride submits to no one. God hates pride because it cries out, "I need nothing. I can manage." God desires that we turn to Him. Pride hinders us from seeking God's presence in our lives. We want to be in control of our own destinies. We want to live life our way. We do not think we need any help.

Being humble means acknowledging our dependence on God and submitting to His authority. Humility also involves respecting other people and not thinking more highly of ourselves than we ought to. It involves looking "not only to [our] own interests, but each of [us] to the interests of the others" (Philippians 2:4). God promises wisdom and grace when we are humble. He will lift us up. Ask the Lord to give you a humble heart today.

Dear Lord, why is it so hard to be humble? Break my independent spirit so that I can receive grace and wisdom from You. Amen.

Day 60

Financial Wisdom

"His master replied, 'Well done, good and faithful servant!
You have been faithful with a few things; I will put you in charge
of many things. Come and share your master's happiness!' "
MATTHEW 25:21

*F*ear can cripple and paralyze. Fear of failure or fear of the future can lead to financial mismanagement. Jesus told a parable about three servants that were given differing amounts of money according to their ability. The master left on a long journey. When he returned, he held each accountable for how they had managed the money they had been given. Two of the servants invested their money wisely and gained even more. But the servant who was given one talent was afraid of losing it, so he buried it. The master was livid.

If fear is crippling you, acknowledge and face it. "Cast all your anxiety on him because he cares for you" (1 Peter 5:7). Then allow the Lord to help you get your finances under control. You will experience a greater sense of freedom and peace. God desires for us to be wise stewards of the resources He has entrusted to us. God will provide.

Dear Lord, in these volatile financial times, it is so easy
to become fearful. Help me turn my fears over to You.
Teach me how to invest Your resources wisely. Amen.

Day 61

Treasures

*"Do not store up for yourselves treasure on earth, where moths
and vermin destroy, and where thieves break in and steal.
But store up for yourselves treasures in heaven, where moths and
vermin do not destroy, and where thieves do not break in and steal.
For where your treasure is, there your heart will be also."*

Matthew 6:19–21

❈

Where is your treasure? Where is your heart? God's Word says
that they are in the same place. Either God is your treasure and
has your heart, or money does. We cannot serve both. We must
choose. These passages are not saying that having money is a problem. The danger comes when money has us—when money trumps
God as the priority in our lives. This is a serious matter to ponder.

We are encouraged to store up treasures in heaven. In other
words, when the Lord is more important than money, our focus
will be spiritual rather than temporal. Material possessions and
money will eventually pass away. Spiritual riches are eternal. Check
your heart. Where is your treasure? May our hearts belong to the
Lord. He is our treasure indeed!

*Dear Lord, many times it is hard to focus on You when we are
surrounded by so many material treasures. Help me to desire
You more than anything else this world has to offer. Amen.*

Day 62

Contentment

But godliness with contentment is great gain.
1 Timothy 6:6

Are you content with what the Lord has blessed you with, or do you often find yourself fantasizing about winning the lottery? What would you buy first? Would you take a lump sum or monthly payments? Would you continue to work or quit your job immediately?

Take heed: "Those who want to get rich fall into temptation and a trap and into many foolish and harmful desires that plunge people into ruin and destruction" (1 Timothy 6:9). The quest for money may tempt us to compromise our values, beliefs, or even the law. If we are constantly chasing after money, we will never be satisfied. Contentment is experienced when we place our trust in the Lord instead of money. He alone gives lasting satisfaction.

Debt occurs when we spend more than we make. Perhaps we have difficulty waiting. We justify a purchase by rationalizing that we "need" it, rather than admitting that we "want" it. The Lord is faithful to satisfy our "needs." He does not always give us everything we "want." We must be willing to wait on Him. Chase the Lord instead of money, and contentment will characterize your life.

Dear Lord, may contentment rule my heart. May I focus on my blessings rather than on what I think I am lacking. Amen.

DAY 63

Practical Financial Wisdom

For the love of money is a root of all kinds of evil.
Some people, eager for money, have wandered from
the faith and pierced themselves with many griefs.

1 TIMOTHY 6:10

$\mathscr{P}$ractical financial wisdom should be based on biblical principles. The Bible has much to say about money and stewardship. Here are some principles to consider:

1. Acknowledge that everything we have comes from God. He has given us the physical and/or mental capacities to earn money. He has opened the doors of opportunity. Thank Him!
2. We have been entrusted with God's money. Take this seriously. We will be held accountable for what we do with what we have been given. God expects us to be good stewards.
3. God has blessed us so that we can be a blessing. Choose to be a conduit that allows His resources to overflow to others.
4. Prayerfully set financial goals. Ask the Lord to help you prioritize your spending. Be willing to let spiritual needs trump temporal wants.
5. Live below your financial means so that you can direct your money instead of having your money control you.

Dear Lord, show me how to apply biblical principles to
my finances. May I manage my finances well so that I
may bless others with what You have given me. Amen.

Day 64

Financial Giving

Calling his disciples to him, Jesus said, "Truly I tell you,
this poor widow has put more into the treasury than all
the others. They all gave out of their wealth; but she, out of
her poverty, put in everything—all she had to live on."

Mark 12:43–44

Each of you should give what you have decided in your heart to give, not reluctantly or under compulsion, for God loves a cheerful giver" (2 Corinthians 9:7). In Mark 12, Jesus draws a contrast between the offering of a poor widow and the gifts of many rich people. It was not the amount that concerned Jesus, but the attitude of the giver's heart. The rich people "threw in large amounts." Perhaps they thought, "There! I have done my part. I feel good about myself!" The poor widow "put in two very small copper coins." Jesus said that it was everything she had to live on. She sacrificed it all and gave what she felt the Lord was asking of her.

What is your attitude about giving? To some degree do you give so others will take note of your generosity? What if the Lord called you to sacrifice as the widow did? Would you be willing to give with a cheerful heart?

Dear Lord, change my heart. Give me the desire to
give financially in order to further Your kingdom.
May my attitude be pleasing to You. Amen.

Day 65

Righteous vs. Unrighteous

*Blessed is the one who does not walk in step with the wicked
or stand in the way that sinners take or sit in the seat of
mockers, but whose delight is in the law of the Lord,
and who meditates on his law day and night.*

Psalm 1:1–2

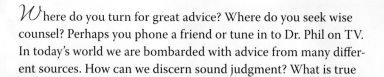

Where do you turn for great advice? Where do you seek wise counsel? Perhaps you phone a friend or tune in to Dr. Phil on TV. In today's world we are bombarded with advice from many different sources. How can we discern sound judgment? What is true wisdom based on?

Check the counsel you receive with what God's Word says. The Bible is truth. Anything that opposes truth is a lie. Be discerning. There is joy in obeying God. God blesses those who refuse to listen to advice from the ungodly. The wicked will lead us down a path that separates us from God. We do not want to follow them down that road.

The righteous mediate on God's Word day and night. They have a firm foundation that cannot be destroyed. They will prosper because they trust God for *everything*. God will be faithful to always watch over the righteous.

*Dear Lord, may I be in Your Word so that I can discern
between godly and ungodly advice. May I run from
those who seek to separate me from You. Amen.*

Day 66

Forgiveness

*If we confess our sins, he is faithful and just and will
forgive us our sins and purify us from all unrighteousness.*

1 John 1:9

*W*hat a great promise! If we confess our sins, God is faithful to
forgive us. He will *always* forgive, regardless of how many times we
have committed the same sin. He will remove our sin as far as the
east is from the west. He will remember it no more.

When we feel guilty, it's as though our conscience is throwing up a red flag signaling trouble. God is our eternal source of truth. Ask Him to help identify the source of guilt. If you have sinned, confess and agree with God. He will forgive. Then make an about-face and ask the Lord to give you strength to proceed in the opposite direction going forward.

We must also forgive those who have hurt us. Forgiveness is essential to spiritual growth. Forgiving others demonstrates our willingness to allow God to be the One to deal with persons who have brought hurt into our lives. Forgiveness is difficult but not impossible with God's help.

*Dear Lord, thank You for forgiving me over and over again. May I
believe that You have truly removed my sin as far as the east is from
the west. May I be willing to forgive others in Your name. Amen.*

Day 67

The Struggle of the Flesh

*So I say, walk by the Spirit, and you
will not gratify the desires of the flesh.*
GALATIANS 5:16

When we come to accept Jesus as our personal Lord and Savior, we are given a new nature—a spiritual one. Unfortunately we still have our fleshly nature to deal with. The fleshly nature opposes God because it would rather be in control than submit. The flesh is revealed in our attitudes, desires, lifestyles, and thoughts. There will always be a constant battle going on. (See the apostle Paul's lament in Romans 7:14–25.)

How do we deal with this continual struggle? The solution is a Christ-centered life as opposed to a self-centered one. Galatians 5:16–26 describes the contrasting results. When we put Christ on the throne of our lives, we give the Holy Spirit control. We submit to His authority. The fruit of the Spirit is evident: "Love, joy, peace, forbearance, kindness, goodness, faithfulness, gentleness and self-control." When we are in control, the following are obvious: "Hatred, discord, jealousy, fits of rage, selfish ambition. . .and envy." Which list characterizes your life? Put Christ on the throne of your heart and experience the abundant life promised in John 10:10.

*Dear Lord, it seems like I struggle most days. I try to run
my own life and then fall flat on my face. Instead, may I
put Christ on the throne and be directed by You. Amen.*

DAY 68

Power over Sin

But because of his great love for us, God, who is rich in mercy,
made us alive with Christ even when we were dead in
transgressions—it is by grace you have been saved.

EPHESIANS 2:4–5

Sin causes death—physical as well as spiritual. Sin separates and alienates us from God. However, when we were powerless because of sin, God sent Jesus to deliver us. Salvation is by faith. There is nothing we can do to earn it. We need only to accept His free gift of eternal life.

Although we may be heaven-bound, we are not sinless. We still struggle with our fallen nature, which is in opposition to God. This fallen nature cannot be improved, disciplined, changed, or redeemed apart from God. Only God can successfully deal with the flesh.

Through Jesus' death and resurrection, He demonstrated power over sin and death. When we accept Him, He imparts that power to us through the Holy Spirit, who resides in every believer. Therefore, we can experience victory over sin in our lives. Just as we rely solely on Jesus to save our souls, we must rely solely on Him on a daily basis to break the chains of sin. Let's walk daily in the victory He has given us.

Dear Lord, thank You for Your grace and
the victory that is mine because of You. Amen.

DAY 69

Temptation

*No temptation has overtaken you except what is common to
mankind. And God is faithful; he will not let you be tempted
beyond what you can bear. But when you are tempted,
he will also provide a way out so that you can endure it.*

1 CORINTHIANS 10:13

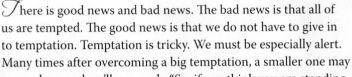

There is good news and bad news. The bad news is that all of
us are tempted. The good news is that we do not have to give in
to temptation. Temptation is tricky. We must be especially alert.
Many times after overcoming a big temptation, a smaller one may
come along and we'll succumb. "So, if you think you are standing
firm, be careful that you don't fall!" (1 Corinthians 10:12).

Pray for a wise and discerning heart. Temptation comes
when we least expect it. Often temptation follows a mountaintop
experience. Perhaps we have become "puffed up" and pride blinds
us from relying solely on the Lord. Or maybe we are experiencing
loneliness, hardship, or grief and we mistakenly conclude that
God has forgotten us. In those times, be alert to your vulnerability.
Look for the "way out" that God is providing for you. Then choose
to take it! He *is* faithful! Allow Him to give you victory over temptation and enable you to stand.

*Dear Lord, may I be aware of my own vulnerability. May I
look to You for the way of escape when I am tempted. Amen.*

Day 70

Jesus Sympathizes

For we do not have a high priest who is unable to empathize with our weaknesses, but we have one who has been tempted in every way, just as we are—yet he did not sin.

HEBREWS 4:15

———✦———

We all face temptation. It's comforting to know that even Jesus was tempted, just as we are. The difference is—He never sinned. He *always* stood firm. He never gave in. That is good news for us! He knows how we feel under the weight of temptation. We are not alone. He is with us. And because Jesus never sinned, He can provide the strength we need to say no to every dark thought or evil imagination. He can give us the power to resist temptation.

God's mighty armor is sufficient for us. The apostle Paul describes the spiritual armor we have been given in Ephesians 6:10–17. "Take up the shield of faith, with which you can extinguish all the flaming arrows of the evil one." Do not become discouraged when you are tempted. Instead, allow your faith to enable you to stand. It is your shield! Confidently come to God and receive grace and mercy to help in your time of need.

Dear Lord, it is comforting to know that You faced the same temptations I face. Help me come to You when I am tempted and receive Your help to stand firm. Amen.

DAY 71

Guilt

If we claim to be without sin, we deceive ourselves and the truth is not in us. If we confess our sins, he is faithful and just and will forgive us our sins and purify us from all unrighteousness.

1 JOHN 1:8–9

The truth is plain: "All have sinned and fall short of the glory of God" (Romans 3:23). So, what do we do with the guilt that is associated with our sin? What if our guilt feels like a huge 18-wheeler bearing down on us? What if, regardless of how fast we run or where we try to hide, we cannot escape the guilt we carry with us?

Guilt indicates that we are still carrying the weight of our sin on our shoulders. We are failing to believe that we have truly been forgiven. Truth asserts that Jesus bore the full weight of our sin on Calvary. He declared, "It is finished."

Jesus died to forgive us and set us free from the penalty of our sin—set us free from guilt. We need to walk in this truth by forgiving ourselves and leaving our guilt at the foot of the cross. We do not have to harbor or hide guilt. It should never rule our life. God has made provision for it through Jesus. Receive His marvelous free gift of grace today!

Dear Lord, there are some things I continually beat myself up about. I replay my sin over and over until guilt overwhelms me. May I believe Your truth: I am forgiven! Amen.

DAY 72

God, Our Creator

LORD, our Lord, how majestic is your name in all the earth!
You have set your glory in the heavens. Through the praise of
children and infants you have established a stronghold against
your enemies, to silence the foe and the avenger. When I consider
your heavens, the work of your fingers, the moon and the stars,
which you have set in place, what is mankind that you are
mindful of them, human beings that you care for them?

PSALM 8:1–4

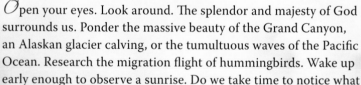

*O*pen your eyes. Look around. The splendor and majesty of God surrounds us. Ponder the massive beauty of the Grand Canyon, an Alaskan glacier calving, or the tumultuous waves of the Pacific Ocean. Research the migration flight of hummingbirds. Wake up early enough to observe a sunrise. Do we take time to notice what God has created? If so, what is our response? Do we give Him praise?

God's splendor is displayed above the heavens; the work of His fingers. He has ordained the moon and the stars. He has placed humans in charge of His creation. We are to rule over the animals and fish of the sea. How majestic is God's name! How awesome is His creation!

Dear Lord, open my eyes. May I see you in creation and marvel at who You are. May I give praise to You as Creator God! Amen.

Day 73

Revival

"If my people, who are called by my name, will humble themselves and pray and seek my face and turn from their wicked ways, then I will hear from heaven, and I will forgive their sin and will heal their land."

2 Chronicles 7:14

The spiritual journey of the Israelites was extremely tumultuous. In times of prosperity and blessing, they would become proud and arrogant. Choosing to live life by their own standards, they would turn their backs on the Lord and forsake Him. In love, God would discipline them and allow hardship to enter their lives. In their pain, the Israelites would cry out to God for relief and mercy. God would faithfully forgive their rebellion, only to have the cycle repeat itself over and over again. Does any of this sound familiar?

God desires revival. He longs for hearts to turn to Him. In order for revival to occur in a church or nation, the following conditions must occur in individual hearts:

1. The people must humble themselves before God.
2. The people must pray.
3. The people must seek God's will.
4. The people must turn from their sinful ways.

Then God will hear, forgive their sin, and heal their land. Let's learn from the Israelites and purpose to walk with the Lord in times of prosperity or peril.

Dear Lord, our churches and nation need You. May we humbly pray and desire to turn from our sinful ways. Bring revival today! Amen.

Day 74

God Reveals Himself to Us

The heavens declare the glory of God; the skies proclaim
the work of his hands. Day after day they pour forth
speech; night after night they reveal knowledge.

PSALM 19:1–2

God reveals Himself to us in many ways. The apostle Paul asserts that creation itself proves that God exists. "The wrath of God is being revealed from heaven against all the godlessness and wickedness of people, who suppress the truth by their wickedness, since what may be known about God is plain to them, because God has made it plain to them. For since the creation of the world God's invisible qualities—his eternal power and divine nature—have been clearly seen, being understood from what has been made, so that people are without excuse" (Romans 1:18–20).

God also reveals Himself through those who proclaim His Word: pastors and teachers. The Bible itself is God's Word. Sometimes God makes Himself known through the circumstances of our lives—good times or difficult ones. Christian friends can speak God's truth to our hearts. Prayer ushers us into God's presence. Jesus Christ is God in the flesh.

Are our spiritual eyes open to "see" God at work around us? Do we declare His glory?

Dear Lord, help me to be aware of You every day. You are constantly
revealing Yourself to me, yet I miss You time and time again. Give me
spiritual eyes to "see" so that I may give You praise! Amen.

Day 75

The Struggle of Unforgiveness

Be kind and compassionate to one another,
forgiving each other, just as in Christ God forgave you.
EPHESIANS 4:32

Do we really understand what God has done for us through Jesus Christ? When it comes to forgiveness, God forgives us on the basis of Christ's finished work on the cross, not on anything we have done or failed to do.

Grace means freely giving us what we don't deserve. We don't deserve forgiveness because we are sinners, yet God imputed Christ's righteousness to us and forgave our sins—that is *grace*. Accept God's forgiveness, which He freely gives.

Mercy means withholding what we do deserve. We deserve death for the punishment of our sin (see Romans 6:23). Instead, God poured out His wrath against sin on Jesus and withheld it from us—that is *mercy*. "But he was pierced for our transgressions, he was crushed for our iniquities; the punishment that brought us peace was upon him, and by his wounds we are healed" (Isaiah 53:5). Forgiveness encompasses both grace and mercy. Since we have been the recipients of God's grace and mercy, let's be quick to extend forgiveness to others.

Dear Lord, sometimes I have been so hurt by others,
it is hard to forgive. But when I am reminded of what
Jesus suffered on the cross on my behalf, it puts my pain
in perspective and enables me to forgive others. Amen.

DAY 76

God's Forgiveness

*But you are a forgiving God, gracious and compassionate,
slow to anger and abounding in love.*

NEHEMIAH 9:17

❦

Forgiveness from God's perspective is immediate. He doesn't make us wait and wonder if He might withhold forgiveness from us this time. The moment we confess, He forgives. Be sensitive to the still, small voice of the Holy Spirit. God's Spirit is moving in our lives. A wonderful blessing comes when we obey the promptings of the Holy Spirit. When convicted, be quick to confess. Desire forgiveness and immediately ask for it. Keep short accounts with the Lord.

God forgives our sin and remembers it no more. It is over and done with! He removes it as far as the east is from the west. And that is far! How *great* is our Lord! He is gracious and compassionate. So refuse to beat yourself up over your shortcomings and regrets. Living in the past affects enjoyment of today. The Lord wants you to learn from your mistakes so that you can move forward in a positive way. Do not allow the failings of your past to impede forward progress today! You are not condemned. You are forgiven! Receive God's forgiveness this very moment.

*Dear Lord, thank You for Your unconditional love!
May I receive Your forgiveness and know in my heart
that You do not count my sins against me. Amen.*

Day 77

Jealousy

And from that time on Saul kept a close eye on David.
1 Samuel 18:9

$\mathcal{D}$avid was a loyal warrior for King Saul. However, when David began receiving more praise than King Saul, Saul quickly became jealous of David (1 Samuel 18:5–16). Over time, King Saul's jealousy escalated to hatred and rage. "Saul was afraid of David, because the LORD was with David but had departed from Saul" (1 Samuel 18:12). Although King Saul made many attempts on David's life, God protected him and spared his life.

Our jealousy may not incite us to want to kill someone, but we can all relate to feelings of jealousy. Someone gets the promotion that we think we deserved. A friend builds his dream home while we're still stuck in our two-bedroom apartment. Our neighbor seems to have the perfect family.

Jealousy leads to irrational behavior. It brings about confusion, bitterness, fear, resentment, and anxiety. Jealousy is an emotion indicating that we are in disagreement over what God is doing in another person's life. The truth of the matter is that we need to concentrate on what God is doing in our own! When a jealous thought enters your mind, confess it. Do not allow jealousy to get a foothold and escalate over time!

Dear Lord, jealousy is a human emotion, yet that does not excuse it. May I rejoice with others rather than become jealous of their accomplishments or successes. Amen.

Humility—
the Divine Antidote for Jealousy

Who is wise and understanding among you? Let them show it by their good life, by deeds done in the humility that comes from wisdom.

JAMES 3:13

*J*ames asserts that godly wisdom produces humility. True humility involves seeing ourselves and others through God's eyes. Paul exhorts us in Philippians 2:3–4 to "do nothing out of selfish ambition or vain conceit. Rather, in humility value others above yourselves, not looking to your own interests but each of you to the interests of the others."

Jealousy is born when we see others through our own eyes. We judge and compare. We decide if life is fair from our perspective. Jealousy is born when we deem ourselves worthier to receive what another has been given.

The divine antidote for jealousy is humility. Humility enables us to want the best for others rather than becoming jealous of what they have been given. The Lord gives and the Lord takes away. We should be content with what He gives us and not jealous of what He might shower upon another. When we lead blameless lives, we can have confidence that God will lead us, protect us, and meet all of our needs.

Dear Lord, may I gain godly wisdom and humility.
May I love my fellow man and be content in You. Amen.

DAY 79

Intimacy with God

*Going a little farther, he fell with his face to the ground
and prayed, "My Father, if it is possible, may this cup
be taken from me. Yet not as I will, but as you will."*

MATTHEW 26:39

Jesus took His disciples to Gethsemane, an olive grove, prior to His arrest. He sought time alone with His heavenly Father as He anticipated the events that would soon unfold. Jesus knew what lay ahead. How did He respond to the intense emotional pain and sorrow He experienced in the Garden of Gethsemane? He went to His heavenly Father in prayer and asked for his disciples to intercede as well. He was honest yet submissive. Although He did not want to face death, He was willing to submit to His Father's will.

If we really want a personal, intimate relationship with God, we too must be humble and open before Him. Although He knows us through and through, He desires for us to be completely honest with Him about our emotions, concerns, and thoughts. Never hold back the details. He is able to handle it! He is the only One who will love us unconditionally, regardless of our emotional state. Let's follow Jesus' example by honestly communicating with our heavenly Father.

*Dear Lord, why do I sometimes hold back with You?
You are omniscient. May I be real with You and
experience Your unconditional love. Amen.*

Day 80

Praising God

When hard pressed, I cried to the LORD; he brought me
into a spacious place. The LORD is with me; I will
not be afraid. What can mere mortals do to me?

PSALM 118:5–6

There are many circumstances in life that can leave us reeling emotionally: a business collapse, terminal illness, divorce, or job termination. We feel forsaken, alone, and afraid. We may not know how to take the next step. We wonder if life will ever be "normal" again.

When life throws us a curve ball, there are spiritual truths we must remember. God is good. His love endures forever. He hears my cries to Him. He has set me free! I will not be afraid because He is always with me. He is my helper.

Trusting God instead of man is the answer. God will never let me down. God will never leave me. God will never forsake me. He is my strength. His right hand has done mighty things. He disciplines me for my own good because He loves me. God will use all things—even what I am experiencing now—for good in my life. As we recount God's promises, we are able to give Him praise. He will see us through!

Lord, the words I utter could never praise You enough!
May my life be an offering of praise to You. Amen.

Day 81

Prayer

Pray continually.
1 Thessalonians 5:17

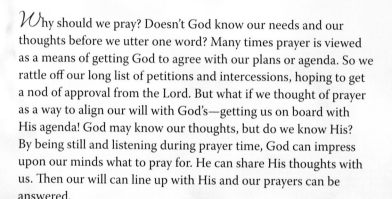

*W*hy should we pray? Doesn't God know our needs and our thoughts before we utter one word? Many times prayer is viewed as a means of getting God to agree with our plans or agenda. So we rattle off our long list of petitions and intercessions, hoping to get a nod of approval from the Lord. But what if we thought of prayer as a way to align our will with God's—getting us on board with His agenda! God may know our thoughts, but do we know His? By being still and listening during prayer time, God can impress upon our minds what to pray for. He can share His thoughts with us. Then our will can line up with His and our prayers can be answered.

God is constantly working in the world around us. He wants us to be involved in His work, too. When we pray and He answers, our faith skyrockets! We catch a glimpse of what He is doing in the spiritual realm. God desires for us to be dependent on Him, trusting that He truly knows what is best. Prayer enables us to grow in our intimacy with Him. Our relationship with God is built on two-way communication. So pray continually and listen intently!

Dear Lord, impress upon my heart the importance
of communicating with You at all times.
Align my will with Yours. Amen.

DAY 82

Doubt

Be strong and courageous, because you will lead these people to inherit the land I swore to their ancestors to give them.

JOSHUA 1:6

After Moses' death, the Lord appointed Joshua to lead the Israelites into the Promised Land. Even though God had prepared Joshua for this assignment, Joshua was afraid that he would not be up for the task. Knowing his fear, God encouraged him by saying, "Be strong and courageous. Do not be afraid; do not be discouraged, for the LORD your God will be with you wherever you go" (Joshua 1:9).

God may not be calling you to lead anyone into the Promised Land, but He has called you to something. Perhaps fear and doubt have gripped your heart because you feel inadequate for the task. There are many reasons for doubt, including sin and guilt, previous failures, negative influence of others, or a wrong focus. Doubt paralyzes our walk with God. When doubt enters our minds, we need to *meditate* on God's Word—read it, study it, and ponder it. As we ask God questions and He answers us, our faith will grow. Fear and doubt will be left in the dust.

Whatever God calls you to do, He will also equip you to carry it out. The same God who was with Joshua is with you! Remember this: "God will be with you wherever you go!"

Dear Lord, You know my struggles with fear and doubt.
Help me meditate on Your Word so that I can
experience Your presence today. Amen.

DAY 83

Persistence

*"So I say to you: Ask and it will be given to you; seek and
you will find; knock and the door will be opened to you."*

LUKE 11:9

$\mathcal{A}$sk. Seek. Knock. These verbs in the original text mean "keep
on asking, keep on seeking, and keep on knocking." Persistence
is one of the major keys to answered prayer. Yet how often do
we become discouraged when our prayers are not immediately
answered? God answers our prayers in one of three ways: yes, no,
or maybe. Many times we misinterpret "maybe" to mean "no."
"Maybe" could simply mean "yes, but not right now."

" 'For my thoughts are not your thoughts, neither are your
ways my ways,' declares the LORD. 'As the heavens are higher than
the earth, so are my ways higher than your ways and my thoughts
than your thoughts' " (Isaiah 55:8–9). Trust that there are reasons God might delay answering your prayer. Never give up or
lose hope. Keep on asking. Keep on seeking. Keep on knocking.
Eliminate impatience by recognizing that God's timing is for your
best. Trust that He will bring about His perfect will in His perfect
timing. No plan of God's can be thwarted.

*Dear Lord, may I pray with persistence. Help me trust
that in Your perfect timing You will answer my
prayers according to Your perfect will. Amen.*

DAY 84

Intercessory Prayer

For this reason, since the day we heard about you, we have not stopped praying for you. We continually ask God to fill you with the knowledge of his will through all the wisdom and understanding that the Spirit gives.

COLOSSIANS 1:9

$\mathcal{D}$o you enjoy praying for others? The apostle Paul viewed intercessory prayer as a privilege. He was always praying specifically for fellow believers that he had met on his missionary travels.

Paul prayed for the believers at Colosse. The following list of requests found in Colossians 1:9–14 are excellent examples for us to use when praying for others:

1. That they be filled with the knowledge of God's will.
2. That they may walk in a manner worthy of the Lord.
3. That they may bear fruit in every good work.
4. That they may increase in the knowledge of God.
5. That they may be strengthened and sustained with the power of God.
6. That they may give thanks for all things.
7. That they may have great endurance and patience.

When we pray scripture, we don't have to wonder if it's in accordance with His will. His Word is truth. Let's boldly pray, and watch God intercede!

Dear Lord, may I be faithful to pray for others.
Thank You for those in my life who pray for me! Amen.

DAY 85

God's Pruning

*"I am the true vine, and my Father is the gardener. He cuts off
every branch in me that bears no fruit, while every branch that
does bear fruit he prunes so that it will be even more fruitful."*
JOHN 15:1–2

Many times Jesus used examples in everyday life to illustrate
spiritual truth. His audience could relate to tending sheep, fishing,
and gardening. In this passage of scripture, Jesus says that He is the
vine and His heavenly Father is the gardener. We are branches that
require pruning. Just what does that mean?

Gardeners use pruning shears to remove dead branches. Fruitful branches must be pruned in order to stimulate new growth. In
the same way, our heavenly Father is the vinedresser of our lives.
He removes old habits, attitudes, and desires that prove harmful
and sinful. God prunes fruitful areas of our lives so they may become even more productive.

Spiritual pruning is painful. But take heart. God only prunes
what is necessary for a vital and healthy spiritual life. He desires for
us to produce abundant spiritual fruit. We see new growth as our
relationship with Him is nurtured. Are we allowing God to prune us?

*Dear Lord, may I submit to Your pruning. Although it is painful,
may I know at the same time that "it is good." Amen.*

Day 86

A Focused Life

Fixing our eyes on Jesus, the pioneer and perfecter of faith.
For the joy set before him he endured the cross, scorning its shame,
and sat down at the right hand of the throne of God.

HEBREWS 12:2

After feeding five thousand people, Jesus sent His disciples in a boat to the other side of the Sea of Galilee. He then dismissed the crowd and went off by himself to pray. During the night, Jesus decided to join the disciples by walking on the water toward them. The disciples were terrified! Yet once Peter knew it was Jesus, he wanted to walk out to Him. Everything was fine until Peter's eyes were diverted. You probably know the rest of the story (see Matthew 14:22–36).

Prayerful devotion is essential if we are to live a spiritually focused life. We must keep our eyes on Jesus. When our attention is diverted, we easily fall into trouble by succumbing to our circumstances. Remember Peter? As long as he kept his eyes on Jesus, he was able to walk on water. But when he allowed the waves and wind to distract him, Peter quickly began to sink.

When we focus on Jesus in *all things*, we will be free from worry and doubt. We are assured that He has the complete ability to take care of our every need. Because He loves us, He has promised abundant blessings. Let's learn from Peter and keep our eyes fixed on Jesus during the storms of life.

Dear Lord, may I always keep my eyes on You and not on my circumstances. Thank You for Your love and provision. Amen.

A Lamb without Blemish

For you know that it was not with perishable things such as silver or gold that you were redeemed from the empty way of life handed down to you from your ancestors, but with the precious blood of Christ, a lamb without blemish or defect.

1 Peter 1:18–19

Passover is the most important Jewish holiday. It speaks of God's redemption and the deliverance of His chosen people. The Israelites found themselves in Egypt because of a great famine. Over time, the Egyptians enslaved them, forbidding them to return to their homeland. Studying about the Passover in Exodus 12–14 helps us understand our faith in a deeper way.

The blood of an unblemished lamb was put over the doorposts of each Israelite home. When the angel of death "passed over" those houses, the lives of the firstborn male children were spared. In contrast, every firstborn son in Egypt died. Only then did Pharaoh consent to let the Israelites go.

Over 1,400 years later, when John the Baptist saw Jesus approaching him, he proclaimed, "Look, the Lamb of God, who takes away the sin of the world!" (John 1:29). Jesus is our Passover Lamb! When we accept Jesus as Savior, His blood covers our sin. The angel of death will "pass over" us. We have been given eternal life! Hallelujah!

Dear Lord, thank You for sending your Son, Jesus, as the lamb without blemish. Thank You that I have been given eternal life through Him! Amen.

Day 88

The Resurrection

*But Christ has indeed been raised from the dead, the firstfruits
of those who have fallen asleep. For since death came through a
man, the resurrection of the dead comes also through a man.
For as in Adam all die, so in Christ all will be made alive.*

1 Corinthians 15:20–22

Three days after Jesus was crucified, He rose from the dead! He
then spent forty days on earth before ascending to heaven. During
that time Jesus walked through a locked door to show Thomas the
scars on His hands. He cooked breakfast for the disciples on the
beach and reinstated Peter. These occurrences are proof that Jesus
was indeed raised from the dead!

Just as death came through one man, Adam, eternal life comes
to us through another man, Jesus Christ. The spiritual condemnation that we inherited through Adam was settled at Calvary's cross.
Through Christ's death and resurrection, all of our sins have been
forgiven—past, present, and future. God raised Jesus from the
dead. Jesus now sits at His Father's right hand in heaven. Someday,
we, too, will be raised to live with Him forever.

This profound truth should impact our daily lives. If we know
where we are going, the future should hold no fear. If we know to
whom we belong, the past should hold no regret. We can live in
the present with hope and thanksgiving.

*Dear Lord, may I truly comprehend all that Your
resurrection means. Thank You for making an
eternal difference in my life! Amen.*

Day 89

Our Resurrected Bodies

There are also heavenly bodies and there are earthly bodies;
but the splendor of the heavenly bodies is one kind,
and the splendor of the earthly bodies is another.

1 Corinthians 15:40

There is much about heaven and our resurrected bodies that is not revealed in scripture. Perhaps God in His wisdom knew that we would be unable to comprehend it all. It would be like trying to describe our present life to an unborn baby. However, we can glean some understanding by looking at Jesus' resurrected body.

After Jesus' resurrection He appeared to His disciples. He reinstated Peter and showed His scars to "Doubting Thomas." Although His body was flesh and bones, He had the ability to walk through locked doors. Jesus ate a piece of broiled fish in their presence. He could appear and disappear. Jesus was recognized when He broke bread with His disciples. There is no reason to think that our resurrected bodies will be any different.

Just because we cannot comprehend this marvelous mystery does not make it any less true. By faith we can embrace all that the Lord has for us!

Dear Lord, my finite mind cannot comprehend all that You
have in store for me. Help me trust You with truths that I cannot
fully understand. May I rejoice in the knowledge that, like You,
someday I, too, will have a resurrected body! Amen.

DAY 90

He Is Risen!

In their fright the women bowed down with their faces to the ground, but the men said to them, "Why do you look for the living among the dead? He is not here; he has risen!"

LUKE 24:5–6

After Jesus' death, women took prepared spices and perfumes to His tomb. Upon arriving they noticed that the stone had been rolled away, so they entered the tomb. But His body was gone! Could this mean that someone had stolen Jesus' body? As they were wondering about this, an angel appeared to confirm Jesus' resurrection!

" 'Death has been swallowed up in victory. Where, O death, is your victory? Where, O death, is your sting?' The sting of death is sin, and the power of sin is the law. But thanks be to God! He gives us the victory through our Lord Jesus Christ" (1 Corinthians 15:54–57).

Christ's resurrection is a glorious reality! His resurrection solidifies our faith. We are guaranteed our own resurrection someday. Death has been destroyed! His resurrection brings us hope and assurance. If Jesus were still in His grave, our faith would be futile and we would be objects of pity. Hallelujah, He is risen!

Dear Lord, You have indeed risen! You are alive!
Death has been defeated once and for all. Thank You for
giving me life through Your death and resurrection. Amen.

DAY 91

Remain

*"I am the vine; you are the branches. If you remain in me and I in
you, you will bear much fruit; apart from me you can do nothing."*
JOHN 15:5

If a branch becomes severed from a tree, it ceases to remain
alive. The leaves wither and the wood rots because it is no longer
connected to its life-giving source. This illustration from nature
reminds us of spiritual truth. Jesus is our life-giving Vine. We must
remain in fellowship with Him in order to produce spiritual fruit.
We can do nothing that is of spiritual value in our own strength.
Apart from Him, we are dead.

The greatest hindrance to our peace and victory is the flesh.
When we become absorbed in our own troubles, cares, rights, or
wrongs, our focus becomes physical rather than spiritual. We lose
communion with God. It's as if we have severed ourselves from
the vine. A cloud of darkness falls over our spirits. There is *nothing*
we can do to remove it. But praise be to God Almighty! He can
and will restore our fellowship if we but seek Him. It is *all* for the
asking! Return to the life-giving Vine.

*Dear Lord, I want to abide with You at all times. Yet sometimes
I become so absorbed in my own troubles that I forget to focus
on You. Help me, Lord! I desperately need You! Amen.*

DAY 92

Intimacy with God

Jesus answered, "I am the way and the truth and the life.
No one comes to the Father except through me.
If you really know me, you will know my Father as well."

JOHN 14:6–7

*H*ow do we become intimate with God? Get to know Jesus—He is the way to God. God created man to be in relationship with Him. Unfortunately Adam's sin created a huge chasm between a Holy God and sinful man. But God, in His love, sent His Son, Jesus, to bridge that gap. We can now come into a relationship with our heavenly Father.

Like any relationship, we grow closer to Jesus by spending time with Him. Prayer is our form of communication. Bible reading immerses our minds with His thoughts and truth. Meditation allows the Holy Spirit to whisper to our heart.

The visible result of an intimate relationship with God is the bearing of spiritual fruit. As we grow in our knowledge of Jesus, we are conformed to His image. Our thoughts and actions emulate His. We gain understanding and compassion. Because we are never alone, we can continually pour out our hearts to Him. Our lives will show evidence that Jesus has complete control.

Dear Lord, thank You that I can have an intimate
relationship with You because of Jesus. Continue
to conform me to the image of Your Son. Amen.

God Is Our Keeper

I lift up my eyes to the mountains—where does my help come from?
My help comes from the LORD, the Maker of heaven and earth.
PSALM 121:1–2

Where do we go for help? If our tire suddenly goes flat while driving, we call roadside assistance. When we get sick, we make an appointment with the doctor. We call the plumber for a clogged drain. But what happens when life is spinning out of control? Where do we go for help when our world seems to be falling apart? Who is the expert in matters of life?

Why not cry out to the Author of life? There is never a time when we are outside the loving care of our heavenly Father. We never face our trials alone. He stands guard over our lives. He is our keeper. He is the beginning and the end—the Alpha and Omega.

We may fall asleep, but God never does. He does not sleep nor slumber. He preserves our souls. His love is unconditional. God has promised victory and blessing to all who trust Him with their lives. Rest in the arms of your heavenly Father today, and know that you are well cared for!

Dear Lord, thank You for watching over me at all times.
May I rest safe and secure in Your loving arms. Amen.

Day 94

Delight in the Lord

Take delight in the LORD, and he
will give you the desires of your heart.

PSALM 37:4

———※———

*W*hat exactly does this verse mean? To delight in the Lord means to take pleasure in His presence—to enjoy spending time together and growing in our relationship. His priorities become our priorities. We typically conclude that if we delight ourselves in Him, then He will give us what we desire. In other words, He will grant us our desires because we have delighted in Him. Possibly.

But what if the desires came from Him instead of from us? In other words, when our delight is in the Lord, He imparts desires within our hearts. This interpretation is consistent with Jesus' words in Matthew 6:33: "But seek first his kingdom and his righteousness, and all these things will be given to you as well." If we delight in the Lord, we seek His kingdom above all else. He then gives us desires in our hearts that are consistent with His will. His desires become our desires. We are fulfilled and satisfied. We are in the center of His will. Let's delight in the Lord today!

Dear Lord, may I truly find my delight in You.
Then my desires will be Your desires. May it be so! Amen.

What Is of Value?

*But whatever were gains to me I now consider loss for the sake of
Christ. What is more, I consider everything a loss because of the
surpassing worth of knowing Christ Jesus my Lord, for whose sake I
have lost all things. I consider them garbage, that I may gain Christ.*

PHILIPPIANS 3:7–8

❧

From an earthly perspective, Saul had every reason to brag.
He was a Jew from the tribe of Benjamin. As a Pharisee, he had
meticulously kept the law. Saul had education and determination.
The world was at his fingertips. Then Saul met Jesus on the road to
Damascus, and in an instant everything changed. He became the
apostle Paul and later declared that knowing Jesus was greater than
any worldly achievement or birthright.

What achievements do you value? Our accomplishments here
on earth are of no consequence unless they are in the service of His
name. A relationship with Christ surpasses *everything* we've ever
done. May we be willing to lay aside those things that only have
temporal value in order to gain eternal riches. Knowing the Lord is
the greatest treasure we could ever possess.

*Dear Lord, search me. Am I more excited about my earthly
accomplishments or the fact that I know You? Help me
realize that You are my most valuable gift. Amen.*

DAY 96

How to Know God Intimately

I want to know Christ—yes, to know the power of
his resurrection and participation in his sufferings.
PHILIPPIANS 3:10

God longs for us to know Him intimately. He sent His Son, Jesus Christ, so that a personal relationship with us could be possible. God reveals Jesus throughout scripture. The Old Testament prophesies His coming, while the New Testament reveals the fulfillment of that prophecy. If we desire to know God, we can begin by studying the Bible and getting to know Jesus.

Spending time alone with God in prayer and meditation also draws us close. Talking and listening are both components of prayer. Meditation involves pondering and thinking about truth, digesting it with our minds. God's truth can then begin to move from our heads to our hearts.

Once truth is planted in our hearts, we can step out in faithful obedience. Trusting the Lord in *all* things enables us to see Christ in every circumstance. He imparts power and gives grace amid suffering. Let's desire to know God intimately. Open your Bible today, and allow Him to speak to your heart. The more time you spend with Him, the deeper your relationship will grow.

Dear Lord, I do want to know You more. Help me set aside
time to read the Bible and pray. Help me step out in
obedience. Grow my relationship with You! Amen.

Day 97

A Doer of the Word

Do not merely listen to the word,
and so deceive yourselves. Do what it says.

James 1:22

James uses an illustration of a mirror to make a point about obedience. He says that listening to God's Word and failing to obey it is like looking at yourself in the mirror and then forgetting what you look like the second you turn away from the mirror. God's Word needs to make such an indelible impression on our minds that we live it out in obedience. Truth needs to move from our heads to our hearts.

We may know truth, but when we are facing a difficult trial, obedience may seem impossible. Yet that is the very moment when obedience is necessary. We obey as an act of our will, even though we may not feel like it.

Our true character is revealed when we are under pressure. Keep in mind that God uses trials to test our faith. Perseverance is learned. Spiritual maturity is the result. When we understand that there is a spiritual purpose behind our trials, we are able to rejoice because God is working in our lives. God will bless us when we are doers of His Word!

Dear Lord, I want to know Your Word and obey it. Change my heart to desire to obey You even in the midst of the trials I face. May I see the bigger picture so that I can appreciate Your purposes. Amen.

DAY 98

False Teachers

For certain individuals whose condemnation was written about
long ago have secretly slipped in among you. They are ungodly
people, who pervert the grace of our God into a license for
immorality and deny Jesus Christ our only Sovereign and Lord.
JUDE 4

Jude warns about false teachers and scoffers in the last days. Paul says: "For the time will come when people will not put up with sound doctrine. Instead, to suit their own desires, they will gather around them a great number of teachers to say what their itching ears want to hear. They will turn their ears away from the truth and turn aside to myths" (2 Timothy 4:3–4).

We do not have to look very far. False teachers are rampant in our society: practicioners of Scientology, New Age spirituality, and Christian Science do not base their doctrine on biblical truth. Even some Christian churches have twisted God's Word to suit today's culture. False teachers are exposed in the light of God's Word. The Bible is the authority on which truth stands. Be aware. Be bold. Seek sound doctrine. Speak the truth in love. God is able to keep us from falling. He has all power, authority, majesty, and glory!

Dear Lord, help me recognize false teachers and
be willing to take a stand for Your truth. Amen.

Day 99

A Passion for Serving

For we are God's handiwork, created in Christ Jesus to do
good works, which God prepared in advance for us to do.

Ephesians 2:10

Moses led the Israelites out of Egypt. Solomon built God's temple. The apostle Paul established churches in Asia Minor. Have you ever wondered what assignment the Lord might have for you? You are God's handiwork. God has prepared in advance good works that only you can do.

God desires to use you in mighty ways for His kingdom. Allow Him to direct you along a path that is pleasing to Him. Be open to God's call on your life. God has uniquely created us with different gifts, talents, and abilities. He gives us an assignment that is specifically suited for us.

We should not expect a "Damascus Road" experience like Paul had. Be careful not to compare yourself with others. Sometimes we may view our assignment as insignificant. However, sometimes serving behind the scenes is the most important. God has gifted you in unique ways. Be open to ways that He might be calling you to serve. Many times God will speak His will through our circumstances. Listen. Serve.

Dear Lord, help me believe that You can use me for Your
service. Thank You for equipping me. Help me step
out in faith to serve others in Your name. Amen.

DAY 100

Living a Spirit-Filled Life

For sin shall no longer be your master,
because you are not under the law, but under grace.
ROMANS 6:14

*S*in is the biggest deterrent to living a Spirit-filled life. But, as believers, we do not have to allow sin to control us. Paul states in Galatians 2:20: "I have been crucified with Christ and I no longer live, but Christ lives in me. The life I live in the body, I live by faith in the Son of God, who loved me and gave himself for me." Like Paul, we too have been crucified with Christ. Just as Christ was raised from the dead, we, too, have been given eternal life. Because we live under the grace that God has freely given us, sin is no longer the master of our lives.

Every believer possesses the indwelling Holy Spirit, the manifestation of God's presence. The Holy Spirit is our Counselor. He empowers us to say no to sin. But we must desire to have victory over sin. Ask for God's help. Turn your back on sin. Submit to God's authority instead. This is a not a "once and for all" choice we make, but a choice we consciously make on a moment-to-moment basis.

Dear Lord, I realize that sin should not be the master of my life,
yet many times I let sin control me. Give me the desire to yield to the
Holy Spirit so that I may have daily victory over sin in my life. Amen.

Day 101

Firstfruits

But Christ has indeed been raised from the dead,
the firstfruits of those who have fallen asleep.

1 Corinthians 15:20

Several of Israel's feasts included firstfruits offerings. God was to receive His portion first—before anyone tasted a bite of the harvest. This principle applied to everything that the soil produced.

The apostle Paul applied the principle of firstfruits to Christ's resurrection. This is a wonderful reminder that Christ's victory over death is the promise of our resurrection when He returns! Before Jesus ascended into heaven, He reassured His disciples in John 14:2–3, "My Father's house has many rooms; if that were not so, would I have told you that I am going there to prepare a place for you? And if I go and prepare a place for you, I will come back and take you to be with me that you also may be where I am."

This truth is meant for us as well. Heaven is real! Jesus has gone ahead of us and is preparing our place. Someday we will join Him for all eternity. This spiritual reality is not diminished just because it's difficult to wrap our heads around this truth. Jesus proved heaven is real by going first!

Dear Lord, thank You for reminding me not only of
the reality of Jesus' resurrection but of my own!
May I look forward to being in Your presence. Amen.

Day 102

Serving God

I press on toward the goal to win the prize for which
God has called me heavenward in Christ Jesus.

PHILIPPIANS 3:14

❈

Saul was passionate, yet his efforts were misdirected. He was obsessed with persecuting Christians until the Lord stopped him dead in his tracks on the road to Damascus. Following his conversion, Saul became the apostle Paul. Christ became his passion, and serving Him his life goal.

Have you ever thought about the purpose of your life? Why are you here? Many goals are noble, but only one is best. Serving the Lord is the highest calling; the only one with eternal rewards. The wonderful news is that regardless of your career, age, or gender, you can serve the Lord right where you are. Be a witness for Him at work, school, or play!

We must always move forward in serving God. Although mistakes will be made, we have a forgiving God. Let passion compel us to serve Him, not in our own strength but in the power of His Spirit. The key to fruitful service is to place *God first*. Our goal should be to bring honor and glory to Him, not ourselves. This is accomplished by allowing Christ to work through us.

Dear Lord, may I be about Your business. Help me to
keep focused on You wherever I am. Use me. Amen.

Sharing God's Truth

"Therefore go and make disciples of all nations, baptizing them
in the name of the Father and of the Son and of the Holy Spirit,
and teaching them to obey everything I have commanded you.
And surely I am with you always, to the very end of the age."
MATTHEW 28:19–20

⸺⸺❧⸺⸺

The verse above is known as the Great Commission, Jesus' parting words to His disciples just prior to His ascension into heaven. Had the eleven disciples (Judas had already betrayed Jesus) not taken this charge seriously, Christianity would have quickly died out. Jesus' command is just as pertinent for us today. Think about it: Christianity is always just one generation away from extinction.

God wants us to share with the world the knowledge of His saving power and grace. We are *not* to keep these truths buried in our hearts. Personally testify to others about what the Lord is doing in your life. Allow your life to serve as an example of the difference Jesus has made. Teach a Sunday school class or assist with church functions. Look for opportunities to use whatever platform the Lord has given you to share His truth with others.

Dear Lord, sometimes I get so caught up with my own daily agenda
that I fail to see the "big picture." I have been entrusted with Your
truth. Help me to faithfully share that truth with others. Amen.

Day 104

A Spirit-Filled Believer

*To this end I strenuously contend with all
the energy Christ so powerfully works in me.*

COLOSSIANS 1:29

What are the characteristics of a Spirit-filled believer? The apostle Paul is a great example of a life led by the Holy Spirit. Paul would admit that he was weak. He endured shipwrecks, beatings, and imprisonment. How was he able not only to endure but to advance God's kingdom against insurmountable opposition? He refused to depend on his own strength, power, and abilities. Paul totally depended on the power of the Holy Spirit to do God's work in and through him. He was sold out for the cause of Christ.

We would do well to emulate Paul's passion, focus, and perseverance. When we accept Jesus as our Lord and Savior, we experience a dramatic change from within like Paul did. This transformation should compel us to talk about the difference Jesus has made in our lives. In your weakness, rely on God's strength and power. Allow Christ to work in and through you. When we "proclaim" Christ, as Paul did, we will experience inexpressible joy, even in the midst of turmoil and tribulation!

*Dear Lord, may I follow Paul's example of living a Spirit-filled life.
I am wholeheartedly Yours. Help me to depend solely on
Your power and strength each and every day. Amen.*

DAY 105

Waiting for the Lord

"Be still, and know that I am God; I will be exalted
among the nations, I will be exalted in the earth."

PSALM 46:10

$\mathcal{D}$o you have a friend who is notoriously late? You always seem to be waiting for them to show up. Sometimes it may seem like we're waiting the Lord. But in reality we expect God to be on our timetable, and when He's not, we think He's late. The truth is God is *always* right on time. His timing is perfect. Perhaps we need to adjust our watch to His time.

Waiting on the Lord requires *patience*. How often do we lose patience and try to remedy things on our own? The hard, sobering truth is this: no matter how harsh the storm or how deep the grief or trouble, God is in control. Although our emotions may have difficulty embracing that truth, it is truth just the same.

Trust—it's as simple as that. It's an act of the will. It's a choice. Relax. Take a deep breath. Wait in expectation that God will equip and sustain you during the storm. God *is* faithful. He knows the beginning from the end. Make up your mind right now to *trust Him*. Realize that He is always right on time!

Dear Lord, I feel so fragile at times. I am easily frightened
and fearful. Help me remember that You are indeed in control.
Give me patience. May I choose to trust and wait for You. Amen.

DAY 106

Burdens

"Come to me, all you who are weary and burdened, and I
will give you rest. Take my yoke upon you and learn from me,
for I am gentle and humble in heart, and you will find rest
for your souls. For my yoke is easy and my burden is light."
MATTHEW 11:28–30

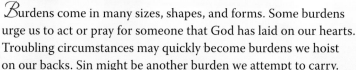

*B*urdens come in many sizes, shapes, and forms. Some burdens
urge us to act or pray for someone that God has laid on our hearts.
Troubling circumstances may quickly become burdens we hoist
on our backs. Sin might be another burden we attempt to carry.
Regardless of the burden, the longer we carry it, the heavier it becomes. It weighs us down physically, emotionally, and spiritually.

The Lord never intended for us to carry our own burdens.
He is our burden-bearer. Jesus tells us to come to Him and put on
His yoke. He is stronger. As we allow Him to bear our burdens,
our load will become lighter and we will experience rest. What
burdens are you carrying? Come to Jesus. Lay your burdens at His
feet. Allow Him to carry your burdens. Find rest for your soul.

Dear Lord, why do I insist on carrying burdens when
You desire to give me rest instead? I am coming to You,
asking that You be my burden-bearer. Amen.

The Mind of Christ

Set your minds on things above, not on earthly things.
COLOSSIANS 3:2

*T*he slogan "A mind is a terrible thing to waste" was part of a campaign used years ago by the United Negro College Fund. This profound statement is applicable to all of us. Our mind has great capabilities, yet we can squander its potential.

Our mind is a battleground where our thoughts are often under attack. What will we choose to dwell on? Where will we focus our thoughts? The apostle Paul stated his choice: "We take captive every thought to make it obedient to Christ" (2 Corinthians 10:5). We need to set our minds on things above, not on earthly things.

When we know Jesus, we begin to develop the mind of Christ through the indwelling Holy Spirit. We begin to process spiritual truth and see the world through His eyes. That's when Satan steps in to attack our minds. "Be alert and of sober mind. Your enemy the devil prowls around like a roaring lion looking for someone to devour" (1 Peter 5:8). God has equipped us to stand firm by providing His spiritual armor (see Ephesians 6:10–17). The victory is ours, yet we must commit to dwell on truth and dismiss lies from our minds with the strength that God provides.

Dear Lord, may I be aware of my thoughts throughout the day. When they do not line up with Your Word, help me dismiss them immediately from my mind. Amen.

DAY 108

The New Covenant

*"I will put my law in their minds and write it on their hearts.
I will be their God, and they will be my people. . . . For I will
forgive their wickedness and will remember their sins no more."*

JEREMIAH 31:33–34

The old covenant focused on laws and rules. Jesus came not to abolish the laws, but to fulfill them. "Do not think that I have come to abolish the Law or the Prophets; I have not come to abolish them but to fulfill them" (Matthew 5:17).

Jesus has come! The new covenant has been ushered in! Jesus inaugurated the new covenant with His blood. We are recipients of the blessings of this new covenant. The full benefits are still in the future for Israel, but we can enjoy the provisions of this wonderful gift from God today.

There are many benefits of this covenant that Jesus makes with us. God has written his law in our minds and on our hearts. We can worship Him in spirit and in truth. Through Jesus' sacrificial death on the cross, God has forgiven our sins and remembers them no more. Let us rejoice in this blessing! Let us appropriate this truth!

*Dear Lord, thank You for Your forgiveness and
grace in my life. May I not take Your gift for granted,
but live boldly in Your presence. Amen.*

DAY 109

Holy Living

And whatever you do, whether in word or deed, do it all in the name of the Lord Jesus, giving thanks to God the Father through him.
COLOSSIANS 3:17

We must ask ourselves this difficult question: Are we living for God or living for self? The answer to that question is reflected in our daily choices and priorities. Our lives produce fruit that indicates our choice. Either our lives will reflect kindness, humility, gentleness, patience, and forgiveness, or greed, anger, malice, slander, and lies will characterize our lives. God has given us free will. The choice is ours to make.

Since we have been raised with Christ, we are encouraged to set our hearts on things above, where Christ is seated at the right hand of God. We should choose to put to death whatever belongs to our earthly nature. Whatever we do, we are to do it all in the name of the Lord Jesus, *always* giving thanks to God through Him.

When we live for the Lord, peace will rule our hearts. We will be filled with gratitude and thankfulness. A life lived for the Lord will be a life with no regrets.

Dear Lord, I want to live for You, yet many times I fall back into my selfish ways. Give me victory! Help me to live a life pleasing to You. Amen.

Day 110

Backsliding

Why did you despise the word of the
Lord by doing what is evil in his eyes?
2 Samuel 12:9

King David had an adulterous affair with Bathsheba and then
tried to cover it up by having her husband, Uriah, killed. The
prophet Nathan then confronted King David with these piercing
words found in Second Samuel.

Our Christian walk can sometimes seem like two steps forward and one step back. Setbacks are humbling. Yet humility is
an essential component to spiritual maturity. Take heart. David,
Elijah, and Peter all experienced spiritual setbacks. David gave in to
lust. Elijah's fear left him hopeless. Peter denied Christ when fear
overwhelmed him. God understands our human frailties yet loves
us still.

Backsliding happens. It is a faith failure. It begins by doubting
God's promises and ends by stepping outside of His will. How do
we return to God and resume our close relationship with Him?
Repentance is the first step. Then we recall the many blessings God
has given us in the past, refocus our attention on God's power,
remember His promises, and resolve to trust God completely.

Dear Lord, how can You still love me even when
I turn my back on You? May Your love compel me
to quickly repent and trust You completely. Amen.

Day 111

God's Unconditional Love

For I am convinced that neither death nor life, neither angels nor demons, neither the present nor the future, nor any powers, neither height nor depth, or anything else in all creation, will be able to separate us from the love of God that is in Christ Jesus our Lord.

Romans 8:38–39

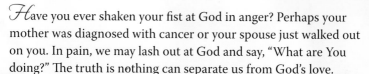

Have you ever shaken your fist at God in anger? Perhaps your mother was diagnosed with cancer or your spouse just walked out on you. In pain, we may lash out at God and say, "What are You doing?" The truth is nothing can separate us from God's love.

Even if we express anger toward God, His love for us never wavers. He does not turn His back when we raise our fists. He does not reject us when we do not understand His ways. He stands by us in our hour of anguish and waits. He allows us to wail, question, and express our anger. He continues to love us as He always has and always will. God meets us in the depths of our despair. He holds us. He understands our pain. He desires that we continue to trust Him even as we walk through our deepest valleys. As we turn to Him, He will peacefully bring us through. His love is unconditional. Turn to Him today.

Dear Lord, nothing can separate me from Your love—even my own emotions. You couldn't love me any more or any less than You always do. That is amazing love! Thank You! Amen.

DAY 112

Tug of War

*"Do not store up for yourselves treasures on earth, where moths
and vermin destroy, and where thieves break in and steal.
But store up for yourselves treasures in heaven, where moths
and vermin do not destroy, and where thieves do not break in and
steal. For where your treasure is, there your heart will be also."*

MATTHEW 6:19–21

When we come to know Jesus as our personal Lord and Savior, He also becomes our Friend. He takes hold of our hand and beckons us to follow Him. However, the world quickly grabs our other hand and pulls in the opposite direction. We have a choice to make. Which hand do we continue holding and which hand do we drop? When we attempt to hold on to both, we are caught in a tug-of-war.

The hand of the world offers a taste of "The Good Life"—worldly pleasures that are experienced through our five senses. The list is endless: successful jobs, dream homes, fancy cars, sculpted bodies, and five-star resorts. Although the things of this world may seem so appealing, they are temporary at best.

The hand of Jesus offers us a taste of "The God Life"—spiritual blessings that are experienced through faith. These fruits of the Spirit are eternal: love, joy, peace, patience, gentleness, kindness, faithfulness, and self-control (see Galatians 5:22–23). Many times we are asked to let go of worldly priorities in order to follow Jesus. We cannot love the things of the world and the things of God equally. Which has your heart?

*Dear Lord, what worldly strongholds have found
their way into my life? Give me the strength to let
go and hold tightly to Your hand instead. Amen.*

DAY 113

Basket Case

Do not be anxious about anything, but in every situation,
by prayer and petition, with thanksgiving, present your requests to
God. And the peace of God, which transcends all understanding,
will guard your hearts and your minds in Christ Jesus.
PHILIPPIANS 4:6–7

Moses was a Hebrew baby born in Egypt at a time when the Israelites were being oppressed by the Egyptians. When the king issued an edict to kill all male Hebrew babies, Moses' mother hid him. After three months she was unable to hide him any longer, so she placed him in a papyrus basket among the reeds of the Nile River. God miraculously rescued Moses. He grew up in Pharaoh's own household where God prepared him to lead the Israelites out of Egypt forty years later (see Exodus 1–4).

Being a "basket case" usually carries negative connotations. We use it to describe feeling at the end of our rope, about to break or unable to handle one more thing. We feel anxious and fearful. But what if we viewed being a "basket case" in a different light? What if we emulated Moses' mother and trusted the Lord completely, believing that our circumstances had divine purpose?

Have faith that God will bring about His will in your life. Just as God protected Moses, He will protect you. Just as God provided for Moses, He will provide for you. God can be trusted. Place your life in His hands.

Dear Lord, when I feel like I am losing control,
may I place my life in Your hands. Guard me as You
guarded Moses. You are my hope and help! Amen.

DAY 114

Our Spiritual Gardens

"But the seed falling on good soil refers to someone who hears the word and understands it. This is the one who produces a crop, yielding a hundred, sixty or thirty times what was sown."

MATTHEW 13:23

*M*any times Jesus used parables to illustrate spiritual truth. The parable of the sower is no exception. Jesus described a farmer who went out to sow his seed. The seed fell on various types of soil—pathways, rocks, thorns, and good soil. The soil itself determined whether the seed would grow and produce a crop.

Our hearts are the soil on which the Lord sows spiritual seed. What type of soil is your heart: hard, rocky, thorny, or good? Good soil receives the sown seed because it is not hard, but well watered. Jesus is the Living Water. Daily Bible reading and prayer allow the Living Water to saturate our souls. The Lord also uses circumstances and people to stimulate spiritual growth, much like fertilizer enriches the soil. Well-watered soil promotes germination. Let's allow the seed of truth to penetrate the good soil of our hearts so that we will yield spiritual fruit!

Dear Lord, You are the Living Water. I cannot live spiritually without You. Help me tend my spiritual garden as I should and be watered daily by You. Amen.

DAY 115

Discipline Produces Fruit

No discipline seems pleasant at the time, but painful.
Later on, however, it produces a harvest of righteousness
and peace for those who have been trained by it.
HEBREWS 12:11

Spiritual growth begins when our heart receives Jesus. But, like a vineyard, our growth is balanced with pruning so that optimal fruit can be produced. The Lord prunes and disciplines us by "cutting off" areas of harmful growth in our lives and "cutting back" areas of good growth in order to stimulate even more. Although pruning is painful at the time, it produces abundant growth and maturity.

Weeding out sin is also mandatory. Sin can quietly invade our hearts and put down roots. Once established, it spreads rapidly and chokes out everything good. We must diligently look for sin that has crept under the garden gate of our hearts. Like weeds, sin needs to be dealt with early. Confess sin immediately and receive forgiveness. Do not allow Satan to establish a foothold. Has your spiritual garden been neglected? Make tending your heart a priority so that you will produce a fruitful harvest for the Lord.

"Search me, God, and know my heart; test me and know my
anxious thoughts. See if there is any offensive way in me,
and lead me in the way everlasting" [Psalm 139:23–24]. Amen.

Day 116

Serving Others

*Whatever you do, work at it with all your heart, as working
for the Lord, not for human masters, since you know that
you will receive an inheritance from the Lord as a reward.
It is the Lord Christ you are serving.*

COLOSSIANS 3:23–24

The Pharisees were the religious leaders in Jesus' day. They were
notorious for outward acts to impress others, yet their hearts
were far from God. Jesus admonished them and accused them of
being like whitewashed tombs—beautiful on the outside but full of
dead men's bones. The Pharisees were motivated by man's praise,
not God's approval. Jesus called them hypocrites (see Matthew
23:25–28).

When we examine our motives for serving others, what is
revealed? Do we serve in order to feel better about ourselves or
to have others think more highly of us? Are we called by "duty" or
obligation? Do we secretly want to be admired for our generosity?
Jesus came to humbly serve, not to be served. He had no hidden
agenda. His motives were pure. Love and love alone compelled
Him to lay down His life for others. When we serve with the same
attitude, we demonstrate to a watching world what true love looks
like. Serve others in Jesus' name.

*Dear Lord, help me serve others with Your attitude and with the
strength that You provide. May I desire to seek Your approval
alone. May love compel me to serve others in Your name. Amen.*

Day 117

God Loves Me

*For God so loved the world that he gave his one and only Son,
that whoever believes in him shall not perish but have eternal life.*
JOHN 3:16

Although God's love for us never changes, we may not always
"feel" His love. We might mistakenly conclude that prosperous
times indicate that God loves us, while trials communicate His
displeasure. Some trials, like being diagnosed with cancer, have
nothing to do with God's discipline. We live in a fallen world where
sickness, disease, and death occur. Even amid the greatest struggles
in this life, God's love is still present. God promises, "Never will I
leave you; never will I forsake you" (Hebrews 13:5).

God's love is unchanging—immutable. Nothing can separate
us from His love. It is constant and eternal. His love is not based
on our actions, neither is it dependent on the circumstances of life.
God could not love us any more or any less than He always does!
That is truth. We never have to fear that God will withdraw His
love from us.

*Dear Lord, help me remember that when I am going through a
rough time, it does not mean that You have forsaken me. May I
experience Your love and peace in tangible ways today. Amen.*

DAY 118

Throw a Lifeline

God is our refuge and strength, an ever-present help in trouble.
Therefore we will not fear, though the earth give way and the
mountains fall into the heart of the sea, though its waters roar and
foam and the mountains quake with their surging.

PSALM 46:1–3

In her book *The Atonement Child*, Francine Rivers writes, "One person standing on the Rock can throw a lifeline to others drowning in the sea." We are surrounded by people on the brink of disaster. They are holding on to life preservers they mistakenly think will keep them afloat: children, spouses, careers, money, homes, health, and beauty. But when children leave, spouses betray, financial markets plummet, and health fails, they quickly begin to sink. They need a lifeline!

Jesus Christ is the only life preserver that keeps us afloat amid life's greatest storms. He's the lifeline. Those who cling to Him will not drown. How should we respond when we see someone drowning? Share the truth of Jesus in their hour of need. Testify that because He has rescued and saved you, He is able to do the same for them. The Lord has given you His lifeline. Throw it to others!

Dear Lord, may I be attuned to the cries of those who are
drowning because they are clutching faulty life preservers.
May I stand on the Rock (Jesus) and throw them a lifeline. Amen.

DAY 119

Bargaining with God

And we know that in all things God works for the good of those
who love him, who have been called according to his purpose.

ROMANS 8:28

Whether or not we care to admit it, most of us have tried to bargain with God. Subconsciously we attempt to manipulate God so that *our* will might be done. Mistakenly we believe that we know best. We want life to turn out the way we think it should.

Here's proof: Have you ever been extremely disappointed and said, "But, Lord, I did such and such, so You should have done so and so"? When life doesn't turn out as we had planned, we blame God. We thought we had an unspoken agreement with Him. But in reality, God had never agreed to our deal in the first place. God is God. We are not.

The truth remains: God knows what is best. His will is perfect. We are to live for Him and leave the results of our lives to Him. Trust God. Do not allow fear to drive you to manipulation. God is in the business of bringing beauty from ashes. God uses everything for good in the life of the believer. So when life takes an unexpected turn, trust Him. God is ultimately working everything out for your good.

Dear Lord, may I live my life with You in control.
Help me to surrender to Your greater purpose
and desire Your will above my own. Amen.

Day 120

Root-Bound

That person is like a tree planted by streams of water,
which yields its fruit in season and whose leaf does
not wither—whatever they do prospers.
Psalm 1:3

Have you ever seen a root-bound plant? Yellow leaves indicate new growth has ceased. Intertwining roots have displaced the soil. Repotting must be done or the plant will surely die.

Christians can become spiritually root-bound. Growth is stifled when we become comfortable and complacent in our protected environment. Sometimes the Lord has to take us out of our "comfort zone" and break up our tightly woven roots. He replants us in new soil to facilitate our reliance on Him. This may happen when we relocate, encounter a job change, welcome a new baby into the family, or go on a mission trip.

It may be scary to leave our well-known environment, but spiritual growth takes place when we do. Change is difficult, yet it helps transform us from being self-reliant to being God-reliant. So embrace change from the Lord! Allow the Lord to divinely intervene so that you can continue to flourish spiritually. Don't be content to stay in your root-bound pot. Grow where the Lord plants you!

Dear Lord, when we are walking with You, change is always
in our favor [Camilla Seabolt]. *Have Your way with me*
so that I can continue to grow and flourish. Amen.

Day 121

Fearfully and Wonderfully Made

For you created my inmost being; you knit me together in my mother's womb. I praise you because I am fearfully and wonderfully made; your works are wonderful, I know that full well.

PSALM 139:13–14

Wint if we viewed our bodies as God does? Would we stop obsessing about our nose, wrinkles, weight, or hair? We are beautiful in God's sight! We are fearfully and wonderfully made by our Creator. God loves us just as we are because we are His creation. He created us for an eternal purpose.

Our bodies were made by Him and for Him. When He looks at our bodies, He doesn't see any physical flaws that we may zero in on. God doesn't focus on our appearance. He is more concerned with our heart and how we use our bodies. So, it stands to reason that we should care for our bodies with proper rest, exercise, and nutrition so that they are in optimal condition to be used by Him. "Offer your bodies as a living sacrifice, holy and pleasing to God— this is your true and proper worship" (Romans 12:1). Embrace the body the Lord has given you. Care for it properly. Do not focus on your appearance, but on how you may be used by Him.

*Dear Lord, help me see my body as You do
and consecrate it for Your use. Amen.*

Day 122

Shattered Dreams

As for God, his way is perfect: the LORD's word
is flawless; he shields all who take refuge in him.
PSALM 18:30

*D*reams. Hopes. Aspirations. We have them for ourselves as well as for others. What happens when our dreams are shattered, our hopes go up in smoke, or our aspirations vanish? The longer we live, the more we realize that life rarely turns out as we had envisioned. We humbly acknowledge that we are not in control. God alone is sovereign.

We have a choice. We can continue to hold on tightly to our dreams, allowing our hands to become clenched fists raised in anger to God. Bitterness is the end result. Or we can open our hands and give God our shattered dreams. He can bring forth beauty from ashes. He uses all things for our good. We can trust His plan above our own. Regardless of how things may appear from our perspective, He loves us and has our best interests at heart. As we trust Him, He will confirm that truth to our hearts. When our dreams are shattered, we can stand on the Rock, Jesus Christ. We will stand secure. We will have hope. We will experience peace.

Dear Lord, my shattered dreams of today can
become the victories of tomorrow when I trust You.
Help me believe and trust You more. Amen.

Day 123

Content by Your Side

Jesus replied, "Anyone who loves me will obey my teaching.
My Father will love them, and we will come to
them and make our home with them."
John 14:23

Jesus makes a sobering statement: If we love Him, we will obey Him. Sometimes we make the correct decision to obey the Lord. Yet at other times we may choose to disobey and go our own way. Unfortunately we may foolishly think that walking with the Lord is too restrictive. In our desire for "freedom," we become blinded to the dangers that await us. Like the parable of the lost sheep, the Lord seeks us, finds us, and carries us home. The Lord disciplines us for our own good and brings us back to Himself.

The Lord always has His eye on us. He loves us and wants to protect us. That's why He desires that we walk near Him in obedience, content by His side. As our love relationship with the Lord grows deeper, so does our desire to obey. We begin to understand that "true freedom" comes through Christ. We desire a closer walk so that we can hear His voice and follow. Our relationship has progressed from obedience training to deep abiding. Lord, may it be so!

Dear Lord, thank You for Your patience in calling me back to
Yourself time and time again. You truly know what's best for me.
May I desire to be content by Your side. Amen.

Day 124

God's Embrace

"My sheep listen to my voice; I know them, and they follow me.
I give them eternal life, and they shall never perish;
no one can snatch them out of my hand."

John 10:27–28

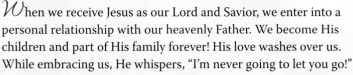

When we receive Jesus as our Lord and Savior, we enter into a personal relationship with our heavenly Father. We become His children and part of His family forever! His love washes over us. While embracing us, He whispers, "I'm never going to let you go!" What comfort! What assurance! He is ours and we are His. Nothing will ever alter that fact.

Unlike in our earthly families, we will never be asked to break away. In fact, just the opposite happens. As we mature, we draw closer and closer to Him. We learn to depend on Him more and more. We become more dependent on the Lord, not less so.

Have you received the embrace of your heavenly Father? Do you have the assurance that His love is forever? He will never let you go! Do not live life independently, but desire to walk closer with the Lord with each passing day.

Dear Lord, thank You for embracing me with Your love.
Help me to become more and more dependent on You. Amen.

Day 125

Closed Doors

*Jesus replied, "What is impossible
with man is possible with God."*
LUKE 18:27

$\mathcal{N}$o door is closed to the Lord. He can walk through any door—locked or unlocked. Remember how He appeared to the disciples in the upper room after His resurrection? Even though the doors were locked, Jesus stood in their midst and made a believer out of "Doubting Thomas" (see John 20:24–28). The Lord has no boundaries or limitations.

Because of this truth, the Lord can walk through any locked door in our lives and open it for us from the inside. We must remember that His ways and timing are perfect. We must trust that He knows best. He will open the door for us if it is in accordance with His sovereign will. Until that happens, we are to "be still, and know that I am God" (Psalm 46:10). Being still means to cease striving and relax, trust and wait.

Jesus told Thomas to "stop doubting and believe." He encourages us to do the same! What doors in your life seem bolted shut? Sometimes God has closed them because He has something better in store. Ask Him. Or He may want to demonstrate His power by opening locked doors and taking you to the other side. Be still. Trust Him.

*Dear Lord, help me truly believe that nothing is impossible
for You! May I trust You to open the closed doors in
my life according to Your perfect will. Amen.*

Day 126

The Bread of Life

"I am the bread of life. Your ancestors ate the manna in the wilderness, yet they died. But here is the bread that comes down from heaven, which anyone may eat and not die. I am the living bread that came down from heaven. Whoever eats this bread will live forever. This bread is my flesh, which I will give for the life of the world."

John 6:48–51

---

*I*t has been said that sharing our Christian faith is simply one beggar telling another beggar where to find food! Everyone is spiritually hungry. God created us that way. But there is Good News: God also provides the food to satisfy that hunger. He has given us Jesus, the Bread of Life. Jesus is revealed to us through the Bible. So, if we want our spiritual hunger satisfied, we must feed on His Word.

When the Israelites were wandering in the desert for forty years, God provided food by raining down manna from heaven. The manna had to be gathered daily (with the exception of the Sabbath). In the same way, we are to daily feast on the Bread of Life. We cannot store up spiritual sustenance in advance. Have you found spiritual food? If so, share the Good News with others.

Dear Lord, You created me with a spiritual hunger that only You can satisfy. May I be nourished daily by Your Word and share Your food with others! Amen.

Jesus, Our Friend

"I no longer call you servants, because a servant does not know his master's business. Instead, I have called you friends, for everything that I learned from my Father I have made known to you."

JOHN 15:15

Jesus desires a *real* relationship with us. Since He is our Maker, we can be ourselves with Him. Complete honesty is possible because He knows our thoughts even before we speak them. We can admit our mistakes and receive His forgiveness. Although Jesus knows our deepest, darkest secrets, He still loves us. We can share our hopes and dreams while seeking His wisdom.

Joseph Scriven penned the hymn "What a Friend We Have in Jesus" in 1857. Although his life was filled with personal tragedy, he wrote about the friendship he enjoyed with Jesus. The first stanza reads:

> What a Friend we have in Jesus,
> All our sins and griefs to bear!
> What a privilege to carry
> Everything to God in prayer!
> O what peace we often forfeit,
> O what needless pain we bear,
> All because we do not carry
> Everything to God in prayer.

Dear Lord, You are Creator God, yet at the same time I can call You Friend. Although that truth is difficult to fully comprehend, thank You that I can have a real relationship with You. Amen.

Day 128

Rebellion

*"Why do you look at the speck of sawdust in your brother's eye
and pay no attention to the plank in your own eye?"*

Matthew 7:3

Why is it easier to spot rebellion in others than to recognize it in ourselves? A story is told of a woman who was constantly complaining about her neighbor's dirty windows. She blamed her marred view on her neighbor. One day she decided to set an example by washing her own windows. Perhaps, she thought, her neighbor would take the clue and finally wash hers. To her shock and amazement, once her windows were cleaned, so were her neighbors! The whole time she was the one with the dirty windows.

Focusing on another's rebellion can blind us to the fact that we ourselves may not be following the Lord. Perhaps we have rebellious teenagers who are making poor life choices. We see them headed for disaster, so we allow worry, anxiety, and fear to rule our heart. We may blame our sleepless nights on their rebellion. But, are *we* choosing to live up to the truth that we know? Are we praying without ceasing? Are we trusting the Lord with all our heart?

The truth we know in our head must penetrate our heart. We will not be held responsible for the rebellion in others. But God will hold us accountable for our own choices. Concentrate on living up to the truth that we have been given, and leave the rest to the Lord.

*Dear Lord, take the log out of my eye so I can see clearly.
May I concentrate on my own walk with You. Amen.*

Day 129

Sticks and Stones

He heals the brokenhearted and binds up their wounds.
Psalm 147:3

❧⟨≋⟩❧

Although sticks and stones may break our bones, emotional pain is equally damaging. Rejection, betrayal, and abuse leave invisible scars. Since these scars are easier to hide, we often deny, suppress, or ignore the pain. Healing from emotional scars is not easy. But take heart: Jesus is the Great Physician! He is the One who can give you the power to forgive others, believe His truth, and begin the healing process.

Jesus understands your emotional pain even when no one else does. In the Garden of Gethsemane, the night before His crucifixion, He felt such intense emotional pain that his sweat was like drops of blood falling to the ground. He wanted His disciples' prayer support, but they fell asleep instead.

Others may not understand your pain, but Jesus does. Nothing is too hard for Him. Nothing is beyond His capabilities. Nothing is outside His area of expertise. He brings joy where there is pain, hope where there is discouragement, and peace where there is anguish. Cry out to Him. The Great Physician will wipe your tears and mend your heart.

Dear Lord, heal the emotional pain that I have kept hidden deep within my heart. As I acknowledge my pain before You, I ask for Your power to help me forgive. Restore and heal me, Lord. Amen.

DAY 130

Captive or Free?

*The Spirit of the Sovereign LORD is on me, because the LORD
has anointed me to proclaim good news to the poor. He has
sent me to bind up the brokenhearted, to proclaim freedom
for the captives and release from darkness for the prisoners.*

ISAIAH 61:1

Although we yearn to be free, many things can hold us captive.
Addictions, destructive relationships, personality weaknesses, or
sinful habits can rule our lives. Jesus came to set the prisoners
free—that includes you! The price for freedom has been paid once
and for all when Jesus died on the cross. Although we have been
given freedom, we may have difficulty experiencing it. What is
holding us back?

In some strange way, stepping out of captivity into freedom
may be scary. Captivity, though not desired, may have become "familiar." Freedom would require stepping "out of our comfort zone."
Take heart! There is hope! Not only did Jesus pay the price for our
freedom, He is the One who gives us the power and strength to
embrace that freedom. As we depend on His power *daily*, His victory is ours! Live in the freedom that the Lord has won for you.

*Dear Lord, thank You for setting me free! Help me to
walk in that freedom daily as I rely on You. Amen.*

DAY 131

Blocks

Therefore let us stop passing judgment on one another.
Instead, make up your mind not to put any stumbling
block or obstacle in the way of a brother or sister.

ROMANS 14:13

Would you rather be a building block or a stumbling block?
Building blocks enable others to draw closer to the Lord by encouraging and facilitating spiritual growth. By contrast, stumbling blocks are obstacles that cause tripping and stumbling in another's spiritual journey. The choice is ours. We can either aid or hinder others in their relationship with Christ.

How can we act as building blocks in someone's life? Focus on the Lord and others. Be humble and real. Be a godly example in word and deed. Extend forgiveness. Intercede in prayer to communicate genuine care and concern. Take time to listen and demonstrate unconditional love. Share scripture to remind someone of God's truth. Lay your life down for another.

In contrast, we become a stumbling block when we focus on ourselves rather than the Lord. We develop a critical, judgmental spirit. Forgiveness may be withheld. Hypocrisy and pride are present. Unfortunately when we stumble, others will follow. Let's move closer to the Lord ourselves so we can be used to help others do the same.

Dear Lord, as Your ambassador, may my life be a building
block that enables others to draw closer to You. Amen.

Day 132

A Mother's Love

A mother's love,
how great the worth,
born sweet in labor's pain—
that, only the beginning of
her life of loss for gain.

She gives herself away each day
to those within her care,
to nourish and to watch at play
and wipe away each tear.

Those tiny hands raised up to her
will find her warm embrace;
her calming love to reassure
resides upon her face.

Her tears, she hides
behind her smile,
as, off to school, she waves
her little ones who look so small,
as, in her eyes, they gaze.

With each new year, a letting go,
a rending of her heart;
but, wisdom causes her to know,
they must, of need, depart.

A mother's love of tendrils sure
can span all space and time,
and cause a weary heart endure
when life has lost its rhyme.

A mother's love,
how great the cost!
Can one, her source deplete?
All that she owns,
she counts as loss
to see her child complete.

My mother's love reflects the
love of Jesus unto me.
Our hearts will be enjoined
above for all eternity.

JENNY MATHEWS

DAY 133

A Diamond in the Rough

I praise you because I am fearfully and wonderfully made;
your works are wonderful, I know that full well.

PSALM 139:14

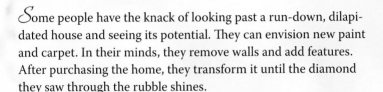

Some people have the knack of looking past a run-down, dilapi-dated house and seeing its potential. They can envision new paint and carpet. In their minds, they remove walls and add features. After purchasing the home, they transform it until the diamond they saw through the rubble shines.

When God looks at us, He sees diamonds in the rough. Look-ing beyond our sin and inadequacies, God focuses on our tremen-dous potential. He purchased us with the blood of Jesus. Through His transforming power, the diamonds He created will slowly be revealed. As He pours His love into our lives, we are transformed from the inside out. Beauty is born from ashes.

Transformation is a process that does not happen overnight, but over a lifetime. God will chisel away our rough edges in order to expose the beautiful diamonds He created. The process of being transformed by His love will continue until the day we die. In heaven our glorified bodies will be like perfect diamonds that reflect His radiance!

Dear Lord, may I see myself as You see me. Continue to mold
and shape me to be conformed to the image of Christ. Amen.

DAY 134

The Roaring Lion

Submit yourselves, then, to God.
Resist the devil, and he will flee from you.

JAMES 4:7

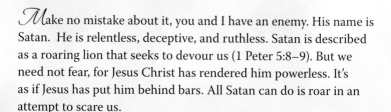

Make no mistake about it, you and I have an enemy. His name is Satan. He is relentless, deceptive, and ruthless. Satan is described as a roaring lion that seeks to devour us (1 Peter 5:8–9). But we need not fear, for Jesus Christ has rendered him powerless. It's as if Jesus has put him behind bars. All Satan can do is roar in an attempt to scare us.

Satan tries to convince us that we are hopeless and defeated. He lies. In fact, Jesus calls him the father of lies. Satan is the one who has been defeated! He has no power over those who are in Christ Jesus. The apostle John assures us in 1 John 4:4 that "the one who is in you is greater than the one who is in the world." God has given us victory. When we stand firm and resist Satan, we are choosing to believe God's truth rather than listen to Satan's lies. Faith replaces fear. Satan must flee in defeat.

Do not let Satan scare you. Stand firm and do not run. You are safe in Christ Jesus. May you remember that truth and walk in victory.

Dear Lord, thank You for the victory You have given me.
May I walk in Your truth and dismiss Satan's lies. Amen.

Day 135

The Trailblazer

*Your word is a lamp to my feet,
a light for my path.*

PSALM 119:105

*L*ike a hike through the woods, there are many divergent paths our lives can take. On the trail of life, we can choose to strike out on our own by taking an unmarked path. Or we can decide to follow a path that has already been marked by Jesus Christ, the trailblazer. He has gone before us to show us the way. He has left signposts to help us stay the course and not get lost. It is our responsibility to take note of these signposts. The Bible lights our path. Circumstances of life nudge us in the right direction. The Holy Spirit counsels us. Other people may serve as our guides.

Perhaps you are at a crossroads. Ask the Lord which path to take. Keep alert to the signposts He has marked for you. Or maybe you have gotten off track and are lost. Cry out to Him. The Lord knows exactly where you are! You are not lost to Him. He will come to you and lead you back on the right path. Let's have courage to follow the Lord on the road less traveled.

*Dear Lord, You are the way. When I follow You,
I will be on the best possible path for my life. Amen.*

Day 136

Be Still

Be still before the LORD and wait patiently for him;
do not fret when people succeed in their ways,
when they carry out their wicked schemes.

PSALM 37:7

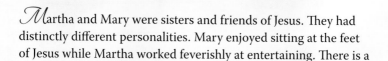

Martha and Mary were sisters and friends of Jesus. They had distinctly different personalities. Mary enjoyed sitting at the feet of Jesus while Martha worked feverishly at entertaining. There is a balance. The secret is knowing when to work and when to be still.

When life is confusing or painful, we need to be still. When our hearts are grieving or hurting, we need to be still. When tomorrow is filled with uncertainty or dread, we need to be still. To be still means to cease striving. Quit trying to figure out all the answers. Quit trying to understand incomprehensible things. Quit trying to be God.

We can experience rest and peace when we are still. Being still demonstrates that we believe that God is God—that He is in complete control. In times of waiting, the Lord gives us all we need to know: "Be still, and *know that I am God*" (Psalm 46:10, emphasis added). When we need to know more, He will reveal it to us. In the meantime, may we simply *be still* before Him. Let's learn from Mary and sit at the feet of Jesus.

Dear Lord, being still is so difficult! Grow my faith so that I can be still. May I simply, yet completely, trust You at all times. Amen.

DAY 137

Soar Like Eagles

But those who hope in the LORD will renew their strength.
They will soar on wings like eagles; they will run and
not grow weary, they will walk and not be faint.

ISAIAH 40:31

Eagles fly by gently flapping their wings and using the air currents to soar. They do not appear frantic in flight, but peaceful and calm. What if we could go through life with such poise and strength? This passage from Isaiah states that it is possible when we put our hope in the Lord.

God is God. We are not. If we are honest with ourselves, most of us have difficulty being still and waiting on God. Foolishly believing that we are in control, we may jump into action. Many times prayer is the only action the Lord desires of us. Prayer demonstrates our belief in His sovereignty. God is at work whether or not we see His plan unfolding. When we trust God rather than ourselves, we are able to be still, knowing that He is faithfully working on our behalf.

As we humble ourselves before the Lord, we receive His peace. We can then respond rather than react to life's circumstances. The Lord renews our strength and enables us to soar on wings like eagles!

Dear Lord, I desire Your peace and strength.
May I pray, wait, and be still before You. Amen.

DAY 138

The Abundant Life

"The thief comes only to steal and kill and destroy;
I have come that they may have life, and have it to the full."
JOHN 10:10

———— ❈ ————

What did Jesus mean by those words? Jesus was crucified and buried. But the story does not end there. Three days later Jesus demonstrated victory over death by coming back to life! His resurrection assures us that same victory—eternal life. Eternal life begins the moment we accept Jesus Christ as Savior, and continues in heaven, our final destination.

We must remember that before Christ was victorious, He had to suffer and die. Christ willingly went to the cross. Although He asked that the cup pass from Him, He submitted to His heavenly Father by saying, "Not my will but yours be done." We are called to follow Christ's example by desiring God's will above our own. The abundant life on earth is experienced when we submit to God's will. Jesus not only came to give us eternal life in heaven, but also abundant life on earth!

Dear Lord, sometimes it is so difficult to submit to Your
will. Help me believe that Your way is best so that I can
experience the abundant life You desire for me. Amen.

Day 139

Spiritual Victory

"Death has been swallowed up in victory. Where, O death,
is your victory? Where, O death, is your sting?" The sting of
death is sin, and the power of sin is the law. But thanks be to
God! He gives us the victory through our Lord Jesus Christ.
1 Corinthians 15:54–57

After Jesus' death, His body was bound in grave clothes and hidden in a dark tomb for three days. During that time God's power was at work transforming and giving life. That same power is available to us. Metaphorically, we can enter the tomb, shed our grave clothes, and emerge victorious. Grave clothes could represent earthly entanglements that bind and hold us captive—sinful habits or past hurts. God begins His transforming work in those areas. Be patient. Transformation takes time. But just as Jesus experienced spiritual victory when He shed His grave clothes, we too can celebrate the victory He claimed for us.

Satan viewed the cross and tomb as his means of victory. But God had a better plan. Satan may attempt to hold you captive. But God has a better plan! Allow the Lord to do His work and unbind those things that hinder. Then you can leave your grave clothes behind and experience spiritual victory by the power of the Holy Spirit.

Dear Lord, transform me and give me new life in You.
By Your power, may I shed those things that have held me captive.
May I walk in freedom and spiritual victory today! Amen.

DAY 140

The Counselor

*"But very truly I tell you, it is for your good that I am
going away. Unless I go away, the Advocate will not
come to you; but if I go, I will send him to you."*

JOHN 16:7

The disciples were filled with grief as Jesus shared the news that
He would be leaving them. Over the past three years, they had
become accustomed to spending quality time together. How would
they cope if He suddenly disappeared? Jesus explained that unless
He left, the Holy Spirit could not come. The Holy Spirit would be
their Comforter and Counselor. He would guide them into all truth
and correct their course when they went astray.

When Jesus was on earth, He could only be in one place at any
given time. Today we have the benefit of the indwelling Holy Spirit.
God's presence lives inside every believer! What a privilege to have
the Holy Spirit as our sure compass. He always responds to our
prayers and faith. Let us continually listen to the guiding voice of
the Holy Spirit and follow His lead.

*Dear Lord, I take for granted that You are with me
in the presence of the Holy Spirit. What a privilege!
May I listen and yield to the Counselor of my soul. Amen.*

Day 141

The Good Shepherd

The LORD is my shepherd, I lack nothing. He makes me lie down in green pastures, he leads me beside quiet waters, he refreshes my soul. He guides me along the right paths for his name's sake.

PSALM 23:1–3

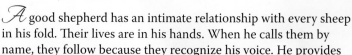

A good shepherd has an intimate relationship with every sheep in his fold. Their lives are in his hands. When he calls them by name, they follow because they recognize his voice. He provides for all of their needs. He protects them from wild animals and rescues them if they wander off. They are able to rest because they feel safe and secure. A good shepherd identifies with his sheep by experiencing life together. He never abandons them because he is committed to his sheep forever.

We have a Good Shepherd. His name is Jesus. Our lives are in His hands. He calls us by name, and we *can* recognize His voice. He desires to lead us along paths of life that will satisfy our souls. He meets our every need. Jesus felt sorrow and rejection. He endured pain and suffering. Therefore He is able to help us in our time of need. Jesus finds us when we stray and protects us against Satan's schemes. He has given us victory by laying down His life for us. He is committed to us for eternity!

Do you have a personal relationship with the Good Shepherd? If not, why not ask Him into your heart right now. If you do know the Good Shepherd, can you recognize His voice? Ask for discernment. Listen intently. Then obey. The more we obey, the more we will be able to discern His voice.

Dear Lord, thank You for being my Good Shepherd.
Give me spiritual ears to hear and recognize Your voice.
Then give me the desire to obey and follow You. Amen.

DAY 142

Yield

*Trust in the LORD with all your heart and lean not on
your own understanding; in all your ways submit to him,
and he will make your paths straight.*

PROVERBS 3:5–6

The Lord has equipped us with everything we need to successfully navigate through life. The Bible serves as our road map to
prevent us from getting lost. We need to open it, read it, and obey
it. Not only do we have a road map, we have been given the Holy
Spirit as our personal Guide and Counselor. He is with us in every
situation. We need to listen and heed His instructions.

How are we doing? Do our lives feel like they're spinning out of
control? Do we often run ahead of the Lord or lag behind? The secret to walking in step with the Lord is found in our ability to "yield."
To yield means to submit, defer, or give way to someone. When we
yield to other drivers on the road, we acknowledge that they have the
right-of-way by allowing them to go first. To the extent that we learn
to yield to the Holy Spirit, we will be able to discern God's will.

Learning to stop, listen, yield, and follow are essential if we
want to be on God's path for our lives. Practically speaking, do not
make hasty decisions without praying for guidance first. Be willing
to wait until the Lord makes something clear through His Word,
other people, or your circumstances. Then be willing to step out
and follow Him.

*Dear Lord, it is very difficult to yield to the Holy Spirit
but so necessary for spiritual maturity. Help me defer
to You and not barge full-speed ahead in life. Amen.*

DAY 143

Dark Storm Clouds

We are hard pressed on every side, but not crushed;
perplexed, but not in despair; persecuted,
but not abandoned; struck down, but not destroyed.
2 CORINTHIANS 4:8–9

*M*any childhood fears can be attributed to the lack of wisdom. As adults, fear can still grip us because we lack God's wisdom. In the midst of trials, we may feel as though we're enveloped in dark storm clouds. Gloom and heaviness are inescapable. Fear whispers that we are about to be swallowed up by despair. In times like these, we must run to the Lord. He will remind us of spiritual truth. The dark storm clouds we experience in life are temporary. Beyond the clouds are clear blue skies, constant like the Lord's presence. The clouds may change and move, but the Lord remains the same.

As we trust God in the midst of the storm, He will give us sustaining hope. Our faith allows the dark clouds to part ever so slightly, permitting us to catch a glimpse of the blue sky beyond. God allows us to see things from His perspective—the spiritual realm. We then have confidence to persevere. Fear vanishes when we remember that the Lord is with us and will see us through. When dark storm clouds come our way, let's fix our eyes on Jesus so that we can see the patch of blue sky beyond.

Dear Lord, when life is scary, help me keep my eyes on You.
Give me hope that better days are ahead.
May I trust You instead of giving in to fear. Amen.

Day 144

Forgiveness

If we confess our sins, he is faithful and just and will forgive us our sins and purify us from all unrighteousness. If we claim we have not sinned, we make him out to be a liar and his word is not in us.

1 John 1:9–10

*M*uch like rain cleansing the air, God's forgiveness cleanses our souls. It washes away sin and guilt, bringing forth renewal and refreshment. Receiving God's forgiveness is the first step in our spiritual journeys. There is no sin *so great* that God's grace cannot cover it. Remember Saul? He persecuted Christians yet later became the apostle Paul, God's first missionary! Conversely, there is no sin *so small* that we do not need His forgiveness. God does not rank sin as man does. Sin is sin and God hates it all because it required the death of His one and only Son.

We must keep short accounts with God by quickly admitting our sin and receiving the forgiveness He offers. Once our fellowship with God is restored, we can then extend forgiveness to others. Our spiritual growth depends on it. When we refuse to forgive others, we wither and dry up spiritually. Our soul becomes parched and hard. Let's receive God's forgiveness and extend it to others. Experience renewal and refreshment for your soul!

Dear Lord, thank You for forgiving all my sins. May I be quick to forgive others as You have forgiven me. Amen.

Day 145

How Big Is Your Boat?

He replied, "You of little faith, why are you so afraid?" Then he got up and rebuked the winds and the waves, and it was completely calm. The men were amazed and asked, "What kind of man is this? Even the winds and the waves obey him!"

Matthew 8:26–27

Would you rather ride out a tropical storm on a cruise ship or in a tiny rowboat? Jesus' disciples encountered a terrifying experience on the Sea of Galilee in a small boat when a furious storm quickly developed. The disciples feared for their lives while Jesus slept soundly. After being abruptly woken up, Jesus rebuked the waves and then rebuked the disciples' lack of faith. Had they *truly understood* who slept in their midst, they would have felt secure despite the storm.

When we are in the midst of life's storms, remember: Jesus is in our boat! Circumstances may indicate that He is sleeping, but He knows *exactly* what is happening. Creator God is able to rebuke the raging waters and offer us peace. Trust Him. If we are just starting our spiritual journey, even life's smallest trials can rock our boat. Take heart! Our faith grows as we continue to trust Him during those moments and experience His faithfulness. As we look back, we realize that our faith has grown. We are now navigating life's waters in a cruise ship instead of in a rowboat.

*Dear Lord, may I truly understand who You are—
the great I AM. Your presence alone brings me peace.
Help me to trust You more. Amen.*

DAY 146

Spiritually Malnourished

Then Jesus declared, "I am the bread of life.
Whoever comes to me will never go hungry,
and whoever believes in me will never be thirsty."

JOHN 6:35

❧

*S*wollen bellies. Sunken eyes. Skeleton bodies. The signs of physical malnutrition are hard to miss. For most of us, it is difficult to fully comprehend physical starvation. Yet this is the devastating plight of millions around the world.

Physical malnutrition may not be an issue in your neighborhood, but spiritual malnutrition is. Just as our bodies crave physical sustenance, our souls yearn for spiritual food. Spiritual satisfaction eludes us when we seek spiritual food in the physical realm. We may mistakenly conclude that material possessions, successful careers, accomplished children, or perfect bodies can satisfy the yearning of our souls. The truth is only Jesus—the Bread of Life and the Living Water—can quench spiritual hunger and thirst.

Physical malnutrition does not suddenly disappear after one nutritious meal. A healthy body results from eating a balanced diet for weeks, months, and years. In the same way, we must feed on God's Word daily—for weeks, months, and years. How would you access your spiritual health? If a picture were taken of your soul, would you be diagnosed with spiritual malnutrition?

Dear Lord, may I look to You alone for spiritual satisfaction.
"As the deer pants for streams of water, so my soul
pants for you, my God" [Psalm 42:1]. Amen.

Day 147

When Love Hurts

But God demonstrates his own love for us in this:
While we were still sinners, Christ died for us.
ROMANS 5:8

$\mathcal{S}$ometimes love hurts. God powerfully demonstrated His love for us by sending His only Son to save a lost world. Jesus suffered a horrific death as He was nailed to the cross. He died to give eternal life to all who would believe in Him. How has the world responded to His ultimate sacrifice? Has everyone received the love He offered? Unfortunately, many have rejected Him. Although we may have received His love for eternal salvation, we still turn our backs on Him daily when we choose to go our own way. Jesus knows the pain of rejection.

Perhaps you have experienced rejection by someone you love—a child, spouse, parent, or friend. Take heart. Jesus knows *exactly* how you feel. And because of that, He is able to comfort you and give you the strength you need to carry on. He imparts hope that tomorrow will be brighter. Take one day at a time. Allow the Lord to mend your heart. Accept the love that He is offering You.

Dear Lord, whenever I am hurt and rejected by those I love, help me remember the cross and what You endured on my behalf. My betrayal pales in comparison. I receive Your unfailing love. Amen.

DAY 148

Following Christ

*From this time many of his disciples
turned back and no longer followed him.*
JOHN 6:66

❈

*D*uring Jesus' earthly ministry, great crowds followed Him initially. They were curious about the miracles He performed. They may have been intrigued by His teachings. Perhaps they enjoyed the food He miraculously produced when He fed the five thousand. Yet, as time went by, many of His followers fell by the wayside.

When we first met Jesus, we may have been excited and enthusiastic. We couldn't wait to tell everyone about our changed heart and our assurance of heaven! We were fired up! What has happened as the years have passed? Is the fire still burning, or is the flame dying out? Are we still following Jesus, or have we turned away?

A true follower of Christ will be sensitive to the Holy Spirit. This sensitivity is developed and nurtured by faithful obedience to Christ's commands. A true follower of Christ will want to serve others. A true follower of Christ is willing to sacrifice. A true follower of Christ will separate from the world. A true follower of Christ endures suffering, knowing that God will see us through it all. Let's follow Christ to the end!

*Dear Lord, I am challenged to be a true follower of Yours.
Show me how to practically live that out today. Amen.*

DAY 149

A Second Chance

"Then neither do I condemn you," Jesus declared.
"Go now and leave your life of sin."
JOHN 8:11

---

*O*ne day while Jesus was teaching in the temple courts, the teachers of the law and Pharisees brought in a woman caught in adultery. The punishment for adultery was stoning. They asked Jesus a question, hoping to trap Him and accuse Him of breaking the law. Knowing their devious motives, Jesus challenged them to examine their own hearts. If they were without sin, they could throw the first stone. Everyone eventually walked away—everyone except Jesus! He was the *only one* without sin. He "could have" thrown a stone but chose to forgive instead. Incredible! Jesus told the woman to go and leave her life of sin (see John 8:1–11).

When we sin, there are consequences. Galatians 6:7 warns, "Do not be deceived: God cannot be mocked. A man reaps what he sows." Yet we have a God who is merciful and forgiving. His love for us overcomes all. He gives us a second chance. He is always there to pick us up, brush us off, and send us back into the world. He will not condemn, but forgive. God's well of grace is deeper than we could ever imagine! Let's drink from it today.

Dear Lord, I mess up so much, yet You forgive rather
than condemn. Thank You for second chances.
Grant me power to leave my life of sin. Amen.

DAY 150

Praise God!

Let everything that has breath praise the LORD.
Praise the LORD.
PSALM 150:6

*P*raise is a powerful form of worship. God should be praised for who He is—His character. He should also be praised because of what He does. The good news is that we can praise Him anywhere and anytime! We do not need to be in a church setting. Praise is an attitude of the heart—so it knows no limits or boundaries!

We are called to praise God with all that we are and with all that we have. It might be easier to praise God when times are good. Yet God is worthy of our praise in bad times as well. That doesn't mean we feign elation when experiencing difficulties. But we can praise God because He is with us. He will never leave nor forsake us! We can praise Him for giving us strength and grace to endure. His mercy is new every morning. His faithfulness endures forever. We can praise Him for His peace and presence. When we focus on Him in good times and bad, our lives will be filled with praise! Praise the Lord, O my soul!

Dear Lord, You and You alone are worthy of my praise!
Do not let temporary trials rob me of my joy
in You and my praise of You! Amen.

DAY 151

Life's Difficulties

The LORD is my shepherd, I lack nothing.
PSALM 23:1

Shepherds lead their sheep to clean, fresh water and green, lush pastures. They tenderly care for each sheep in their fold. At night the sheep can rest peacefully because they know their shepherd is sleeping across the gate of their pen to protect them from wild animals.

Jesus is our Good Shepherd. We are the sheep in His pasture. Like sheep we can easily become frightened. We wander off and get lost. We desperately need a shepherd to meet our every need.

Take heart! When we are scared, He is there. We can be confident during life's difficulties because of His presence, His power, and His provision. Jesus is the One who dispels fear and provides comfort. He carries us through every experience—good or bad. He is trustworthy and *always* faithful. He *knows* all that is happening to us. He knows our thoughts and fears. Jesus is there for us. He shows mercy and love in many tangible ways. He guides and leads us in the right paths. We should have no cause for anxiety, because our Good Shepherd is always watching over us. He has a plan for us. Complete trust is what He desires from us—total surrender.

Dear Lord, I trust You as my Good Shepherd.
Calm my anxious thoughts.
May I rest in Your loving arms. Amen.

Day 152

Suffering

*Praise be to the God and Father of our Lord Jesus Christ,
the Father of compassion and the God of all comfort, who comforts
us in all our troubles, so that we can comfort those in any trouble
with the comfort we ourselves have received from God.*

2 Corinthians 1:3–4

No one is exempt from suffering. Although it is painful at the time, we must remember that our suffering does have divine purpose. We can count on God's comfort and strength to help us endure. The apostle Paul reminds us that because we experience God's comfort during trials, we can offer that same comfort to others when they encounter suffering. We don't have to go through the exact same trial as another to be able to offer comfort. Since God has been faithful to deliver us, He will be faithful to deliver them. That is the hopeful news that we can enthusiastically share with others!

We are encouraged to pray for one another when suffering hardships. "The prayer of a righteous person is powerful and effective" (James 5:16). The Lord will intervene. He will answer prayer and impart power. God's strength is sufficient for any trial.

Dear Lord, I must admit, I hate to suffer. Transform my suffering into joy as I turn to You for comfort. Remind me to pray for others and to offer them comfort in their time of need. Amen.

Day 153

Stewardship

For who makes you different from anyone else?
What do you have that you did not receive? And if you
did receive it, why do you boast as though you did not?
1 Corinthians 4:7

The self-made man or woman is highly regarded in today's society. Rags to riches success stories captivate us. It's the American Dream. As our culture subtly creeps into the church, boasting and bragging become commonplace. God gets left out of the picture as we pat ourselves on the back.

Stop and think for a moment. Everything we have has been given to us by God—our lives, families, material possessions, time, and abilities. God has entrusted us to manage the resources He has given us. In light of all that we have been given, how should we respond? We should freely offer everything back to Him as a gift of love.

It is important to be faithful. Since God owns everything, we must not hold on tightly to our time or money if God asks us to part with it. Ask the Lord how He wants you to spend the money, time, and talents He has given you. Then listen to His answer and be ready to obey.

Dear Lord, somehow I mistakenly think that everything I
am and have is due to my own efforts. Forgive me of my
arrogance. Help me see spiritual truth. May I give You
control of my finances, time, and talent. Amen.

DAY 154

Confession

*If we confess our sins, he is faithful and just and will forgive
us our sins and purify us from all unrighteousness.*

1 JOHN 1:9

The sacrificial death of Jesus Christ cleanses us from all our
sins—past, present, and future. Why, then, do we need to confess
our sins? Confession is simply agreeing with God that we have
fallen short of His perfect standard. We have "missed the mark."

"Sins of commission" may be easy to identify—lying, gossiping,
coveting, stealing, and so forth. But what about "sins of omission"—
those things we fail to do? "If anyone, then, knows the good they
ought to do and doesn't do it, it is sin for them" (James 4:17). Perhaps we failed to make a phone call when the Holy Spirit prompted.
Or we were too busy to take time to listen to a friend in need.

Ask the Lord to bring to mind sin in your life—especially sin
you may not even be aware of. Then confess those sins. Confession
restores intimacy with God. Our daily communion with God is
vital to maintaining a Spirit-filled life. Confession releases us from
guilt. Take responsibility for your sins. Receive the forgiveness and
grace that Christ offers.

*Dear Lord, although You are aware of my sins, make me aware also.
May I readily confess my sins and receive Your forgiveness. Amen.*

DAY 155

Forgiving One Another

*Be kind and compassionate to one another, forgiving
each other, just as in Christ God forgave you.*
EPHESIANS 4:32

*F*orgiveness is something we all want for ourselves but find difficult to extend to others. Why is that? Do we feel that our shortcomings are not as grievous as someone else's? Or maybe we want them to suffer for the pain they have inflicted. Whatever the reason, we are only hurting ourselves when we refuse to forgive.

An unforgiving spirit is like a cancer—it often steals a person's joy for years. What is the remedy? First, ask the Lord to forgive you of your unforgiving spirit. Acknowledge that your attitude is wrong. Receive God's forgiveness for yourself.

Then ask Him to help you extend forgiveness to the person you have in mind. *Release* the debt you feel they owe you. This is an act of the will. Acknowledge that the person's wrongdoing toward you exposed a weakness in your life. Forgiveness is a process. You may not be able to instantaneously move past the feelings of pain, hurt, and resentment. Each time the offense is brought to mind, ask the Lord to give you the strength to forgive. In time God will heal your heart. Remember how many times God has forgiven you, and be encouraged!

*Dear Lord, many times I am quick to receive Your forgiveness
yet slow to extend it to others. Forgive my prideful heart.
Transform my heart to be more like Yours. Amen.*

Day 156

Rejoice in Hard Times

Though the fig tree does not bud and there are no grapes on the vines, though the olive crop fails and the fields produce no food, though there are no sheep in the pen and no cattle in the stalls, yet I will rejoice in the LORD, I will be joyful in God my Savior.
HABAKKUK 3:17–18

Job was blameless and upright. He feared God and shunned evil. Yet Job quickly became acquainted with suffering and hard times. One minute he was prosperous and enjoying life with his large family, and the next minute he was knocked to his knees. He lost his oxen, donkeys, sheep, camels, servants, house, and children all in one day(chapter one of Job)!

Perhaps we are walking closely with the Lord yet are suffering greatly. We look around and see others having a much easier time. Evil is all around us. It appears that the unrighteous are in control. We may wonder why God permits such things. We must remember that we have a just God who *will* judge the wicked. Justice will be served in God's timing.

God allowed Job to be tested to prove that his faith was genuine. Perhaps God is permitting the same thing in your life. What must you do in the meantime? Cling to the Lord. He will restore you. Rejoice in the Lord, and be joyful in the God of your salvation! This is an act of the will that results in true worship.

Dear Lord, You are God in the good times and bad.
In that truth I can rejoice! Amen.

DAY 157

God Makes All Things New

For the LORD your God is God in
heaven above and on the earth below.

JOSHUA 2:11

---

*B*efore Joshua captured the town of Jericho, he secretly sent spies into the city. Rahab, the prostitute, had heard how the God of Israel had led His people out of Egypt. She believed that the Lord was "God in heaven above and on the earth below." Rahab acted on that belief by hiding the Israelite spies that had infiltrated the town of Jericho. Not only did the Lord reward Rahab by sparing her life, but she can be found in the genealogy of Jesus!

Nothing from our past can keep us from coming to God and becoming a member of His family. Rahab was a prostitute. David was an adulterer. Saul (apostle Paul) was a murderer. When we accept Jesus as Lord and Savior, all the heartaches of our past are forgiven and forgotten. "As far as the east is from the west, so far has he removed our transgressions from us" (Psalm 103:12).

Is your past preventing you from receiving God's forgiveness? Nothing is permanent with God. He is the Master of change! Allow Him to come into your life and change you from the inside out. "Therefore, if anyone is in Christ, the new creation has come: The old has gone, the new is here!" (2 Corinthians 5:17).

Dear Lord, regardless of my past, You love and accept me.
May I leave my past behind so that I can grow
in my relationship with You. Amen.

DAY 158

Forgiveness Extended

Then Peter came to Jesus and asked, "Lord, how many times
shall I forgive my brother or sister who sins against me?
Up to seven times?" Jesus answered, "I tell you,
not seven times, but seventy-seven times."
MATTHEW 18:21–22

How does one forgive a spouse that throws in the towel on your marriage? How about a child who runs away from home and squanders your money? Or a coworker who spreads lies about you and receives the promotion that should have been yours? Life is painful. At times it is very difficult to forgive others.

Forgiving someone once is hard enough—but *seventy-seven times*? This seems impossible until we grasp how many times the Lord continues to forgive us! God blesses a true spirit of forgiveness. Reconciliation is what God desires. Only God can grant us a forgiving heart and spirit.

To forgive someone means to agree not to hold anything against them. Here's how you know when you have truly forgiven someone:

1. The feelings you had against them are no longer present.
2. You can accept them.
3. Your concern about the person who wronged you supersedes your concern about what they did to you.

Dear Lord, You forgive me over and over. Give me
the ability to extend that kind of forgiveness to
others from my heart. Heal me today. Amen.

DAY 159

Forgiveness

But Joseph said to them, "Don't be afraid. Am I in the place of God?
You intended to harm me, but God intended it for good to
accomplish what is now being done, the saving of many lives."
GENESIS 50:19–20

*J*oseph had every right to hold a grudge against his brothers, but he didn't. They had sold him into Egyptian slavery. Joseph became Potiphar's attendant but found himself serving three years' jail time after being falsely accused of sexual misconduct by Potiphar's wife. Through it all Joseph never became bitter. Why? Joseph had faith that God was working behind the scenes. He was right! Joseph eventually became Pharaoh's right-hand man. At Joseph's reunion with his brothers, Joseph was able to extend forgiveness to them because the suffering they had imposed was overshadowed by God's greater purposes.

When we are walking with God, we, too, will prosper and fulfill His purposes. The Lord will turn evil into good. However, when we refuse to forgive others, God will not honor us. Forgiveness is not based on feelings—it is an act of the will. We must believe that God is in control and act on that belief by extending forgiveness. We will be held accountable for an unforgiving spirit. However, our lives will be blessed when we choose to forgive.

Dear Lord, help me follow Joseph's example of faith and
forgiveness. You are working in my life, too. Help me
demonstrate that belief by forgiving others. Amen.

DAY 160

Forgiving Ourselves

The LORD is compassionate and gracious, slow to anger,
abounding in love. He will not always accuse, nor will
he harbor his anger forever; he does not treat us as our
sins deserve or repay us according to our iniquities.

PSALM 103:8–10

*W*e may be able to forgive others, but do we forgive ourselves? Perhaps we replay our mistakes over and over again in our minds and beat ourselves up with every remembrance. Forward progress can only be made when we put our sin in the past and leave it there. Every time we drag it back up, we will stumble and fall.

Refusing to forgive ourselves is in essence refusing to believe God's Word. When God forgives us, He erases our sin forever. He never recalls our sin or holds it over us. God forgets that it even happened! "If we confess our sins, he is faithful and just and will forgive us our sins and purify us from all unrighteousness" (1 John 1:9). Believe God's Word. You have been declared "not guilty" because of Jesus' sacrifice. The debt has been paid once and for all. Forgive yourself. He has!

Dear Lord, sometimes I'm my own worst enemy. Help me believe
Your Word and forgive myself. Against You have I sinned.
So, if You have forgiven me, I am forgiven! Amen.

DAY 161

Spread the Word

I am not ashamed of the gospel, because it is the
power of God that brings salvation to everyone
who believes: first to the Jew, then to the Gentile.

ROMANS 1:16

*S*amantha was a home healthcare nurse. At a staff meeting one day, the subject of death and dying was being discussed. The following question was thrown out to the group: "Do you believe in life after death? Why or why not?" If you had been Samantha, how would you have responded? Many times we are hesitant to speak up about our faith. Why?

The apostle Paul was not ashamed of the good news of Jesus Christ. We may not be called to the foreign mission field, but we can proclaim the Gospel right where we are. As believers, we hold God's saving truth in our hearts. Therefore, we have an obligation to be shining lights to those around us who are stumbling in the dark.

God expects every believer to help spread the good news of His saving grace. As we pour our lives into our children or grandchildren, interact with coworkers, or relax with friends, God's truth can be lovingly shared with others. God plants the seed of faith in us that carries us from death into life. Let's not shrink back, but share His life-giving truth with others!

Dear Lord, give me boldness to share the Gospel message
with others. You have given me eternal life. May I
not keep Your Good News to myself. Amen.

Day 162

Generous Giving

Remember this: Whoever sows sparingly will also reap sparingly,
and whoever sows generously will also reap generously. Each of
you should give what you have decided in your heart to give,
not reluctantly or under compulsion, for God loves a cheerful giver.
2 Corinthians 9:6–7

God blesses us so that we can be a blessing to others. When we sow generously, we will also reap generously. A cyclical pattern of sowing and reaping develops whereby our lives act as conduits through which God's grace flows. In other words, God's blessings flow through our lives and spill over into the lives of those around us. The more we sow, the more we reap. God's glory is the end result.

We can generously give of our money, time, and talents. Seek the Lord's counsel on what He desires for you to give financially. This principle also applies to our time and talents. We cannot meet every need we encounter. Ask the Lord how He wants you to spend your time and talents. Then see how He supplies your needs so that you can generously give to others. The Lord will be praised when we generously give!

Dear Lord, help me see beyond myself. I am not
to hoard Your blessings. Teach me to give generously
to others so that You receive glory. Amen.

Day 163

Greed

The greedy bring ruin to their households,
but the one who hates bribes will live.

Proverbs 15:27

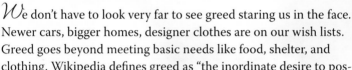

*W*e don't have to look very far to see greed staring us in the face. Newer cars, bigger homes, designer clothes are on our wish lists. Greed goes beyond meeting basic needs like food, shelter, and clothing. Wikipedia defines greed as "the inordinate desire to possess wealth, goods, or objects of abstract value with the intention to keep it for one's self, far beyond the dictates of basic survival and comfort."

Why does God warn against greed? Greed is the opposite of generosity. A greedy heart focuses on self, while a generous heart focuses on others. Greed is never satisfied—it always desires more. Greed tempts us to buy what we cannot afford, while withholding from those in need. Debt ultimately follows, and financial bondage is the end result. This is not God's will for us.

God warns us against all forms of greed. Be on guard to the temptations of greed. Ask the Lord to change your heart. Replace greed with generosity. Count your blessings. Be content with what the Lord has given you.

Dear Lord, so many times I run after things I "think" I must have. Break the hold that greed has on my heart. Instead, may I be content, grateful, and generous with what You have given me. Amen.

DAY 164

Deeds

But someone will say, "You have faith; I have deeds."
Show me your faith without deeds,
and I will show you my faith by my deeds.
JAMES 2:18

Salvation cannot be earned through our good works. Ephesians 2:8–9 states, "For it is by grace you have been saved, through faith—and this not from yourselves, it is the gift of God—not by works, so that no one can boast." So, what is our motive for doing good works?

We may do good deeds to make ourselves feel better or to receive accolades from others. In the end, selfish motives leave us feeling empty—there is no real reward. Or perhaps we are attempting to gain favor from the Lord through all of our hard work. However, grace cannot be earned. It can only be received.

Serving God because we love Him is the purest motive for good works. We serve God when we serve others. Because the Lord has given us eternal life, our good deeds are in response to His grace. Therefore, good works prove that our faith is genuine. Faith that is demonstrated by good deeds will reap eternal blessings.

Dear Lord, thank You for my salvation. You paid the ultimate price for my gift of grace. May I respond by demonstrating my faith through good works. May they be a love offering back to You. Amen.

Day 165

God's Promises

Let us hold unswervingly to the hope we profess,
for he who promised is faithful.
Hebrews 10:23

God has given us more than four thousand promises in the Bible. These promises can be limited or general, conditional or unconditional. General promises are for all people: "But God demonstrates his own love for us in this: While we were still sinners, Christ died for us" (Romans 5:8). Conditional promises require something of the believer: "And we know that in all things God works for the good of *those who love him*, who have been called according to his purpose" (Romans 8:28, emphasis added). Unconditional promises require nothing of the believer: "Never will I leave you; never will I forsake you" (Hebrews 13:5).

How many promises of God are you familiar with? Sometimes God's promises are all we have to cling to during times of trials and difficulties. God remains faithful. He will keep His promises! Read the Bible so that you will know the promises He has written for you. God's promises become the anchor in the storm—the hope we can cling to. Trust in His faithfulness and hang on tight!

Dear Lord, You have been so faithful to keep Your promises. Help me search Your Word diligently so that I can trust You more. Amen.

DAY 166

Claiming God's Promises

But do not forget this one thing, dear friends: With the Lord a day is like a thousand years, and a thousand years are like a day. The Lord is not slow in keeping his promise, as some understand slowness. He is patient with you, not wanting anyone to perish, but everyone to come to repentance.

2 PETER 3:8–9

---

*A*lthough this truth is difficult to comprehend, it is true just the same. Our timetable is not God's. His ways are higher than our ways. Yet many times we may secretly demand that the Lord fulfill His promises on our timetable—which usually means now!

Before claiming God's promises, ask yourself these questions: Does it meet my particular need or desire? Is it in submission to God's will? Will it honor God? Would it harm or hurt someone else? Does the Holy Spirit bear witness with my spirit that God is pleased? Does it conflict with God's Word? Will it fulfill my spiritual growth if God fulfills it? God honors His promises and always has our best interest at heart. The fulfillment of God's promise may require a wait. Be patient and trust Him.

Dear Lord, You are patient with us, desiring that everyone come to repentance. Help me submit to Your perfect timing. Give me patience and peace as I wait on You. You are faithful! Amen.

Day 167

Words

"For the mouth speaks what the heart is full of."
MATTHEW 12:34

*A*s Julie was growing up, her mother constantly told her, "It's not what you say, but how you say it." Julie always wondered how her mom could detect when she had a negative or bad attitude. Our mouth may speak words, but attitudes are also easily conveyed.

Words are but a reflection of our heart. Assess your speech. Are your words generally positive or negative—uplifting or critical—trusting or fearful—humble or proud? Words reveal the condition of our hearts. If our speech is to be pleasing to the Lord, we need to get to the root of the problem—our heart!

Only the Holy Spirit, who indwells every believer, can cleanse our hearts and fill us with new attitudes and motives. As our hearts are transformed over time, our words will also reflect this change. Since we will be held accountable for the words we speak, let us ask the Holy Spirit to change our hearts. Then our words will edify others and glorify the Lord. May it be so!

Dear Lord, sometimes I focus on trying to change the words
that come out of my mouth rather than confessing the
sinful attitudes in my heart. Change my heart so that
my words will be pleasing to You. Amen.

DAY 168

The Benefits of Prayer

*Do not be anxious about anything, but in every situation,
by prayer and petition, with thanksgiving, present your requests to
God. And the peace of God, which transcends all understanding,
will guard your hearts and your minds in Christ Jesus.*

PHILIPPIANS 4:6–7

Jesus was God's Son, yet He took time to get off by Himself and pray. Why did He need to pray? Didn't He know everything? He certainly didn't have any sin to confess. Jesus had a personal relationship with His heavenly Father, and so He wanted to talk with Him. Jesus wanted to carry out God's will. If Jesus saw the importance of prayer, shouldn't we?

Prayer is simply communicating with our heavenly Father. Eloquent words are not necessary, but transparent hearts are a must. Prayer is not about getting God to grant us our will, but to align our hearts with His.

Spending time with God in prayer enlarges our relationship with Jesus. We develop a passion to follow God in obedience. As we seek God's will for our lives, unique changes will occur. God will guard our hearts (emotions) and mind (thoughts). The pressures of life begin to dissolve when we lay down our burdens before Him. Our anxious hearts will find rest and experience peace. Let's follow Jesus' example and make time to pray today.

*Dear Lord, may I come to You throughout the day with
a humble, open heart. Align my will with Yours. I want
to exchange my anxiety for Your peace. Amen.*

DAY 169

Sharing Our Faith

"In the same way, let your light shine before others, that they may see your good deeds and glorify your Father in heaven."

MATTHEW 5:16

---

*D*arkness is the absence of light. Even the tiniest bit of light dispels darkness. Jesus is the Light of the World. When we know Jesus, His light radiates from our lives. Our lives—our light—are supposed to shine in the darkness so that He is revealed.

Our lives speak volumes. God desires that they be a powerful witness for Christ to those around us. He calls us to be shining lights on a hill that attract others to Himself. Unfortunately sometimes we become glaring spotlights that blind and repel instead.

How do we become a shining light? How do we pass on our faith to others? Begin by asking God to prepare you to be used by Him. Spend time with God in prayer so that you are sensitive to opportunities that He brings across your path. Live a consistent spiritual life. Learn to truly listen to others as they share their hurts. Be patient and long-suffering. Love others unconditionally. Your life will then stand out in stark contrast to the world. Others will not only see Jesus in you but will want to know Him also.

Dear Lord, help me to be a shining light rather than a glaring one. I want to share my faith with others so that they may come to know You. Amen.

Day 170

Passing on Our Faith

I have been reminded of your sincere faith, which first
lived in your grandmother Lois and in your mother
Eunice and, I am persuaded, now lives in you also.
2 Timothy 1:5

*W*ould you consider yourself a leader or a follower? Even if you are content to follow, there is someone in your life that you are leading—a child or grandchild, a neighbor, a coworker. You may be oblivious to your influence. But rest assured, they are observing your life and learning from you all the time.

Timothy was a third-generation believer. The apostle Paul points out that Timothy's grandmother Lois and mother, Eunice, had been godly examples to young Timothy. How was their walk with the Lord so influential in his life? They must have consistently lived out their genuine faith before him. They must have "walked the talk." He undoubtedly wanted what they possessed—Christ.

Our faith must be so ingrained in us that it automatically comes out when we are with others. Does God's love flow through us? Showing unconditional love brings courage and hope to the most fearful hearts. God has given us a spirit of power, love, and self-discipline. Since we, like Timothy, have received this gift of faith, may we be compelled to pass it on to those following close behind.

Dear Lord, may I be cognizant of those in my sphere of influence.
May I "walk the talk" so that I can pass on my faith to them. Amen.

DAY 171

Power, Love, and Discipline

For the Spirit God gave us does not make us timid,
but gives us power, love and self-discipline.
2 TIMOTHY 1:7

*T*imid is an adjective that means "showing a lack of courage or confidence; easily frightened." As Christians we have not been given a timid spirit; one that is easily frightened. Instead, we have been given the powerful Holy Spirit. When the apostle Paul pleaded with the Lord three times to remove his thorn in the flesh, the Lord responded by saying, "My grace is sufficient for you, for *my power* is made perfect in weakness" (2 Corinthians 12:9). Therefore Paul concluded in verse 10 of 2 Corinthians 12: "For when I am weak, then I am strong." The secret to power and courage is to rely on the Holy Spirit rather than ourselves.

To the extent that we allow the Holy Spirit control, fruit of the Spirit will be produced: love, joy, peace, forbearance, kindness, goodness, faithfulness, gentleness, and self-control (see Galatians 5:22–23). God's love shines through us as we serve others. Self-control, or discipline, is also evident in our lives. Is your life characterized by power, love, and discipline? If not, receive them by yielding to the Holy Spirit.

Dear Lord, may I yield more of my life to the control
of the Holy Spirit so that I can live a life that is
full of power, love, and discipline. Amen.

Day 172

Acceptance of Suffering

*"Come to me, all you who are weary and burdened,
and I will give you rest. Take my yoke upon you and learn from
me, for I am gentle and humble in heart, and you will find rest
for your souls. For my yoke is easy and my burden is light."*
MATTHEW 11:28–30

Whatever God puts on our shoulders, we must be willing to accept. Accepting our suffering is an important step toward healing. When we acknowledge that He has permitted suffering to come into our lives, we can easily turn to Him for help. Jesus was no exception. Although Jesus did not want to suffer and die, He submitted to God's will and prayed for the strength to endure. Acceptance does not mean jubilation. Jesus was not elated that He would suffer and die, yet He was at peace, knowing that He was in the center of God's will.

The Lord may allow suffering to come into our lives. We do not have to feign happiness. However, we can know that the Lord is there with us in the midst of our suffering. As we come to Him and are yoked to Him, He carries our load and gives us peace. He will never leave nor forsake us. He is with us all the way!

*Dear Lord, may I come to You in my times of suffering.
Carry my burdens, Lord, and grant me Your peace. Amen.*

DAY 173

Criticizing Others

*"Do not judge, or you too will be judged. For in the same
way you judge others, you will be judged, and with
the measure you use, it will be measured to you."*
MATTHEW 7:1–2

"Those parents must not supervise their children or they wouldn't have been busted for drugs." "The new boss is clueless!" "Can you believe what she's wearing?" The list of subjects to criticize others about is endless. Criticism runs the gamut from trivial to monumental matters.

What motivates us to criticize or judge others? Perhaps we put others down to make ourselves look better. Or maybe we are retaliating for an offense that was committed against us. Whatever the reason, there is never an appropriate time to judge others.

The Holy Spirit is the only One in the proper position to convict. It is impossible to have fellowship with God with a critical spirit. When we judge someone else, the sin of pride has reared its ugly head. Humility, not pride, should characterize our lives. We are not superior to anyone. God alone is above all. Let's confess our critical spirit and allow the Lord to take the logs out of our eyes.

*Dear Lord, even when I don't outwardly criticize others,
You know my heart. Break the sin of pride that creeps
in and compels me to sit in judgment of others. Amen.*

Day 174

Temptation

No temptation has overtaken you except what is common to mankind. And God is faithful; he will not let you be tempted beyond what you can bear. But when you are tempted, he will also provide a way out so that you can endure it.

1 Corinthians 10:13

Temptation presents itself to us in one of three ways: the lust of the flesh, the lust of the eyes, or the pride of life. Jesus was tempted in every way, just like we are, yet was without sin (see Matthew 4:1–11). Anything that separates us from God—habits, desires, feelings—is evidence that temptation has gotten a foothold.

The good news is that we do not have to succumb to temptation! We have a choice. We can say no! Jesus withstood temptation by quoting scripture. God is faithful. When we turn to Him in our hour of temptation, He will provide the way of escape. The question we must ask ourselves is this: Do we want to take God's way out? Temptation is an opportunity for obedience that in turn leads to blessing. Choose to take the way out!

Dear Lord, even though I am tempted, I can choose not to sin. In that moment, help me turn to You and choose obedience instead. Thank You for Your faithfulness to provide a way out. Amen.

DAY 175

Obedience

But Samuel replied: "Does the LORD delight in burnt offerings and sacrifices as much as in obeying the LORD? To obey is better than sacrifice, and to heed is better than the fat of rams."
1 SAMUEL 15:22

*S*ometimes sacrifice is easier than obedience. We can check something off and feel good about ourselves. Yet God's Word is clear: the Lord desires obedience rather than sacrifice. Obedience requires walking God's way, internally (in the attitude of our heart) and externally (in outward words and actions). The two must match. God is not deceived. Halfhearted obedience is disobedience.

As the Israelites wandered in the desert, they learned obedience by following the cloud—God's presence. When the cloud lifted, they broke camp and followed. When the cloud settled, they set up camp and stayed put.

We, too, must learn to wait on God's timing. Obediently waiting demonstrates trust. Conversely, impatience indicates that fleshly desires are active. Obedience may mean going forward even when the way appears unclear. Our willingness to step out of our "comfort zone" confirms our belief that God is in control. Facing suffering and trials with the strength God provides can be another step of obedience that allows us to grow spiritually. Are you willing to be obedient?

*Dear Lord, You want me to trust and follow You.
Help my heart desire obedience whether I'm waiting
on You or stepping out in faith. Amen.*

DAY 176

Sin

For I do not do the good I want to do,
but the evil I do not want to do—this I keep on doing.
ROMANS 7:19

*H*ave you ever said, "I'm not going to do *that* again!"—and then immediately do the very thing you vowed you'd never repeat? Or have you ever purposed to do something good but just couldn't carry it out? Welcome to the human race!

We all struggle with sin. Although we may want to do what's right, we don't always follow through. Today's passage reveals that even the apostle Paul experienced inner struggles with sin. Although we're forgiven, Christians still wrestle daily with the sinful nature that we all possess.

Refusing to acknowledge our sinful nature just sets us up for disaster. We must reconcile ourselves to the fact that our human relationships are flawed by sin. None of us is perfect. Paul concludes these verses by saying in Romans 7:24–25, "What a wretched man I am! Who will rescue me from this body that is subject to death? Thanks be to God, who delivers me through Jesus Christ our Lord!" Because of our sinful nature, we *all* need the Lord! He is the only One who can rescue us.

Dear Lord, I am utterly hopeless without You! May
Your Holy Spirit empower me to live the life that You
have called me to. You dealt with my sin on the cross;
please deal with my sinful nature today! Amen.

Day 177

God Meets All of Our Needs

*For we do not have a high priest who is unable to empathize
with our weaknesses, but we have one who has been tempted in
every way, just as we are—yet he did not sin. Let us then approach
God's throne of grace with confidence, so that we may receive
mercy and find grace to help us in our time of need.*

Hebrews 4:15–16

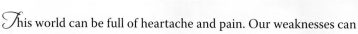

This world can be full of heartache and pain. Our weaknesses can
be exposed in an instant. Illness can wreak havoc with our body.
Job loss can send us into a financial tailspin. Divorce can leave us
an emotional wreck. Where can we go when feeling vulnerable
and weak?

Jesus is our empathetic, approachable great High Priest. He
sympathizes with our weaknesses. Although He endured temptation like us, He never succumbed to sin. This is great news,
because it means He is able to give us victory and meet all of our
needs. We must confidently come to Him to receive mercy and
grace.

God is *always* there for us when we need Him. He desires to
bear our burdens and help us. The Lord should be our first option
in times of trials and tribulations. He knows us and can relate to
our circumstances. He gives us assurance. Why would we go anywhere else?

*Dear Lord, when no one else can relate to what I am going
through, You can. May I come boldly to You with confidence.
Meet my every need. Amen.*

DAY 178

Agape Love

This is love: not that we loved God, but that he loved us and
sent his Son as an atoning sacrifice for our sins. Dear friends,
since God so loved us, we also ought to love one another.

1 JOHN 4:10–11

*P*atrick grew up in a home with conditional love. When he
brought home As, he experienced his father's love. But when Patrick failed to measure up, love was withdrawn. If you can relate to
Patrick, agape love may be difficult to comprehend or emulate.

"God is love" (1 John 4:8). God's love does not depend on our
performance. He always loves us—period. His love is unconditional and self-sacrificing. God's love cannot be earned. It is freely
given, not because of who we are or what we do, but because of
who He is! Once we receive and experience God's love, we are
commanded to love others in the same way.

Jesus wants us to demonstrate agape or unconditional love.
This kind of love involves sacrifice and surrender of self for the
sake of another. Agape love puts others' needs above our own, calling us to forsake our own desires. "This is how we know what love
is: Jesus Christ laid down his life for us. And we ought to lay down
our lives for our brothers and sisters" (1 John 3:16).

Dear Lord, it is impossible to love as You do in our own strength.
Give me Your power to love others as You have loved me. Amen.

Day 179

The Future

Whatever your hand finds to do, do it with all your might,
for in the realm of the dead, where you are going, there is
neither working nor planning nor knowledge nor wisdom.

Ecclesiastes 9:10

*A*ll humans will experience two significant days in their lives—
their birthday and the day of their death. God already knows them
both. Psalm 139:16 states, "All the days ordained for me were written in your book before one of them came to be." In our culture,
many times death is a taboo subject. Yet death is inevitable. Even if
we remain in denial, no one will escape physical death. In light of
this truth, how should we then live?

We are not to retreat from life, but rather to enjoy the gifts
that God has given us today. Each day is special because it presents
new opportunities to serve and please the Lord. There is much joy
in walking daily with God and living according to His principles.
We may not know what our immediate future holds, but we do
know *who* holds our future! Trust Him. He is in control. In life or
death, we are securely held. How wonderful!

Dear Lord, I do not have to fear the future. Even in death,
You will walk with me. Thank You for Your guiding presence.
May I celebrate each day of life in You! Amen.

Day 180

Basic Economics

*Be sure you know the condition of your flocks, give careful
attention to your herds; for riches do not endure forever,
and a crown is not secure for all generations.*

Proverbs 27:23–24

The Lord appeared to King Solomon in a dream and said, "Ask for
whatever you want me to give you." Instead of asking for wealth,
Solomon asked the Lord for a discerning heart to govern the Israelites. The Lord granted him wisdom like no other. King Solomon
also became an exceptionally wealthy man.

The book of Proverbs is thought to have been written by Solomon. In these verses he exhorts the reader to "know the condition
of your flocks." We may not have flocks, but we might have invest-
ments, savings accounts, or other assets. We are to be knowledge-
able about our financial situation. This is imperative if we are to be
good stewards of the resources God has entrusted to our care.

Feigning ignorance is not a valid excuse for incurring debt.
We must deal with financial reality in order to make wise, financial
decisions. When we "know the condition" of our finances, we can
answer questions such as: Can we afford to buy this now, or should
we wait? God will provide for our needs. We must be responsible
to manage His assets well.

*Dear Lord, help me get a handle on my finances.
Hold me accountable to wisely manage the material
blessings You have bestowed on me. Amen.*

DAY 181

Our Earthly Body

*Therefore we do not lose heart. Though outwardly we are
wasting away, yet inwardly we are being renewed day by day.
For our light and momentary troubles are achieving for
us an eternal glory that far outweighs them all.*

2 CORINTHIANS 4:16–17

$\mathcal{D}$oes getting older depress you? Although we might desperately
attempt to slow down the aging process, our bodies deteriorate
with each passing year. There is just no way around it! Yet, despite
our physical limitations, God does not want us to lose heart.

Although our bodies may slow down, our spirits can be constantly renewed. This is great news, because someday our earthly
bodies will return to the dust, but our spirits will live forever. Ask
the Lord to help you shift your focus from the physical to the
spiritual.

When we experience temporary suffering, we can look forward to an eternity that is glorious and beyond anything we now
know. We can live confidently today because we know that death
will usher us into the Lord's presence. When we are walking with
the Lord, it's a win-win situation. Are you allowing the Lord to
renew your spirit with each passing day?

*Dear Lord, help me fix my eyes "not on what is seen,
but on what is unseen, since what is seen is temporary,
but what is unseen is eternal" [2 Corinthians 4:18]. Amen.*

DAY 182

Grow Up

*...until we all reach unity in the faith and in the knowledge
of the Son of God and become mature, attaining to
the whole measure of the fullness of Christ.*

EPHESIANS 4:13

*S*piritual maturity is a process whereby we become more and
more Christlike. Not only will we know truth, but we will be able
to speak that truth into the lives of those around us. Here are some
signs of spiritual growth:

1. We become more aware of our own sinfulness and our
   weaknesses.
2. We respond quickly to sin. Genuine repentance is present.
3. Although spiritual battles are more intense, we are still
   able to rejoice.
4. We see trials and temptations as opportunities for spiritual
   growth.
5. Service to the Lord is an honor, not a burden.

Are you growing up, or are you content to remain an infant in
the Lord? Let's press on to maturity so that we will not be
vulnerable. "Then we will no longer be infants, tossed back and forth
by the waves, and blown here and there by every wind of teaching
and by the cunning and craftiness of people in their deceitful schem-
ing" (Ephesians 4:14).

*Dear Lord, grow me up to spiritual maturity. Give me
discipline to read the Bible daily so that Your Word is
planted in my heart. Then may it take root and grow. Amen.*

Spiritual Maturity

Instead, speaking the truth in love, we will grow to become in every respect the mature body of him who is the head, that is, Christ.
EPHESIANS 4:15

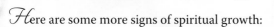

$\mathcal{H}$ere are some more signs of spiritual growth:

1. We view God as sovereign, acknowledging that everything that comes into our lives has passed through His fingers: He has either brought it or allowed it.
2. Our faith is growing stronger. More time is spent in praise and worship.
3. The desire for obedience becomes more intense.
4. We are more aware of His presence at all times.
5. Quiet time and Bible study are priorities.
6. We have an eagerness to share with others what Christ is doing in our lives.

Do not become discouraged if you do not see these signs in your own life. Start with baby steps. Read the scripture references in these devotionals. Meditate on spiritual truth. Ask the Lord to help you apply it today. Then do the same thing tomorrow. As we walk with the Lord each day, maturity will happen over time. Be patient. God is!

Dear Lord, I want to be mature right now, but I know that spiritual maturity does not happen overnight. As Your seed of truth is planted in my heart each day, may it take root and grow. Amen.

DAY 184

Testing Our Spiritual Growth

For those God foreknew he also predestined to be
conformed to the image of his Son, that he might
be the firstborn among many brothers and sisters.
ROMANS 8:29

Children develop characteristics of their parents; similar mannerisms, values, and speech are a few examples. In the same way, Christians should take on the characteristics of Christ. This doesn't happen automatically. We must spend time with Him.

The Christian life is never stagnant—we are either moving forward or backward in our relationship with the Lord. We move forward when we are obedient to His Word and follow Him. We draw closer because we are listening and obeying, like sheep following their shepherd. Conversely, when we ignore His truth or go our own way, we move further from Him. Sin and rebellion have put a wedge in our relationship. It has been said, "If you don't feel close to God, guess who moved?"

There are times when you might be following the Lord yet "feel" stagnant. Take heart! Emotions can fool you. God is working out His perfect plan in His perfect timing. Rest right where you are until He reveals the next step. Studying His Word and spending time in prayer each day are crucial. God will be faithful to draw you to Himself and conform you to the likeness of His Son.

Dear Lord, I want to grow closer to You. May I study the
Bible so that I can follow in faithful obedience. Amen.

Day 185

Praying for Our Nation

*"If my people, who are called by my name, will humble
themselves and pray and seek my face and turn from
their wicked ways, then will I hear from heaven,
and I will forgive their sin and will heal their land."*

2 Chronicles 7:14

After the dedication of the temple, the Lord appeared to Solomon and spoke these words from 2 Chronicles. Israel had a rocky history of rebellion followed by repentance and restoration. Although Israel was God's chosen people, they did not always walk in His ways. During prosperous times, they became arrogant and proud. God had to discipline them in order to bring them back to Himself. This pattern repeated itself over and over again.

The United States' history is not as long as Israel's, yet as Christians we are called to intercede for our nation. "Let everyone be subject to the governing authorities, for there is no authority except that which God has established" (Romans 13:1). Prayers for our nation and leaders are important. God hears. Nothing is impossible with God's help. May we not forsake the Lord. We need revival. Lord, may it be so!

*Dear Lord, our country has gotten so far away from
biblical truth. It is never too late to turn back to
the principles that our nation was founded upon.
Help me faithfully pray for You to heal our land. Amen.*

A Man after God's Own Heart

*But now your kingdom will not endure; the LORD has sought out
a man after his own heart and appointed him ruler of his people,
because you have not kept the LORD's command.*

1 SAMUEL 13:14

Saul was thirty years old when he became king over Israel. He
reigned for forty-two years. While Saul was king, the Philistines
assembled to fight Israel. The prophet Samuel was late in coming
and Israel was outnumbered, so Saul panicked and offered up the
burnt offering himself. When Samuel arrived, he confronted Saul
with the piercing words in the passage above. God would give
Saul's kingdom to David.

David was truly a man after God's own heart. What does this
mean? David's heart was bent toward God. He sought to know
Him, serve Him, obey Him, and seek His will. This does not mean
that David never sinned—he did. David was human just like we
are. However, when he sinned, he turned toward God with a repentant heart and received forgiveness.

Would God say that your heart is inclined toward His? Commit
to seek the Lord in all things. Desire His will for your life above your
own. Ask Him to direct your paths. Repent when you have sinned.
Receive His forgiveness. Hearts seeking God will be blessed.

*Dear Lord, "As the deer pants for streams of water,
so my soul pants for you, my God" [Psalm 42:1]. Amen.*

Victories in the Battles of Life

"The LORD who rescued me from the paw of the lion and the paw of the bear will rescue me from the hand of this Philistine."

1 SAMUEL 17:37

Have you ever felt like the odds were stacked against you? Perhaps you felt like a little shepherd boy facing a giant. Be reminded of David, and be encouraged!

It was an unlikely scenario: a young shepherd boy killing a giant warrior. The odds were stacked against David, yet God was on his side, and that made all the difference. David was not afraid to face the Philistine giant. In fact, he confidently proclaimed that the Lord would deliver him! Most of us know the rest of the story: David's small stone hit Goliath in the forehead, killing him instantly.

We must remember that the battles we face are the Lord's, too! Nothing is too hard for Him. We must have a servant's attitude and spend time in His Word to develop an intimacy with Him. Sometimes when we least expect it, God gives us victory. Like David, we must rely on God's power and not our own. Our faith must be unswerving, inexhaustible—a total trust in God for everything. He gives us victory!

Dear Lord, help me be bold and confident like David in the battles I face. Help me rely solely on Your power to give me victory. The battle is Yours! Amen.

Day 188

Friendships

One who has unreliable friends soon comes to ruin,
but there is a friend who sticks closer than a brother.
PROVERBS 18:24

❖

God created us to be relational. We thrive when we foster relationships with other people by spending time together and sharing from the heart. True friendships are built on mutual respect, emotional love, and genuine commitment. Friendships take time to develop. Rarely do two people become best friends overnight.

Not only were we created to be in relationship with one another, but there is also an innate desire in each one of us to know our Creator. A personal relationship with our heavenly Father is possible because of Jesus Christ. He is our truest friend. He will never leave us nor forsake us. We can respect Him as being wise and just. We feel safe and secure in His presence.

Do you know Jesus? If not, open your heart to Him today and meet the greatest friend you'll ever have. If Jesus already is your best friend, nurture your relationship. Spend time in His Word. Communicate through prayer. Share your heart, and listen to His. Jesus is always available. He responds to our cries for help. He sticks closer than a brother!

Dear Lord, I am so blessed to call You friend.
May I not take my relationship with You for granted. Amen.

DAY 189

The Struggle

For our struggle is not against flesh and blood, but against the rulers, against the authorities, against the powers of this dark world and against the spiritual forces of evil in the heavenly realms.

EPHESIANS 6:12

The apostle Paul describes our human struggle. He opens our eyes to the fact that our real battles are not physical, but spiritual in nature. An unseen spiritual battle is raging all around us. Although it is invisible, it is real just the same. We need not be afraid, but we do need to be aware.

We are constantly being tempted. When the seeds of temptation germinate in our hearts, they sprout and choke our relationship with God. Temptation can gain a foothold when we are more concerned about what the world thinks than about what God thinks, or when our focus turns to self.

With a transparent heart, we are to trust and obey God. This allows Him to fight our battles. God has equipped us with spiritual armor—the belt of truth, breastplate of righteousness, shield of faith, helmet of salvation, and the sword of the Spirit (see Ephesians 6:13–18). Let's put on the full armor of God so that we can be victorious over temptation!

Dear Lord, help me to be aware of the spiritual battle I am in. May I turn to You so that I can be assured of the victory that You have already won for me. Amen.

DAY 190

Life and Death

*This day I call the heavens and the earth as witnesses against you
that I have set before you life and death, blessings and curses.
Now choose life, so that you and your children may live and that
you may love the LORD your God, listen to his voice,
and hold fast to him. For the LORD is your life.*

DEUTERONOMY 30:19–20

*B*efore entering the Promised Land, the Lord warned the Israelites through Moses that they had two choices: life or death—
blessings or curses. The choice was theirs. If they loved the Lord
and walked in His ways, they would live.

If you were given the choice between life and death, which
would you choose? Jesus holds out eternal life to each one of us.
But we must receive His gift in order to live spiritually. Many
people postpone making that decision. Unfortunately, by default,
they are choosing death. The time to make this choice is now—in
this life. Once we take our last breath, it is too late. If we have not
chosen Jesus in this life, we will not be with Him in the next. Hell is
living apart from God for all eternity.

Jesus is offering you eternal life. Accept Him today and live.
You will also receive a relationship with the Creator of the universe, peace in the midst of life's greatest storms, joy that knows
no bounds, a Friend who will never leave your side, purpose and
direction for your life, and a home in heaven! Choose life today!

Dear Lord, I receive Jesus. I choose life. Amen.

Day 191

Know Thyself

In the spring, at the time when kings go off to war,
David sent Joab out with the king's men and the whole
Israelite army. They destroyed the Ammonites and
besieged Rabbah. But David remained in Jerusalem.

2 Samuel 11:1

King David should have been off to war with his men, but he remained in Jerusalem instead. One evening he got up from bed and walked around on the roof of his palace. There he spotted Bathsheba bathing. After seeing her beauty, he wanted her. You probably know the rest of the story.

We, too, have vulnerable moments. Know yourself; we are all unique. Be especially diligent when outside your norm or routine. Avoid situations that tempt you to sin—don't even flirt by getting too close to the fire—you *will* get burned. Surround yourself with godly role models who can help keep you accountable.

However, despite our best efforts, temptation will still present itself. Jesus Himself was tempted. But, like Jesus, we do not need to succumb to sin. When we put on the full armor of God and pray, God will give us the strength we need to resist (see Ephesians 6:10–17).

Dear Lord, help me to be aware of my own vulnerabilities.
May I rely on Your armor and strength to keep
me strong during times of temptation. Amen.

Day 192

Our Priority

*Jesus replied: " 'Love the Lord your God with all your
heart and with all your soul and with all your mind.'
This is the first and greatest commandment."*

MATTHEW 22:37–38

*O*ur relationship with God should be our number one priority in
life. Isn't it interesting that this commandment from Jesus cor-
responds to the first of the Ten Commandments that God gave
Moses: "You shall have no other gods before me" (Deuteronomy
5:7)? God repeats and highlights important truth throughout the
Bible that He wants us to grasp.

If something or someone else has preeminence, an idol has
usurped God's rightful place as Lord. Idols could be ideals, people,
relationships, or material things of this world. Idols can even be
"good," but when they become more important than God, we need
to reevaluate our priorities.

Why is God so concerned about being first in our lives? Idols
prevent us from knowing God intimately and loving Him with all
our hearts, souls, and minds. Idols limit us from becoming all that
God intended—all that He created us to be. Idols circumvent God's
design for our lives. What idols have pushed God aside in your life?
Commit to reestablish the Lord on the throne of your heart today.

*Dear Lord, show me the idols in my life.
Give me the desire to love You most of all. Amen.*

DAY 193

Love Speaks Volumes

*"A new command I give you: Love one another. As I have
loved you, so you must love one another. By this everyone
will know that you are my disciples, if you love one another."*
JOHN 13:34–35

What was Jesus' strategy for spreading the Gospel? How did He envision the disciples passing on their faith to the next generation? Jesus did not focus on communicating doctrine. He did not emphasize following specific laws. Jesus simply told His disciples to love one another. Their love would be enough to turn the world upside down!

Love is powerful. It speaks volumes. Jesus epitomized love when He died on the cross on our behalf. After His death and resurrection, His disciples followed suit by living lives of love. When we emulate His love, we demonstrate that we are also His disciples. Jesus is our example. Love enables us to be transformed into the image of Christ.

God's unconditional love compelled Him to forgive, redeem, and restore us. As we love others unconditionally, we help point them to Christ. Loving our enemies is impossible without the power of the Holy Spirit. Yet, when we love our enemies, the world takes notice. Love speaks volumes! God is love!

*Dear Lord, may I love my neighbor as You have loved me.
Give me Your eyes to see others as You do. Amen.*

Day 194

Meditation

One generation commends your works to another; they tell of your mighty acts. They speak of the glorious splendor of your majesty— and I will meditate on your wonderful works.

Psalm 145:4–5

The word "meditation" conjures up many different meanings in today's world. Buddhist monks and Yoga enthusiasts alike meditate. Is this the same kind of meditation that is mentioned in the Bible? Meditation involves quieting the body and mind so that thoughts become focused.

It greatly matters what we choose to meditate on. David meditated on God's wonderful works. God-centered meditation focuses on God's Word so that we can know Him better. We learn about His will, His work, His ways, and His person. Truth is absorbed into our minds and digested into our hearts. Meditation that enables truth to be lived out in our daily lives makes a profound difference.

How do we get started? Read the Bible daily. Then pray over the scripture. Ponder it throughout the day. Ask the Lord to show you ways to apply His truth to your life. As we meditate on God's Word, truth moves from our heads to our hearts.

Dear Lord, meditation is an act of my will—a choice to think about Your Word instead of other things. Help me discipline my mind so that Your truth can be lived out in my life. Amen.

DAY 195

Time with God

That person is like a tree planted by streams of water,
which yields its fruit in season and whose leaf does
not wither—whatever they do prospers.

PSALM 1:3

*D*oes that verse describe you? The secret to God's blessings are found in the preceding verses: "Blessed is the one who does not walk in step with the wicked or stand in the way that sinners take or sit in the company of mockers, but whose delight is in the law of the LORD, and who meditates on his law day and night" (Psalm 1:1–2). We must forsake worldly counsel and spend time in God's Word if we want our lives to flourish.

Set aside time each day to spend with God. Habits are formed quicker if we can get into a predictable routine—the same time and place each day. Our spirits need to be still and silent by eliminating distractions. In these moments we can listen to God's voice speak truth to our hearts. Time with God quiets our spirits and purifies our hearts. When we hunger for His Word, we are given a clearer sense of direction. Let's make time to be alone with God. It will indeed be time well spent!

Dear Lord, I am pulled in so many directions each day.
Help me to make spending time with You a priority. Amen.

The Lamb of God

The next day John saw Jesus coming toward him and said,
"Look, the Lamb of God, who takes away the sin of the world!"
JOHN 1:29

————⋙⋘————

Many Jews in Jesus' day thought John the Baptist was the promised Messiah or the prophet Elijah. After denying this time and time again, John the Baptist quoted the words of the prophet Isaiah and said, "I am the voice of one calling in the wilderness, 'Make straight the way for the Lord ' " (John 1:23).

One day John was baptizing in the Jordan River and Jesus came to be baptized. As Jesus approached him, John the Baptist proclaimed that Jesus was the Lamb of God who takes away the sin of the world! Like a Passover lamb, Jesus' death gave life. When the Israelites covered their doorposts with the blood of an unblemished lamb, the angel of death "passed over" them during the night (see Exodus 12:1–30). When we are covered with the blood of Jesus, we are not only given life but given life everlasting!

God accepts us, loves us, and grants us access to Him in prayer—not because of anything we have done to deserve His favor, but because of the blood of Jesus. We became children of God the moment we accepted Christ as our Lord and Savior and trusted in His sacrificial death as atonement for our sins. We were bought with the blood of Jesus, the Lamb of God.

Dear Lord, You are indeed the Lamb of God!
Thank You for laying down Your life for me. Amen.

Justification

*But God demonstrates his own love for us in this: While we
were still sinners, Christ died for us. Since we have now
been justified by his blood, how much more shall we
be saved from God's wrath through him!*

ROMANS 5:8–9

Justification is a big-sounding theological word that is difficult
to explain to children. In an attempt to simplify its meaning, it
has been said that justification means, it's "just as if" never sinned.
The dictionary's definition is: "the action of declaring or making
righteous in the sight of God." When we accept Christ as our Savior,
God immediately justifies us. We are declared "not guilty." When
God looks at us, He sees Jesus' righteousness and imputes it to our
account. We are acceptable to God because of Jesus.

"If God is for us, who can be against us?" (Romans 8:31).
God accepts us and does not condemn us. In light of His love, we
should have no reason to suffer from poor self-esteem. Catch a
glimpse of how the God of the universe looks at you! Do not allow
other people to judge or condemn you. You are justified before
God. Let the shackles fall! Walk in the freedom that has been purchased for you.

*Dear Lord, You have set me free. I am free indeed!
Help me walk in that freedom. Amen.*

DAY 198

My Relationship with God

*"Yet I hold this against you: You have
forsaken the love you had at first."*

REVELATION 2:4

It is heartwarming to see a couple celebrating their fiftieth wedding anniversary, especially if their love has grown even stronger over the course of time. Every newlywed couple with stars in their eyes assumes that their love will automatically deepen over the years. With the divorce rate over 50 percent, unfortunately this is not the case. A strong, lasting marriage requires effort. What about our love relationship with God?

Has your relationship with God grown cold and distant? Or is it still vibrant, full of new growth and revelation? Long-lasting relationships require effort from both parties. Be assured that the Lord has not reneged on His commitment to us. If our relationship with God is in need of an overhaul, most likely we are the ones who have allowed an idol to usurp His rightful place.

Think back to the enthusiasm and joy you had when you first came to know Jesus. Rekindle that love relationship by confessing anything that has come between you and the Lord—other priorities, relationships, materialism, sin. Then ask God to change your heart. We need God's help in serving Him like we used to.

*Dear Lord, help our relationship flourish as the years go by. You are
always faithful. May I keep You on the throne of my heart. Amen.*

DAY 199

Interference

*"For my thoughts are not your thoughts, neither are your
ways my ways," declares the Lord. "As the heavens are
higher than the earth, so are my ways higher than
your ways and my thoughts than your thoughts."*

ISAIAH 55:8–9

Interference means to hinder, intervene, or intrude upon. *Interference* is a word commonly used in sports. A defensive back may interfere with a wide receiver attempting to catch a pass. A runner must stay in his lane to prevent interference with another runner.

Are we ever guilty of running interference with God? Do we try to hinder God's plans? The temptation to interfere comes when the unfolding of God's plan appears to be in direct conflict with our own. This may be especially true with children or spouses. It is difficult to accept the fact that it could be God's will for them to experience valleys, trials, or pain in order to draw them closer to Himself. So we bail them out to prevent them from falling.

Interference may temporarily interrupt God's plans, but His plans cannot be thwarted. "I know that you can do all things; no purpose of yours can be thwarted" (Job 42:2). Perhaps God could fulfill His perfect plan easier if we would get out of the way. Instead of trying to convince God that He should go along with our plans, we need to go along with His!

*Dear Lord, may I allow Your plans to succeed without
trying to interfere. Help me trust You more! Amen.*

Refuse to Interfere

Trust in the Lord with all your heart and lean
not on your own understanding; in all your ways
submit to him, and he will make your paths straight.
PROVERBS 3:5–6

❈

*A*braham refused to interfere with God's plans even though it could have cost him the life of his son Isaac (see Genesis 22:1–14). "By faith Abraham, when God tested him, offered Isaac as a sacrifice. He who had embraced the promises was about to sacrifice his one and only son, even though God had said to him, 'It is through Isaac that your offspring will be reckoned.' Abraham reasoned that God could even raise the dead, and so in a manner of speaking he did receive Isaac back from death" (Hebrews 11:17–19).

When tempted to interfere with God's plans, choose instead to embrace God's truth. Trust Him regardless of how things appear. Believe that God is in control. He is able to turn the bleakest circumstance into victory. Remember Joseph in the cistern, Daniel in the lions' den, and David facing Goliath? What if Mary would have interfered with Jesus going to the cross? From a human perspective, things looked dismal. But God turned those bleak circumstances into great triumphs for His glory! God is aware of every circumstance. His eternal purposes will prevail. Let's trust Him.

Dear Lord, You turn ashes into beauty. With You in control
things are not as they might appear. Help me believe that
Your ways are best so that I can trust You completely. Amen.

DAY 201

Trials

*Blessed is the one who perseveres under trial because,
having stood the test, that person will receive the crown
of life that the Lord has promised to those who love him.*

JAMES 1:12

Life is not random. The sovereign God is in control. He has good plans for us even when He allows trials to come into our lives. Own this truth. Know it in the core of your being. Perseverance and endurance are only possible when we have this firm foundation of truth on which to stand in times of testing.

Every adversity that touches our life has purpose. God does not randomly allow trials to invade our lives. Each test is designed to develop perseverance by exercising our muscle of faith. As our faith matures, our relationship with the Lord deepens.

So do not become discouraged when experiencing trials! God is shaping you for higher purposes. Each trial you overcome prepares you for the next challenge. The Lord has promised you the crown of life when you demonstrate your love for Him by persevering under trial. We achieve the most precious gift of all—an intimate relationship with the Lord Jesus Christ.

*Dear Lord, I love You. Help me persevere when tested
so that my faith matures and I will receive the
crown of life that You promise. Amen.*

Overcoming Temptation

For sin shall no longer be your master,
because you are not under the law, but under grace.

ROMANS 6:14

⌣⌣⌣

*L*et's face it—no one is perfect. We all stumble and fall. Each of us has a breaking point where we are apt to succumb to temptation. We all have areas of weakness and times when we are the most vulnerable.

Jesus' temptation came when He was alone and hungry. Jesus had been in the desert fasting for forty days and forty nights. Satan came and tempted Him three times. Each time Jesus refuted Satan with "the sword of the Spirit"—God's Word (see Matthew 4:1–11). Jesus was tempted in every way, as we are, yet was without sin. That is why He is able to help us in our times of need.

Overcoming temptation begins with identification of your personal weaknesses and times of vulnerability. Acknowledge that discipline and willpower alone are ineffective for overcoming temptation. Fight back with God's Word. Truth asserts that we are weak, but the Lord is strong! Jesus is our *only* source of strength in overcoming temptation. His power enables us to say no and turn from evil. When we ask the Lord to get involved in our fight against sin, His grace enables us to have lasting peace and victory.

Dear Lord, may I not fool myself. I am weak and desperately
need Your help in overcoming temptation. Amen.

Trust in the Lord

*Trust in the LORD with all your heart and lean not
on your own understanding; in all your ways submit
to him, and he will make your paths straight.*

PROVERBS 3:5–6

*S*atan constantly tempts us to rely on our own ability and knowledge. He tempts us to act independently from God. Yet God declares in Isaiah 55:8–9, "For my thoughts are not your thoughts, neither are your ways my ways. As the heavens are higher than the earth, so are my ways higher than your ways and my thoughts than your thoughts."

God calls us to surrender our wills to His because He truly knows what is best for us. His thoughts and ways are higher than our own. He wants to make our paths straight. He does not want us to look back on our life decisions with regret.

In times of waiting, God has not forgotten you. So do not take matters into your own hands. Focus on God's perfect will rather than your own. Trust that He knows best. Acknowledge Him in all things. God will meet your needs when you trust Him. He will make your paths straight.

*Dear Lord, surrendering my will to Yours is so hard
yet so right! May I not lean on my own understanding.
Please make my paths straight. Amen.*

DAY 204

Be Prepared

Therefore, with minds that are alert and fully sober,
set your hope on the grace to be brought to you
when Jesus Christ is revealed at his coming.
1 PETER 1:13

*A*thletes train *before* they compete. Musicians practice *before* they perform. Soldiers march *before* they go to war. Preparation is the key to success.

It is no different in our Christian walk. Peter exhorts us to be prepared for action. The time to prepare for battle is *before* it commences. Once hard times come upon us, it is too late to train. Many times all we can do is just hang on. So how can we prepare ourselves today for what tomorrow may hold?

Get rid of anything that is distorting your mind and attitude. Be immersed in God's truth—the Bible. Trust God for discernment. Remain joyful while suffering, knowing that God has a design and purpose for your trials. Never fall back into a former lifestyle that fulfilled selfish desires rather than God's perfect plan. "Be holy, because I am holy" (Leviticus 11:44). Holiness is not based on our actions, but results from submission to the Holy Spirit. Let's allow the Lord to prepare us today so that we can successfully face tomorrow.

Dear Lord, I want to be prepared for what tomorrow may bring.
May I obey You rather than conform to the world's desires. Amen.

Day 205

My Rock

I love you, LORD, my strength. The LORD is my rock, my fortress
and my deliverer; my God is my rock, in whom I take refuge,
my shield and the horn of my salvation, my stronghold.
PSALM 18:1–2

Israel wanted to be like the surrounding nations, so they asked God for a king. God relented, and the prophet Samuel anointed Saul as their first king. Under Saul's reign, David the shepherd boy killed Goliath and went on to become a mighty warrior. Because of this, King Saul became extremely jealous of David and tried to kill him. Although David hid from King Saul in the rock caves of En Gedi, he credits the Lord for delivering him. God was his strength, fortress, deliverer, rock, shield, salvation, and stronghold. Are we able to say the same thing?

God knows what is happening in every area of our lives. When life presses down on us, do we turn elsewhere for deliverance? God is concerned and cares for us. He delights when fellowship with Him is a priority. During prayer and Bible study He can impart wisdom and help us navigate through life. Seek the Lord. Place complete trust in Him as David did. Then we can humbly proclaim that the Lord is our Rock!

Dear Lord, You are indeed my Rock.
May I take refuge in You today. Amen.

DAY 206

Mighty in Spirit

*They chose Stephen, a man full
of faith and of the Holy Spirit.*
ACTS 6:5

Stephen was known as a man full of faith and the Holy Spirit. He possessed wisdom from God and boldly addressed the Sanhedrin when he was falsely accused of blasphemy (see Acts 7). Stephen even prayed as he was being stoned and asked the Lord to forgive his murderers.

How do we become mighty in Spirit, like Stephen? First, we must have the Holy Spirit residing within us. We receive the Holy Spirit when we receive Jesus as our Savior—the Holy Spirit is His indwelling presence.

Although we may have the indwelling Holy Spirit, there is a choice we make daily—moment by moment. We can either walk in our own strength and power or defer to the Holy Spirit. As we submit to the Lord, the Holy Spirit is in control. His power is manifested in our lives. We are given boldness to testify about the Lord. We are able to forgive others and to show love to all. This cannot come in our own strength. The Holy Spirit is mighty. Like Stephen, we can become mighty in Spirit when we will allow Him control.

*Dear Lord, I confess I am no Stephen! "Mighty in Spirit" does not
seem to describe me at all. Help me remember that the "might"
and "Spirit" come from You. Use me for Your purposes. Amen.*

God's Peace

*You will keep in perfect peace those whose
minds are steadfast, because they trust in you.*

ISAIAH 26:3

———— ❈ ————

Life is full of change—a new job, new baby, new home, new
school. Adversity seems to come out of left field at times—car
accident, health issue, divorce, financial loss. If peace was based
on our circumstances, we'd be on a continual emotional roller
coaster! Anxiety would be the norm. Worry would easily dominate
our thoughts. But thankfully there is a better way to live than being
bounced around by life's circumstances.

God has a solution for the painful interruptions of life—His
unshakable *peace*. How can change and adversity be handled positively? First, recognize our total dependence on God. Relying on
our own strength in difficult times typically brings disappointment
and isolation. Trust Him alone.

Prayer ushers in peace. "Do not be anxious about anything,
but in every situation, *by prayer* and petition, with thanksgiving,
present your requests to God. And the *peace of God*, which transcends all understanding, will guard your hearts and your minds in
Christ Jesus" (Philippians 4:6–7, emphasis added). Prayer serves to
keep our minds steadfast on the Lord, our Prince of Peace. When
we stay focused on Him, peace will be imparted to our hearts.

*Dear Lord, I give You my anxious thoughts.
Please impart Your peace to my heart today. Amen.*

DAY 208

Just Say No!

So, if you think you are standing firm,
be careful that you don't fall!
1 CORINTHIANS 10:12

The sure way to fall is to think that you won't. Becoming self-reliant leads to pride. Pride gives us the false impression that we are above the fray. We rationalize that other people succumb to temptation but we never will. Beware! If you play with fire, chances are you will eventually get burned.

We all have weaknesses that lead us into temptation. In humility, acknowledge those weaknesses. Temptations are different for all of us and come through various forms—sometimes it's the people we associate with or the places we go. Temptation may come through the media. Have a healthy respect for the temptations that assail you. Do not even flirt with them. Stay as far away as possible! Turn the channel, close the magazine, end the friendship. Falling is a possibility for us all.

When we say no to temptation, God rewards our obedience with hope and peace. Never forget that we always have the opportunity to rise above adversity. Believe that God enables us to endure temptation and remain standing.

Dear Lord, forgive me for thinking I can "dabble with sin" and not pay the consequences. You and You alone enable me to say no to sin and remain standing. Help me to desire that! Amen.

DAY 209

The Storms of Life

Cast all your anxiety on him because he cares for you.
1 PETER 5:7

———⚬———

*I*n the Garden of Eden, life was perfect, just as God had designed. Then Satan came on the scene and tempted Eve to disobey God by eating the forbidden fruit. Satan lied to Eve and lured her to question God's love. She became confused and unable to discern the truth from lies. Eve succumbed to Satan's reasoning, and Adam followed her lead.

During the storms of life, be especially alert for Satan's lies. Jesus called Satan "the father of lies" (John 8:44). Satan also tempts us to question God's love. He asserts that if God truly loved us, we would not be going through our present trial. Satan attempts to undermine God's goodness. He interjects thoughts of doubt, worry, and anxiety during times of crisis.

Circumstances may seem confusing. Emotions may be volatile. But God's truth and love remain. We must purpose to keep our eyes on the Lord, knowing that He is in control and His love is immutable. He is our source of strength. The Lord will remove thoughts of anxiety and give us peace in our circumstances. Enter His rest by casting all your anxiety on Him. He cares for you!

Dear Lord, calm my fearful heart. May I know
that You love me and are near even now. Amen.

DAY 210

Pride

At that time the disciples came to Jesus and asked,
"Who, then, is the greatest in the kingdom of heaven?"
MATTHEW 18:1

The disciples were Jesus' closest followers—His inner circle. Yet they had much to learn from Jesus. Because they were human, the disciples wrestled with their pride. One day they wanted to know who would be the greatest in the kingdom of heaven. Perhaps each of them was hoping that Jesus would utter his name.

Instead, Jesus used a humble child to illustrate what their hearts lacked—humility. Children readily accept the truth about Jesus by simple faith. Their intellectual prowess is not a stumbling block to belief, nor does their pride puff them up.

Pride can even infiltrate the hearts of Christians. In fact, we may erroneously believe that because we know Jesus we are better than others. Pride may tempt us to judge and conclude that we'll be among the greatest in the kingdom of heaven. Beware! Jesus admonished the religious leaders of His day.

The antidote to pride is humility. Jesus is our greatest example. (see Philippians 2:5–11). When we imitate Christ's humility, we are freed from the bondage of pride. Let's humbly follow Jesus and learn from Him! The closer we move toward the cross, Jesus becomes bigger—and we become smaller.

Dear Lord, why do I focus on myself so much? Help me to imitate Your humility so that I can learn to be a true disciple. Amen.

Day 211

The Humble Person

*Do nothing out of selfish ambition or vain conceit. Rather,
in humility value others above yourselves, not looking to your
own interests but each of you to the interests of the others.*

Philippians 2:3–4

We live in a "me generation"—me—me—me! Decisions are based on how they affect "me." In relationships—does the person make "me" happy? In business deals—what's in it for "me"? We erroneously conclude that we are the center of the universe and everything revolves around "me"! Children today feel entitled to things that previous generations had to work hard for.

Although it's human nature to instinctively put ourselves first, God's Word tells us just the opposite. Instead of living for self, we are exhorted to live for Jesus first and others next. Humility is a foreign concept to most of us.

Although counterintuitive, humility is necessary in order to live a victorious Christian life. We must follow Jesus, who epitomized humility. Humble people willingly deprive themselves in order to meet the needs of others. In doing so they become a stepping-stone rather than a stumbling block in the lives of others. Humility begins with self-examination and continues with self denial. In the end, humility brings blessing!

*Dear Lord, help me have an attitude of humility.
Show me practical ways to put others first. Amen.*

Day 212

Our Needs

And my God will meet all your needs
according to glory the riches of his glory in Christ Jesus.
PHILIPPIANS 4:19

God is our Creator. He created us with unique needs that are physical, emotional, social, and spiritual in nature. Trying to meet our own needs is tempting. Making demands on others to fulfill our needs is also common. Frustration is the end result when our needs remain unmet. There is a better way! The God who created us is the One who promises to supply all of our needs. Sometimes that may mean waiting on Him. Other times discernment must be asked for.

It is easy to confuse "needs" with "wants." Fortunately God knows the difference. Ask Him for discernment. Be content knowing that what He supplies is enough to meet your need. The apostle Paul had a physical need—"a thorn in the flesh." Three times he pleaded with the Lord to take it away. God's response was, "My grace is sufficient for you, for my power is made perfect in weakness" (2 Corinthians 12:9). Spiritual maturity is evidenced by *total dependency* on God. Let's trust the Lord to meet all of our needs because He knows what they truly are!

Dear Lord, You meet all of my needs. I can trust
You to know the difference between my wants
and my needs. I depend on You alone. Amen.

Day 213

Peace with God

*Therefore, since we have been justified through faith, we have peace
with God through our Lord Jesus Christ, through whom we have
gained access by faith into this grace in which we now stand.*

Romans 5:1–2

"Peace like a river" is desirous yet elusive. Why? At times troubles
barge in and create tumultuous waves in our lives. Our hearts
yearn for peace, yet peace seems impossible to obtain. How did
Daniel have peace in the lions' den or Paul have peace in a jail cell?

God desires that we experience peace in our hearts regardless
of life's circumstances. We may be encountering financial setbacks,
suffering physical ailments, or facing death. Even in our bleakest
moments, His inner peace is still available for those who know
Him. That is His promise.

However, when we drift away from God, His peace eludes us.
Anxiety provides an opportunity for Satan to step in and fill our
hearts with lies about God. Run back to God like the saints of old.
Use the offensive spiritual weapon we've been given—God's Word.
Combat lies with His truth! God's love for us is eternal. He is a
forgiving God. His peace and joy await those who turn to Him.

*Dear Lord, it's amazing that I can experience Your peace even in
my darkest hours. Thank You for that reality. May I choose to walk
close by Your side so that Your peace rules my heart. Amen.*

DAY 214

Acknowledging God's Voice

"My sheep listen to my voice;
I know them, and they follow me."
JOHN 10:27

Jesus likened our relationship with Him to a shepherd and his sheep. If sheep stay close to their shepherd, they can hear him and thus follow. If they run ahead or lag behind, they can easily get lost. The same is true for us. If we want to hear and follow, we must stay close to our Good Shepherd's side.

Jesus made it clear that if we know Him, we will be able to discern His voice. Although it is not audible, it is real just the same. God speaks to us in many ways: through the Bible, nature, other people, and the still, quiet voice of the Holy Spirit. How can we tell when God is speaking to us?

God's voice is always consistent with His Word. That's why diligently studying the Bible is paramount to discerning God's will. God's guidance contradicts the philosophy of the world. "You adulterous people, don't you know that friendship with the world means enmity against God?" (James 4:4). An intimate relationship with God is the key to hearing His voice. Let's walk closely by our Good Shepherd's side so that we can hear Him speak and follow Him.

Dear Lord, give me ears that are attuned
to Your voice so that I may follow You. Amen.

Day 215

Peace of God

Do not be anxious about anything, but in every situation,
by prayer and petition, with thanksgiving, present your requests to
God. And the peace of God, which transcends all understanding,
will guard your hearts and your minds in Christ Jesus.
PHILIPPIANS 4:6–7

Jesus is the Prince of Peace. Ephesians 2:14 declares, "He himself is our peace." Therefore, if we know Jesus, we can experience peace regardless of our circumstances. Then why do Christians sometimes experience anxiety instead of peace? What has happened?

An anxious heart should be a spiritual red flag. Fear and faith cannot coexist. Neither can anxiety and peace. When fear and anxiety have gripped us, the enemy has gotten a foothold. Anxiety has invaded our heart and pushed peace out. Counteract worry with prayer. Experience how God replaces fear and anxiety with His peace.

God wants us to trust Him and enjoy His peace on a daily basis. God promises that even our trials can work together for our good (see Romans 8:28). The heart that finds its identity in Jesus Christ is a heart of peace. Recognize your dependence on Him, and allow the Lord control. When you focus on Him, peace will be the result.

Dear Lord, my heart is anxious and fearful much
of the time. Through prayer, may I lay my burdens
at Your feet and receive peace. Amen.

Day 216

Unshakable Peace

"But seek first his kingdom and his righteousness, and all these things will be given to you as well. Therefore do not worry about tomorrow, for tomorrow will worry about itself. Each day has enough trouble of its own."

Matthew 6:33–34

Large crowds gathered to listen to Jesus' teaching. On one such occasion, Jesus spoke to them about anxiety, a subject He knew everyone could relate to. He told them not to worry about anything—life, food, drink, or clothing. Jesus reminded them that God feeds the birds and clothes the grass. Since we are God's most valued possession, it stands to reason that He will take care of us as well.

Anxiety is still a relatable topic. We are exhorted to *never* worry. Worrying leads to doubt. It undercuts the sovereignty of God. Why do we try to solve our problems in our own strength? Doesn't that make us anxious? Doesn't our focus shift from God to ourselves? God is responsible for providing for our needs. Our responsibility is to seek Him first. Having a spiritual focus demonstrates our belief that God will provide for our physical needs. And He does! The absence of worry is the evidence of true peace.

Dear Lord, the absence of worry in my life is a true litmus test of my walk with You. May I pass the test by seeking You first and trusting in Your provision. Amen.

Day 217

Loved but Lost

For God so loved the world that he gave his one and only Son, that whoever believes in him shall not perish but have eternal life.

JOHN 3:16

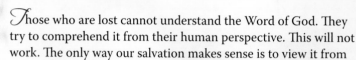

Those who are lost cannot understand the Word of God. They try to comprehend it from their human perspective. This will not work. The only way our salvation makes sense is to view it from God's spiritual perspective.

Take the Romans Road to Salvation:

ROMANS 3:23: "For all have sinned and fall short of the glory of God."

ROMANS 6:23: "For the wages of sin is death, but the gift of God is eternal life in Christ Jesus our Lord."

ROMANS 5:8: "But God demonstrates his own love for us in this: While we were still sinners, Christ died for us."

ROMANS 10:9: "If you declare with your mouth, 'Jesus is Lord,' and believe in your heart that God raised him from the dead, you will be saved."

We are spiritually dead because of sin. Jesus Christ came to give us eternal life by paying the debt we owe. By faith we can accept this gift and be saved. This is the greatest decision anyone could ever make.

Dear Lord, I am a sinner in need of redemption.
I believe that You love me unconditionally and died so
that I could have eternal life. Come into my heart today.
I receive You as my personal Lord and Savior. Amen.

Day 218

Following Jesus

"My sheep listen to my voice;
I know them, and they follow me."

JOHN 10:27

*F*ollowing Jesus begins with listening to His voice. Once we hear, we must decide whether we are going to follow. Many times we are torn because our fleshly desires conflict with what scripture teaches. We naturally choose revenge over forgiveness and anger over biting our tongue.

The truth is we want to go our own way. We would rather lead than follow. We think we know best. So we have selective hearing or claim we do not "hear" Jesus' voice. The problem is, when we cease to follow our Good Shepherd, we quickly become lost. Other paths and pastures may have seemed enticing at the onset, but the farther we move away from Jesus, the more lost we become.

Jesus teaches us to gratify the Spirit rather than the flesh. When we listen and follow Him, we will have true peace. God encourages and builds us up. He loves us and is compassionate toward us. God always wants the best for us. There is no negative with God! He is our trusted Leader!

Dear Lord, why wouldn't I want to follow You? You truly
know what's best for me. Grant me the desire to hear
Your voice and the power to obey when You speak. Amen.

Day 219

The Lost

The Lord is not slow in keeping his promise, as some understand slowness. Instead he is patient with you, not wanting anyone to perish, but everyone to come to repentance.

2 Peter 3:9

What are God's feelings toward the lost—toward those who do not yet know Him? He is compassionate and patient. He celebrates each time someone turns to Him for salvation. After telling the parable of the lost sheep, Jesus said, "I tell you that in the same way there will be more rejoicing in heaven over one sinner who repents than over ninety-nine righteous persons who do not need to repent" (Luke 15:7). God is for us, not against us!

Jesus said in John 3:17, "For God did not send his Son into the world to condemn the world, but to save the world through him." Can you see God's heart? He yearns for a relationship with you. That's why He sent Jesus! Once we accept Jesus, we can enter into a relationship with our heavenly Father. God rejoices over our desire to know Him by studying His Word. He spiritually dries our tears and embraces us. Nothing can be more wonderful than to come close to God. It is His greatest desire!

Dear Lord, You delight in those who fear You and put their hope in Your unfailing love [see Psalm 147:11]. Amen.

DAY 220

Failure: The First Step to Victory

For I do not do the good I want to do,
but the evil I do not want to do—this I keep on doing.
ROMANS 7:19

———※———

The apostle Paul struggled with spiritual failure. Read Romans 7:15–25. The harder he tried, the more he failed. Most of us can relate! Failure should not be condemning. Failure exposes our weaknesses and difficulties. For that reason, failure can actually teach us tremendous lessons. The apostle Paul discovered that weakness can be turned into blessing: "For when I am weak, then I am strong" (2 Corinthians 12:10). Paul knew that this strength came from Christ and not himself.

Many times spiritual failure indicates that we have been operating in our own strength in trying to live the Christian life. This will not work. We will eventually fall flat on our faces. Death to our flesh leads to life in Him. God isn't interested in self-improvement. Sometimes God uses defeat in our lives to fulfill His purposes. We must rely on His power to work in and through us. In our human weakness, we can experience His spiritual strength. Defeat is merely God's way of pointing us to ultimate victory!

Dear Lord, turn my failures into victories.
In my weakness may I be infused with Your
strength and molded into the image of Christ. Amen.

DAY 221

Living above Your Circumstances

*Now I want you to know, brothers and sisters, that what has
happened to me has actually served to advance the gospel.
As a result, it has become clear throughout the whole palace guard
and to everyone else that I am in chains for Christ. And because of
my chains, most of the brothers and sisters have become confident in
the Lord and dare all the more to proclaim the gospel without fear.*

PHILIPPIANS 1:12–14

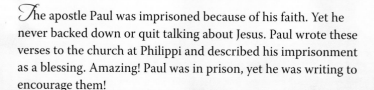

The apostle Paul was imprisoned because of his faith. Yet he
never backed down or quit talking about Jesus. Paul wrote these
verses to the church at Philippi and described his imprisonment
as a blessing. Amazing! Paul was in prison, yet he was writing to
encourage them!

How can we live above our circumstances? It comes down to
our focus. Our focus must be on the Lord and not on the
problem—on the sovereignty of God and not on the will of man.
God works in miraculous ways. Seek God's counsel through His
Word rather than worldly counsel. Focus on positive results, not
personal pain. Ask God for help in learning from the situation and
applying those lessons to your life.

*Dear Lord, I am amazed at Paul's focus when imprisoned
and facing possible death. May I focus on You during
difficulties so that I can have a spiritual perspective. Amen.*

Day 222

False Motives

*But what does it matter? The important thing is that
in every way, whether from false motives or true,
Christ is preached. And because of this I rejoice.*

PHILIPPIANS 1:18

While the apostle Paul was imprisoned, he wrote to the church at Philippi. Paul acknowledged that Christ was being preached out of envy and rivalry by some, and goodwill by others. Paul knew that their motives would be judged by the Lord. Instead, He chose to rejoice that Christ was being preached.

Only God knows someone's heart and true motives. Therefore only He is able to correctly judge what we cannot see. No one likes to be misjudged or misunderstood. How do we react when others judge us? Do we retaliate? Do we suppress the hurt by secretly holding the pain inside? Jesus was often misunderstood. What did He do?

Jesus did not focus on His circumstances. He didn't worry about whether He was liked or admired. He knew His mission and purposed to do God's will. It would serve us well to follow His example. The key is *being* in God's will and *doing* God's will. Then the words and worries of others will never become the focus of our lives. The apostle Paul's main concern was that Christ was being preached. May we rejoice in that also!

*Dear Lord, I hate being misjudged by others.
May I live my life for Your approval only. Amen.*

DAY 223

New Beginnings

*Jesus answered, "Everyone who drinks this water will be
thirsty again, but whoever drinks the water I give them
will never thirst. Indeed, the water I give them will become
in them a spring of water welling up to eternal life."*

JOHN 4:13–14

One day Jesus passed through Samaria on the way from Judea to Galilee. Exhausted from the journey, He sat down by Jacob's well to rest. It was there that Jesus encountered a Samaritan woman as she came to draw water at the well (see John 4:1–42). Although the Samaritans were a despised race, Jesus did not reject her. In fact, He engaged her in conversation by asking her for a drink of water.

Jesus knew this Samaritan woman's heart. Because she was a sinner, she was spiritually thirsty. In the conversation that ensued, Jesus offered her "living water," Himself. She received the "living water" that Jesus offered. Many Samaritans from her town believed in Jesus because of her testimony.

God gives us a new beginning when we seek His forgiveness. Although there are consequences to our sin, He always forgives us. When we turn to Him, God never leaves us in the mess that sin creates. God has a plan for our lives even when we've fallen on our faces. He never gives up on us because He specializes in bringing good out of the worst situations! Like the Samaritan woman, let's drink the "living water."

*Dear Lord, thank You for new beginnings.
You bring beauty from the ashes in my life. Amen.*

Day 224

To Live Is Christ

For to me, to live is Christ and to die is gain.

PHILIPPIANS 1:21

The apostle Paul was writing to the Philippians from jail. He wrote to encourage them to stand firm in the face of persecution and to rejoice regardless of their circumstances. Although Paul was unsure of his future, he reminded them that whether he lived or died, Christ would be exalted. Paul was torn. On one hand, he knew death meant that he would be with the Lord. Yet if the Lord allowed him to live, he could minister to others. For Paul it was a win-win situation.

Most of us will not experience jail time—especially for sharing the Gospel. Yet we may carry burdens or experience severe testing. Are we able to say, "To live is Christ and to die is gain"? When we allow Christ's strength to enable us to live above our circumstances, God preserves His message of hope—eternal life with Him. Our current trials can be used as a powerful testimony. Be willing to tell the reason for our hope: Jesus died so that we may have eternal life. His power that is at work within us enables us to stand!

Dear Lord, the apostle Paul is an example of what it means to be "sold out" to You. May his testimony inspire me to pursue You with passion—whether in life or death. Amen.

Day 225

Accountability

*So then, each of us will give
an account of ourselves to God.*
ROMANS 14:12

*O*ne day each of us will stand before our Maker and give an account of ourselves to Him. This thought is very sobering, yet there is good news. Romans 8:1 assures us, "Therefore, there is now no condemnation for those who are in Christ Jesus." If we know Jesus as our Savior, we will never be condemned!

God will still hold us accountable for our thoughts, words, and deeds. Although nothing is hidden from His sight, He loves us in spite of ourselves. That's amazing! We may rebel and sin against God by inner thoughts or outward actions. Yet He still desires a close personal relationship with us. His love knows no bounds. Once we are His child, there is nothing that we could ever do that would cause Him to withdraw His love.

This should stir a desire within our hearts to draw closer to Him. Pray that the Lord would reveal anything in your life that is displeasing to Him. There should be nothing hidden. Confess your sin and receive forgiveness today.

Dear Lord, "Search me, God, and know my heart; test me and know my anxious thoughts. See if there is any offensive way in me, and lead me in the way everlasting" [Psalm 139:23–24]. Amen.

Day 226

Defeat: A Step Closer to Victory

So I say, walk by the Spirit, and you will not gratify the desires of the flesh. For the flesh desires what is contrary to the Spirit, and the Spirit what is contrary to the flesh. They are in conflict with each other, so that you are not to do whatever you want.

GALATIANS 5:16–17

As Christians we have a choice. We can choose to live by the Spirit or put ourselves in charge. Unfortunately, when we attempt to run our own lives, spiritual defeat is the result. We cannot experience spiritual victory by walking in the flesh. We must walk in the Spirit. But do not be discouraged! The more we experience this type of defeat, the more we realize that we *must* defer to the Holy Spirit for direction. When we ask the Lord for help and depend upon Him, we emerge victorious.

Allowing God to work through us brings spiritual victory every time! Living by the Spirit also produces the fruit of the Spirit: love, joy, peace, patience, kindness, goodness, faithfulness, gentleness, and self-control (see Galatians 5:22–23). Doesn't that sound like a victorious life? Let's choose to live by the Spirit.

*Dear Lord, I mess up so much. Help me learn to let the
Holy Spirit reign in my heart so that my defeats can
be turned into spiritual victories! Amen.*

Day 227

The Things We Say

All kinds of animals, birds, reptiles and sea creatures are being tamed and have been tamed by mankind, but no human being can tame the tongue. It is a restless evil, full of deadly poison.

JAMES 3:7–8

"Sticks and stones can break my bones, but names can never hurt me." Everyone can attest that whoever made up that children's rhyme is dead wrong! Words are powerful. Words can cut deeper than physical trauma, leaving scars that may never heal. James reminds us that words can be poisonous.

Our speech should build others up, not tear them down. We have all experienced the negative consequences when hurtful words have been spoken. Once uttered, those words cannot be taken back. Our speech is crucial to our Christian walk. Our words should be consistent with what we profess to believe. "Do not let any unwholesome talk come out of your mouths, but only what is helpful for building others up according to their needs, that it may benefit those who listen" (Ephesians 4:29).

The Lord wants us to use self-control when it comes to our speech. When you feel the urge to criticize, ask God to silence you. He will. The old adage "If you don't have anything nice to say, don't say anything at all" is a good reminder to all of us.

Dear Lord, guard my tongue. Help me speak encouraging words that depict Your love to others. Amen.

Day 228

Truth

*To the Jews who had believed him, Jesus said, "If you
hold to my teaching, you are really my disciples. Then
you will know the truth, and the truth will set you free."*

JOHN 8:31–32

$\mathscr{F}$reedom is desirous. Unfortunately captivity and bondage are
the plight of many. Ball and chains come in many disguises: work,
materialism, education, athletics, beauty, drugs, alcohol, sex. Many
of these pursuits are not wrong in and of themselves. It's when they
take over and own us that we become enslaved by them. The Lord
desires that we live in the freedom He came to give.

Jesus promised that the truth will set you free. Truth is found
in the Word of God. When we live by fact (truth) rather than feelings, we are set free. We are no longer imprisoned by the world's
lies. We are no longer held captive by our deepest fears. We are no
longer held back by feelings of inadequacy. We are free!

Here is truth: God loved us enough to forgive our sins and
send his Spirit to live inside us. We have been redeemed and justified because of Christ's work. Whatever God requires of us, He
equips us to handle with the help of the Holy Spirit. Walk in the
truth and freedom that Christ has given you!

*Dear Lord, may I walk each day in the truth found in Your Word.
Help me to enjoy the freedom I have in You. Amen.*

DAY 229

Our Position in Christ

But because of his great love for us, God, who is rich in mercy, made us alive with Christ even when we were dead in transgressions—it is by grace you have been saved. And God raised us up with Christ and seated us with him in the heavenly realms in Christ Jesus.

EPHESIANS 2:4–6

*O*ur place in heaven is secure not because of anything we have done on earth, but simply because we know Jesus! Our position in Christ has *nothing* to do with feelings and *everything* to do with facts. The Bible is truth. Trust what it says. We become a child of God by believing in Jesus, His Son—nothing more, nothing less.

God has seated us in the heavenly places in Christ Jesus. At this particular moment, you may not "feel" like you are a child of God, but don't allow feelings to trump fact! Satan attempts to appeal to our emotions. But feelings can change like the wind. Emotions can be deceptive, unreliable, and many times false. Never let emotions cloud truth. None of us are worthy, but Christ is. Our faith in Him means that His righteousness is imputed to us. Stand on that truth today.

Dear Lord, I am clinging to the fact that You love and accept me because I have trusted in Christ—nothing more, nothing less. Amen.

Day 230

A New Creature

*To the church of God in Corinth, to those sanctified in Christ Jesus
and called to be his holy people, together with all those everywhere
who call on the name of our Lord Jesus Christ—their Lord and ours.*

1 Corinthians 1:2

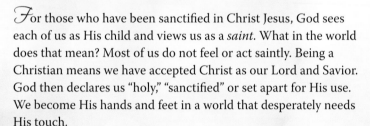

For those who have been sanctified in Christ Jesus, God sees
each of us as His child and views us as a *saint*. What in the world
does that mean? Most of us do not feel or act saintly. Being a
Christian means we have accepted Christ as our Lord and Savior.
God then declares us "holy," "sanctified" or set apart for His use.
We become His hands and feet in a world that desperately needs
His touch.

As Christians, God applied the righteousness of Christ to our
account. As difficult as it may be to believe, God sees us as a saint.
We have been "set apart" for His use. May we take this charge seriously. Ask the Lord how He wants to use you to touch others. Do
you have the opportunity to feed the homeless, teach a children's
Sunday school class, minister to the ill, or simply pray? God can
use you in any way He chooses—big or small. The only prerequisite
is a willing heart. May you answer God's call today!

*Dear Lord, enlighten me. Show me ways that You
have set me apart to be used by You today. Amen.*

DAY 231

Ambassadors for Christ

We are therefore Christ's ambassadors,
as though God were making his appeal through us.
2 CORINTHIANS 5:20

*P*arents are known to remind teenagers that they represent their family as they hop in the car for a night on the town. Their hope is that this gentle reminder will serve a deterrent to making bad choices. When faced with a decision, the teenager will hopefully think about how he is representing other members of his family and choose wisely.

We are members of God's family. Have you ever thought of yourself as Christ's ambassador? You are! Whether or not we acknowledge this fact, believers are ambassadors or representatives for Christ. Do we accurately portray Christ to others through words or deeds? Or do we misrepresent the truth He came to proclaim?

We have been given the responsibility of delivering the message of the living God. The Lord has equipped us to carry out our assignment. Get to know Christ by studying the Bible. Don't be a hypocrite. Live out the truth in God's Word so that Christ will be accurately represented to a watching world that desperately needs Him. Make wise choices so that you can represent Christ well.

Dear Lord, it is truly humbling that You have called me
to be Your ambassador. May I represent You well so
that others will come to know You. Amen.

DAY 232

Let Your Light Shine

"You are the light of the world. A town built on a hill cannot be hidden. Neither do people light a lamp and put it under a bowl. Instead they put it on its stand, and it gives light to everyone in the house. In the same way, let your light shine before others, that they may see your good deeds and glorify your Father in heaven."

MATTHEW 5:14–16

We do not live our lives in a vacuum or bubble. For better or worse, our lives impact those around us. Our influence can be positive or negative. When we let the light of Jesus shine through us, we can bring forth light to everyone we come in contact with.

Letting our light shine means putting every facet of our lives in God's hands. Focus on the Light of the World instead of the darkness of our circumstances. Our purpose in life is to glorify God. When we let our light shine, we are free from the bondage of feelings that can be totally unreliable.

Let go of your circumstances—let your light shine. Am I thankful? Let my light shine. Am I ill? Let my light shine. Am I anxious? Let my light shine.

Dear Lord, it is so difficult to let my light shine when darkness has overtaken me. Help me remember that it is your light that shines through me. In the darkest storms, this is possible as I turn to You. Amen.

Controlling Our Thoughts

We demolish arguments and every pretension that sets itself up against the knowledge of God, and we take captive every thought to make it obedient to Christ.

2 CORINTHIANS 10:5

*O*ur mind is constantly being bombarded with random thoughts. Those thoughts can be positive or negative—uplifting or tempting. While we are not responsible for the negative thoughts that may pop into our heads, we are accountable for dwelling on them. When our minds are surrendered to negative thoughts, we can easily fall into sin. Instead of replaying those thoughts, ask the Lord to help you redirect them.

The apostle Paul in Colossians 3:1–2 states, "Since, then, you have been raised with Christ, set your hearts on things above, where Christ is seated at the right hand of God. Set your minds on things above, not on earthly things." Bring to mind positive, uplifting thoughts. Focus your mind on spiritual truth found in God's Word. Praise the Lord for His faithfulness and goodness in your life. In Philippians 4:8 we are told to think about whatever is true, noble, right, pure, lovely, admirable, excellent, or praiseworthy. Although this takes discipline, controlling our thoughts is possible with the Lord's help.

Dear Lord, I dwell on negative thoughts too much. Help me refocus my thoughts so that joy and peace can rule my heart. Amen.

DAY 234

Worldly Things

You adulterous people, don't you know that friendship with the world means enmity against God? Therefore, anyone who chooses to be a friend of the world becomes an enemy of God.

JAMES 4:4

Those are strong words! What exactly do they mean? Are we not supposed to love the world in which we live? James is exhorting believers not to adopt the world's priorities as their own. Not to allow worldly pursuits to control them. Not to chase after those things that unbelievers live for. "For everything in the world—the lust of the flesh, the lust of the eyes, and the pride of life—comes not come from the Father but from the world" (1 John 2:16).

The world dominates the lives of spiritually lost people. Unfortunately, until Jesus returns, Satan is "the prince of this world" (John 12:31). He has blinded the lost and attempts to destroy those who follow the Lord (see 1 Peter 5:8). Christians should be "in the world" but not "of the world." Although this is a constant battle, Christ can give us victory! Worldliness is a choice that is rooted in pride. May we choose instead to walk *humbly* before our God.

Dear Lord, I have to make daily choices between You and the world. May I choose You and let go of the world's priorities. Amen.

What Counts

Praise be to the God and Father of our Lord Jesus Christ,
who has blessed us in the heavenly realms
with every spiritual blessing in Christ.

EPHESIANS 1:3

Perhaps you have been asked the following question: If your house caught on fire, what three items would you grab on your way out? Pondering this question helps determine what our most valuable possessions are.

Regardless of our material possessions, we possess every spiritual blessing we need. And our spiritual treasures are always with us! So why do we tend to dwell on material riches rather than on possessions that really matter—our possessions in Christ?

God promises to supply all our needs. "And my God will meet all your needs according to the riches of his glory in Christ Jesus" (Philippians 4:19). This promise does not guarantee a six-figure income or an extensive stock portfolio. The Lord wants us to understand that material riches are temporary; spiritual blessings are eternal. The spiritual far outweighs the material. There is no comparison. Regardless of where we are on this earth, we are seated in the heavens with Jesus Christ. Because of that we can praise God today and for all eternity!

Dear Lord, help me to treasure and appreciate the spiritual
blessings You have given me. May I stop obsessing over my lack
of material possessions, which are temporary at best. Amen.

DAY 236

God's Promises

Through these he has given us his very great and precious
promises, so that through them you may participate in the
divine nature, having escaped the corruption in the
world caused by evil desires.

2 PETER 1:4

God's Word is laden with His promises. God is faithful and trust-worthy. He keeps every single promise He makes. "Let us hold un-swervingly to the hope we profess, for he who promised is faithful" (Hebrews 10:23). God has promised us everything pertaining to life and godliness. We have all we need to face life and death.

We cannot know God or His promises without knowing His Word. We must abide and cling to His promises found in the Bible. How many promises can you recall?

ROMANS 8:28: "And we know that in all things God works for the good of those who love him, who have been called according to his purpose."

PROVERBS 3:5–6: "Trust in the LORD with all your heart and lean not on your own understanding; in all your ways submit to him, and he will make your paths straight."

MATTHEW 11:28–30: "Come to me, all you who are weary and burdened, and I will give you rest. Take my yoke upon you and learn from me, for I am gentle and humble in heart, and you will find rest for your souls. For my yoke is easy and my burden is light."

Search the scriptures so that you can cling to His promises!

Dear Lord, may I never become discouraged,
for You are my hope. Your promises are my life. Amen.

Day 237

Believers in Christ

*In him we have redemption through his blood, the forgiveness
of sins, in accordance with the riches of God's grace that he
lavished on us. With all wisdom and understanding.*
EPHESIANS 1:7–8

God accepts us not because of what we have done, but because we know Jesus. Believers in Christ possess everything needed to live a godly, meaningful, and fulfilling life. Jesus Himself said, "I have come that they may have life, and have it to the full" (John 10:10).

Not only have we received eternal life, but we can experience an abundant life on earth as well. What is an abundant life? A life filled to overflowing. A life lived to the fullest. A life that's meaningful and purposeful.

God's grace has been lavished on us. The indwelling Holy Spirit opens our spiritual eyes and gives us the ability to live in the world yet for the Lord. We are given the desire and the ability to walk obediently with the Lord. Because we have access to God through Jesus Christ, we can live our life on earth from a spiritual perspective. This makes all the difference!

*Dear Lord, my life has meaning and purpose because of You.
I rejoice in the eternal life You have given me and the
abundant life on earth that is possible because of You. Amen.*

DAY 238

Leaving a Legacy

*Therefore, since we are surrounded by such a great cloud of
witnesses, let us throw off everything that hinders and the sin
that so easily entangles. And let us run with perseverance
the race marked out for us, fixing our eyes on Jesus.*

HEBREWS 12:1–2

What man or woman has had the greatest impact on your life?
Are they aware of their positive influence? We can be inspired by
those who have gone before us and lived consistent Christian lives.
As we follow in their footsteps, we are acutely aware that we, too,
are leaving a legacy for others to follow. We may be that person
who someone thinks of years from now as having a huge impact on
his or her life.

We can choose to be free from the bondages that have enslaved us by making a conscious decision to believe truth. Throw
off old thought patterns and behaviors that haunt you. Jesus came
to set the captives free! Absorb the deep riches of scripture, asking
God to show you how to apply truth. Claim by faith what rightfully
belongs to you. Trust God with the results. When we keep our eyes
on Jesus and persevere, our walk becomes consistent and easier for
others to follow. We are surrounded by witnesses. May we run the
race of life well!

*Dear Lord, may I keep my eyes on You in this race called life.
May I run in freedom, letting go of sin and worldly
trappings that hinder my progress. Amen.*

DAY 239

Do Not Conform

*Offer your bodies as a living sacrifice, holy and pleasing to God—
this is your true and proper worship. Do not conform to the pattern
of this world, but be transformed by the renewing of your mind.*

ROMANS 12:1–2

$\mathcal{I}$t's human nature to want to fit in and not stand out in the crowd.
So we dress alike, talk alike, and act alike. We're conformists. The
problem is—as Christians we are called to be different. We are not
to look exactly like the world. We are not to conform to its pattern
or adopt its priorities.

The world should not shape us into its mold. Our outward appearance and lifestyle must be consistent with our inner being. In
today's culture, our physical bodies are highly esteemed. Becoming overly obsessed with exercise and diet is common. Christians
should focus less on our bodies and more on how God can use our
bodies for His glory. This is our act of worship.

We are not to conform, but be transformed. Allow your mind
to be transformed by replacing old, erroneous thought patterns
with the truth. When our thoughts are centered on truth, we
become free and confident of our position, personage, and possessions in Christ. May we give the Lord all that we are—body, mind,
and spirit.

*Dear Lord, may You transform my mind with truth so
that I am conformed to Your image and not the world's.
Then I can truly worship You as a living sacrifice. Amen.*

Day 240

Controlling Our Thoughts

*Finally, brothers and sisters, whatever is true, whatever
is noble, whatever is right, whatever is pure, whatever is
lovely, whatever is admirable—if anything is excellent
or praiseworthy—think about such things.*

PHILIPPIANS 4:8

Perhaps you have heard the saying "Garbage in—garbage out."
Certainly what we take in through our five senses affects our
thought life. Our minds are spiritual battlegrounds. Our hearts
may want to dwell on truth, but our enemy is always interjecting
lies in the form of random thoughts that suddenly pop into our
minds. How should we handle this constant bombardment?

We must be proactive and diligent, guarding against what we
allow to enter our minds in the first place. Be selective in media
and entertainment choices. Choose friends wisely. Take notice of
your conversations.

Try not to allow thoughts to wander to places that God has
said are off-limits. When tempting thoughts do enter your mind,
do not dwell on them. Immediately and deliberately ask God to
help you turn them to God-centered thoughts. Pick up your Bible
or a devotional, or call a Christian friend. Do not be discouraged
when you fail. Through discipline and practice, you *can* learn to
focus on God and His glory.

*Dear Lord, help my thoughts to be pleasing to You. May I be
discriminating as to what I allow to enter my mind. Amen.*

DAY 241

Adversity

Consider it pure joy, my brothers and sisters, whenever you face trials of many kinds, because you know that the testing of your faith produces perseverance. Let perseverance finish its work so that you may be mature and complete, not lacking anything.

JAMES 1:2–4

*Y*ears ago the following slogans were meant to encourage exercise: "It hurts so good" and "no pain—no gain." The premise was that even though exercise hurt and was painful, the results would be well worth it!

Adversity is similar in many ways. No one enjoys the pain of adversity. Yet God has a divine purpose for our adversity. The end results are good and beneficial! If we can keep that in mind when experiencing difficulties, adversity can be one of God's most effective teaching tools. Even though trials are painful, we can be assured that the Lord is working on us.

What are some of God's purposes in adversity? It may simply be to get our attention or deal with our pride. Perhaps it may serve to reveal our total inadequacy so that we depend on Him. Spiritual maturity is the end result. Be encouraged! The Lord demonstrates His faithfulness when we turn to Him in our adversity. Hallelujah!

Dear Lord, help me remember that "no discipline seems pleasant at the time, but painful. Later on, however, it produces a harvest of righteousness and peace for those who have been trained by it" [Hebrews 12:11]. Amen.

Day 242

Spiritual Perspective during Adversity

Praise be to the God and Father of our Lord Jesus Christ,
the Father of compassion and the God of all comfort, who comforts
us in all our troubles, so that we can comfort those in any trouble
with the comfort we ourselves receive from God.

2 Corinthians 1:3–4

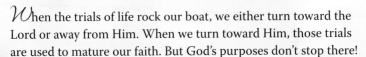

When the trials of life rock our boat, we either turn toward the Lord or away from Him. When we turn toward Him, those trials are used to mature our faith. But God's purposes don't stop there! Our trials can also be used for good in the lives of others.

God's purpose in adversity may be for us to comfort others with the comfort He has given us. The Lord may be preparing and equipping us for future service. The main thing we must *always* remember is that we should view *everything* from God's perspective rather than our own. "If any of you lacks wisdom, you should ask God, who gives generously to all without finding fault, and it will be given to you" (James 1:5).

Ask the Lord for spiritual perspective. Ask Him to reveal spiritual lessons that He wants you to glean from the adversity you're facing. Surrender to the unknown will of God and rest in His trustworthiness to see you through.

Dear Lord, I must admit, I hate adversity. Help me seek
Your spiritual perspective, knowing that You love me and
have a divine purpose for all that I encounter. Amen.

Comparing Our Life with Others

*"For my thoughts are not your thoughts, neither are your
ways my ways," declares the LORD. "As the heavens are
higher than the earth, so are my ways higher than your
ways and my thoughts than your thoughts."*
ISAIAH 55:8–9

———◆———

We may often wonder why some people experience lifelong tragedy while others seem to enjoy smooth sailing. Christian families
may struggle while unbelievers seem to be on the top of the world.
Life seems blatantly unfair at times!

We do not have the whole picture. Only God does. Our per-
ception may not be reality. Millionaires can be miserable. Beauty
queens can lack self-esteem. The confirmed bachelor can be lonely.
Things are not always as they appear.

We don't know how God might be working in another person's life. God's thoughts and plans are unknown to us. God is not
accountable to man. He does not need nor seek our approval for
His actions. He is God. We are not! One thing we can be assured:
He is with everyone who calls on His name. He gives us power and
strength to handle whatever comes our way. We are to trust Him
forever. Remember: God's ways and thoughts are higher than ours.

*Dear Lord, when life from my vantage point seems grossly unfair,
may I trust in You. Help me quit trying to play God. Amen.*

The Wages of Sin

For the wages of sin is death, but the gift of
God is eternal life in Christ Jesus our Lord.
ROMANS 6:23

Unfortunately sin entered the world in the Garden of Eden and severed Adam and Eve's relationship with God. We, like Adam and Eve, are inherently sinful. We all fall short of God's glory. The payment for our sin is death. In His love, God sent Jesus to pay the debt we owe but could not pay. We must choose to either receive or reject Jesus' gift of eternal life. There is no middle ground. By not accepting, we are in essence rejecting.

There is only one way to eternal life—through Jesus Christ our Lord. Jesus himself said, "I am *the way* and the truth and the life. No one comes to the Father except through me" (John 14:6, emphasis added). When we accept the fact that we have been crucified with Christ, we are dead to sin. We can then yield our lives to the Lord to be used for His glory.

Jesus died for the sins of the world. Jesus died for you! He has come to redeem you and give you eternal life. If you have not done so already, accept His gift for you today. Enter into a personal relationship with your heavenly Father through Jesus Christ, His Son. Your life will never be the same!

Dear Lord, You have paid the wages for my sin. May my life be spent in gratitude and praise for that most precious gift! Amen.

Day 245

Blessed Assurance

And this is the testimony: God has given us eternal life,
and this life is in his Son. Whoever has the Son has
life;whoever does not have the Son of God does not
have life.I write these things to you who believe in the name of the
Son of God so that you may know that you have eternal life.

1 John 5:11–13

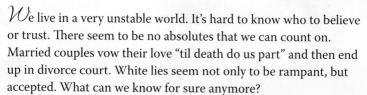

We live in a very unstable world. It's hard to know who to believe or trust. There seem to be no absolutes that we can count on. Married couples vow their love "til death do us part" and then end up in divorce court. White lies seem not only to be rampant, but accepted. What can we know for sure anymore?

There is good news! People may break their promises, but God never does. People may lie to us, but God never will. God is faithful—not just when He feels like it, but always! That is who He is! So, when He assures us of something, we can stake our lives on it. It *will* come to pass.

We can have the assurance of eternal life if we believe in Jesus. It's that simple. No one is worthy of eternal life. Salvation is a gift from God. We are saved by God's grace—His goodness demonstrated toward us. Sin darkens our lives, yet God's grace can permeate every nook and cranny. There is blessed assurance knowing that we possess eternal life. That's something worth believing in!

Dear Lord, I can know that I am Yours and You are mine forever.
May I joyfully rest in that truth today! Amen.

DAY 246

Secure in God's Hand

"I give them eternal life, and they shall never perish;
no one will snatch them out of my hand."
JOHN 10:28

---

*H*ave you ever felt like your sin is so grievous to God that He has disowned you? Peter must have felt that way after denying Jesus three times. I'm sure David could relate after committing adultery with Bathsheba. Both of these men knew better, yet they succumbed to temptation.

Jesus assures His followers that they are secure in His hands. The first step to eternal security is taken when we acknowledge that we are sinful and need a Savior. That Savior is Jesus Christ; God's one and only Son. Once we have accepted Jesus, our eternity is secure.

Although we are heaven-bound, we still succumb to sin. Sin may keep us outside God's perfect will but never outside His eternal love. Restore your relationship by confessing sin and receiving forgiveness. Do not allow feelings of guilt and shame to keep you away from God. Sin never negates God's love for you. Be committed to live by the truth of God's Word. God could not love you any more or any less than He always does!

Dear Lord, Your unconditional love is a hard concept
to grasp. May I live by faith, believing that even my
sin cannot separate me from Your love. Amen.

Day 247

A New Creation

Therefore, if anyone is in Christ, the new creation has come:
The old has gone, the new is here!
2 Corinthians 5:17

*B*elievers are positionally dead to sin yet alive in Christ. "When you were dead in your sins and in the uncircumcision of your flesh, God made you alive with Christ. He forgave us all our sins, having canceled the charge of our legal indebtedness, which stood against us and condemned us; he has taken it away, nailing it to the cross" (Colossians 2:13–14). That does not mean we live a sinless life. Our sinful nature has an appetite that yearns to be satisfied. Satan tempts us to fulfill desires outside of God's boundaries of love. We sin by yielding to those temptations.

Before we came to know the Lord, sin may not have bothered us. Now the conviction of the Holy Spirit leaves us uncomfortable with sin. Because we are new creations, sin brings remorse and calls us back to God. The Lord always forgives and restores. We will never be sinless this side of heaven, but the longer we walk with the Lord, we should sin less and less as we are transformed more and more into the image of Christ.

Dear Lord, help me not succumb to Satan's schemes but live my life
as a new creation in You. Amen.

Day 248

The Belt of Truth

Finally, be strong in the Lord and in his mighty power.
Put on the full armor of God, so that you can take
your stand against the devil's schemes. Stand firm then,
with the belt of truth buckled around your waist.
EPHESIANS 6:10–11, 14

A soldier wouldn't think about going into battle empty-handed. Combat equipment is worn, and offensive weapons are strapped on. An astute soldier would never forget his battle gear—his life depends on it!

Christians are in a spiritual battle. Although it may not be visible, it is real nevertheless. We may have an enemy of our souls, but God has not left us defenseless. He has given us spiritual armor so that we can stand firm when under spiritual attack.

The purpose of a belt is to hold together an entire outfit. The foundation of our Christian faith is Jesus Christ, the Truth. So when we allow the "belt of truth" to hold us together, we will not be defeated. The Word of God is housed in absolute truth. The believer whose life is controlled by truth will defeat Satan, "the father of lies." Don't go into battle without the belt of truth buckled firmly!

Dear Lord, I want to fasten Your belt of truth snuggly around
my waist daily so that I will be able to stand strong in You.
Thank You for providing me with the spiritual armor I need. Amen.

DAY 249

The Sword of the Spirit

Take the helmet of salvation and the sword
of the Spirit, which is the word of God.
EPHESIANS 6:17

Soldiers and police officers take extremely good care of their weapons. Knives are sharpened. Guns are oiled. It's imperative that they become very familiar with handling them and knowing how to use them properly, because these weapons could save their lives someday.

The sword of the Spirit is the Word of God. It is our only offensive spiritual weapon. Jesus used scripture to rebuff Satan's temptations in the wilderness (see Matthew 4:1–11). Jesus was victorious. We can be triumphant also, by following Jesus' example.

We must choose: Do we listen to Satan's lies or God's truth? Truth guides us in life. Without it, we easily become lost. The truth of God keeps us centered on what is real and factual. Becoming familiar with the Bible enables us to know how to use it. Saturating our minds with God's Word helps us discern His truth from Satan's lies. Memorizing scripture enables the Holy Spirit to recall truth in order to counteract the enemy's lies. We have been given the sword of the Spirit. Let's use it!

Dear Lord, You have given me spiritual victory.
May I not retreat in fear, but use the sword of the Spirit
offensively so that I may be victorious today. Amen.

DAY 250

Our Thoughts

For, "Who has known the mind of the Lord so as to instruct him?"
But we have the mind of Christ.

1 CORINTHIANS 2:16

The Secret Life of Walter Mitty is a book about a man with a vivid imagination. Recently it was made into a movie. Although Walter lived a normal life, he allowed his thoughts to take him to another world. As a daydreamer, Walter's thoughts became his escape from reality.

Where do your thoughts drift to the majority of the time? Are you looking for an escape like Walter? Is your mind ever dwelling on the things of God? Our thought lives are extremely important. Our minds may focus on jobs, children, spouses, and homes. Yet believers also have the ability to think about spiritual matters because the indwelling Holy Spirit gives spiritual discernment.

We must be on guard. Satan wants us to focus on negative, self-defeating, and impure thoughts. God must have full control of our thought lives. This takes discipline over time. Do not be discouraged. The more you saturate your mind with truth, the less room the enemy has to gain a foothold in your thought life!

Dear Lord, because of You, I have the ability to dwell on
spiritual truth. Help me take steps to discipline my
thought life so that it is pleasing to You. Amen.

Day 251

Our Time

*Be very careful, then, how you live—not as unwise but as wise,
making the most of every opportunity, because the days are evil.
Therefore do not be foolish, but understand what the Lord's will is.*

Ephesians 5:15–17

How do we spend our time? Perhaps work is all-consuming
or children have us running here and there. Many times we are
controlled by the tyranny of the urgent—frantically trying to put
out one fire after another. At the end of the day, we plop into bed
exhausted!

Think about it—Jesus never hurried anywhere. His life had
focus. He knew where He was supposed to be and what He should
be doing. Peace ruled His days. Does that describe you?

God's desire is that we love and serve Him above all else,
regardless of where we are or what we are doing. When we discern
His will, we can carry it out with calm resolution. Whatever our
circumstances, we can be in God's service. As we worship Him
and meditate on His Word, God reveals His will for us through the
Holy Spirit. Let us spend our time on earth wisely.

*Dear Lord, may I utilize my time on earth wisely. May I be
in the center of Your will where there is rest and peace
regardless of what's happening around me. Amen.*

Our Talents

Each of you should use whatever gift you have received to serve others, as faithful stewards of God's grace in its various forms.

1 PETER 4:10

God has created each individual with unique, natural talents. Imagine if Ludwig van Beethoven never allowed anyone to listen while he played the piano? What if Claude Monet painted only for himself or if *David* by Michelangelo was closed to visitors? God-given abilities and talents are meant to be shared! The world is blessed and God receives glory for the amazing abilities He has given man.

In addition to natural talents, the believer also receives spiritual gifts. The Lord combines these together so that we can reflect His mercy and grace to others. Once we surrender our lives to Jesus Christ, we may discover abilities we never knew we had. When we make ourselves available to God, He will use us. God blesses us with talents and spiritual gifts so that we can be a blessing in other people's lives. Our talents and gifts are not to be kept to ourselves. They are meant to be shared! We may not be a Beethoven or Michelangelo, but God can use us to make a difference in someone's life today!

Dear Lord, although You have given me gifts and talents, sometimes I don't feel like putting forth the effort. Forgive me, Lord. May I use my gifts to bless others and bring glory to Your name. Amen.

DAY 253

Our Treasure

After this, Jesus went out and saw a tax collector by the name of Levi [Matthew] sitting at his tax booth. "Follow me," Jesus said to him, and Levi got up, left everything and followed him.

LUKE 5:27–28

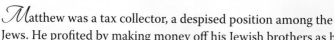

$\mathcal{M}$atthew was a tax collector, a despised position among the Jews. He profited by making money off his Jewish brothers as he collected their Roman taxes. Yet, when Jesus called him, worldly treasures paled in comparison, and he left "everything" to follow Jesus.

Decisions to follow Jesus may present themselves in our lives as well: leaving the corporate world in order to be a stay-at-home mom or declining a promotion because it would compromise your integrity. When the Lord asks you to give up something, make the decision to follow Him.

No financial gain compares to the awesome provision that is ours in Christ. When we leave everything behind and follow Him, we realize the full value of true wealth. Eternal life and unconditional love are the answers to our deepest needs. These can only be found in the person of Jesus Christ. When having to make a choice between money and following Jesus, Jesus is the right choice every time.

Dear Lord, may I let go of anything that is holding me back from following You completely. You are my greatest treasure. May my life be a reflection of that truth. Amen.

DAY 254

Fully Alive

*When you were dead in your sins and in the uncircumcision
of your flesh, God made you alive with Christ.*

COLOSSIANS 2:13

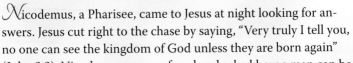

Nicodemus, a Pharisee, came to Jesus at night looking for answers. Jesus cut right to the chase by saying, "Very truly I tell you, no one can see the kingdom of God unless they are born again" (John 3:3). Nicodemus was confused and asked how a man can be born when he is old. Jesus then explained the difference between physical and spiritual birth.

When we accept Jesus, we have been "born again"; born spiritually. We have freedom from sin—both its guilt and its penalty. Because we have been united with Christ in His death, we are also united with Him in His resurrection. Our sin was nailed to the cross. Our debt has been paid in full. We have received eternal life and are spiritually born again.

Our old self is crucified in order that our body of sin might be done away with. We are no longer slaves to sin, but slaves to righteousness instead. We are free to serve Christ. We are fully alive. If Christ has set you free, you are free indeed!

*Dear Lord, I am no longer defined by sin and my
former ways of life. I am alive because of You! Amen.*

The Breastplate of Righteousness

Stand firm then, with the belt of truth buckled around your waist,
with the breastplate of righteousness in place.
EPHESIANS 6:14

❈

A warrior's breastplate protects the heart, the body's most vital organ. Our spiritual breastplate is the righteousness of Christ. We can take our stand against Satan's schemes because of who we are in Christ. His character is our defense. His character protects our heart.

Scripture states that we are a child of the King. We are dearly loved. "What, then, shall we say in response to these things? If God is for us, who can be against us?" (Romans 8:31). "For I am convinced that neither death nor life, neither angels nor demons, neither the present nor the future, nor any powers, neither height nor depth, nor anything else in all creation, will be able to separate us from the love of God that is in Christ Jesus our Lord" (Romans 8:38–39).

He has given us all we need for life and death. He is our all in all. His righteousness covers our most vital organ, our heart. Let's put on our breastplate of righteousness. Let's live in victory today because Christ's righteousness has been given to us! Thank You, Lord!

Dear Lord, You protect my very life. Thank You that I am
secure and safe because of Your righteousness. Amen.

Day 256

Our Treasure

*"Do not store up for yourselves treasures on earth, where moths
and vermin destroy, and where thieves break in and steal.
But store up for yourselves treasures in heaven, where moths and
vermin do not destroy, and where thieves do not break in and steal.
For where your treasure is, there your heart will be also."*

Matthew 6:19–21

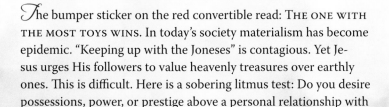

The bumper sticker on the red convertible read: THE ONE WITH
THE MOST TOYS WINS. In today's society materialism has become
epidemic. "Keeping up with the Joneses" is contagious. Yet Jesus urges His followers to value heavenly treasures over earthly
ones. This is difficult. Here is a sobering litmus test: Do you desire
possessions, power, or prestige above a personal relationship with
Jesus?

Examine your checkbook. Evaluate how you spend your time.
Think about what motivates you. When our eyes are set on material gain, our lives are controlled by the desire to acquire more.
However, earthly treasures will never truly satisfy because they
are temporary and will someday pass away. Spiritual treasures are
eternal. There is nothing wrong with possessing material wealth, as
long our hearts don't desire it above the Lord. Jesus is our greatest
treasure! He alone satisfies our souls.

*Dear Lord, I can easily get caught up in earthly treasures.
Help me keep them in their proper place and desire You more
than anything this world can offer. My heart belongs to You. Amen.*

DAY 257

Helmet of Salvation

Take the helmet of salvation and the sword
of the Spirit, which is the word of God.
EPHESIANS 6:17

*H*elmet laws have been passed in many states because statistics show that severe head injuries can be avoided if bicyclists and motorcyclists wear helmets. Likewise, a soldier's helmet protects his head from fatal trauma.

As believers, the helmet of salvation is our spiritual defensive weapon, protecting us from a debilitating blow. Our mind needs to be controlled by God. Symbolically, as we slip on the helmet of salvation, we are asking God to protect our thinking by keeping our minds focused on truth.

Satan tries very hard to get control of our mind by interjecting lies into our thoughts: "You are a failure. Nobody loves you. You'll never amount to anything. You've blown it too many times for God to forgive you." However, when we allow God to control our minds, He whispers truth to our hearts: "I love you unconditionally. I forgive you. You will be victorious because of me."

Don't leave yourself defenseless. Firmly fasten the helmet of salvation on your head. Have your thoughts focused on God's truth. Be encouraged by Jesus' words: "I have told you these things, so that in me you may have peace. In this world you will have trouble. But take heart! I have overcome the world" (John 16:33).

Dear Lord, please control my thoughts so that my
mind is filled with the goodness of Your truth. Amen.

DAY 258

Joy in Trials

*Consider it pure joy, my brothers and sisters, whenever you
face trials of many kinds, because you know that the
testing of your faith produces perseverance.*

JAMES 1:2–3

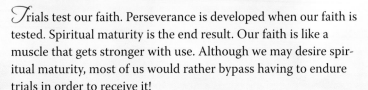

Trials test our faith. Perseverance is developed when our faith is tested. Spiritual maturity is the end result. Our faith is like a muscle that gets stronger with use. Although we may desire spiritual maturity, most of us would rather bypass having to endure trials in order to receive it!

When encountering trials, we must remember that God knows what we are going through and is in control of all things. We must trust God with our circumstances. God is faithful and will never fail us. Do not give up. Trials do not conjure up joy, yet we *can rejoice* that we are drawn closer to the Lord through them. The next time you are being tested, ask God to teach you spiritual truth in the midst of the storm. You will be amazed at what you learn! Spiritual maturity is the result of perseverance. Be encouraged!

*Dear Lord, I desire to be spiritually mature, although I hate going
through trials. Help me see Your good purpose in the trials I face.
May I persevere with inner joy as I draw closer to You. Amen.*

Day 259

Our Testimony

"You are the light of the world. A town built on a hill cannot be hidden. Neither do people light a lamp and put it under a bowl. Instead they put it on its stand, and it gives light to everyone in the house. In the same way, let your light shine before others, that they may see your good deeds and glorify your Father in heaven."
MATTHEW 5:14–16

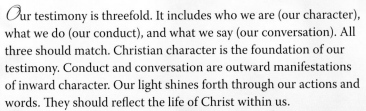

*O*ur testimony is threefold. It includes who we are (our character), what we do (our conduct), and what we say (our conversation). All three should match. Christian character is the foundation of our testimony. Conduct and conversation are outward manifestations of inward character. Our light shines forth through our actions and words. They should reflect the life of Christ within us.

Even the slightest amount of light dispels darkness. We may not feel that the small light of our lives makes a difference, but it does! So don't become discouraged and hide your light. The following question has been asked: If you were put on trial for being a Christian, would there be enough evidence to convict you? Let your light shine brightly today!

Dear Lord, some days I feel as though no one even knows that I am a Christian—a Christ-follower. Help Your light shine through me so that You will receive praise. Amen.

Walk the Talk

*What you heard from me, keep as the pattern of sound
teaching, with faith and love in Christ Jesus. Guard the
good deposit that was entrusted to you—guard it with
the help of the Holy Spirit who lives in us.*

2 TIMOTHY 1:13–14

The apostle Paul was Timothy's mentor in the faith. They had
worked side by side in contending for the Gospel. Now Paul was
encouraging Timothy to put into practice what he had learned
from him. Sound teaching was important in Paul and Timothy's
day. It's just as important in today's world.

All Christians have been entrusted with spiritual treasures. We
have the *truth* of the Living Word—the Bible. Jesus Christ is living
within us in the form of the Holy Spirit. We have been given the
privilege of sharing the Gospel of Christ with others.

We are to uphold our Christian testimony by sharing our spiritual treasures with others. We should be bearing spiritual fruit. "Can
a fig tree bear olives, or a grapevine bear figs? Neither can a salt
spring produce fresh water" (James 3:12). As we allow God's truth to
penetrate our heart and submit to the control of the Holy Spirit, our
spiritual fruit will be consistent with what we profess to believe. May
the treasure in our hearts overflow into the lives of others.

*Dear Lord, I want to "walk the talk" so that others may
come to know the one true and living God. Amen.*

Day 261

Holiness

*You were taught, with regard to your former way of life, to put off
your old self, which is being corrupted by its deceitful desires;
to be made new in the attitude of your minds; and to put on the
new self, created to be like God in true righteousness and holiness.*

Ephesians 4:22–24

Holiness isn't a trait we earn. We are holy because of our position
in Christ. God's Holy Spirit resides within us the minute we accept
Jesus as Lord and Savior. Because of the indwelling Holy Spirit, the
Lord can use us for His service; we have been "set apart" or made
"holy."

God commands us, "Be holy, because I am holy" (Leviticus
11:44). Holiness does not mean sinlessness. It means being "set
apart" to be used by a holy God. We are no longer comfortable
with sin. We no longer take pleasure in walking in the ways of the
ungodly. Instead, we desire to become more like Christ through
the indwelling Holy Spirit.

How does this play itself out in our everyday lives? Make a
conscious decision to turn your back on your old way of life and
turn toward the Lord. Allow God to change your selfish attitudes
and desires to reflect His. This inner transformation will be reflected
outwardly as God uses you for His glory.

*Dear Lord, holiness seems unattainable to me. Yet You would not
ask the impossible from me. You have given me the Holy Spirit so
that I can be set apart for Your use. What a privilege! Amen.*

DAY 262

The Need for Honesty

*When I kept silent, my bones wasted away through my groaning all
day long. For day and night your hand was heavy on me;
my strength was sapped as in the heat of summer. Then I
acknowledged my sin to you and did not cover up my iniquity. I
said, "I will confess my transgressions to the LORD."
And you forgave the guilt of my sin.*

PSALM 32:3–5

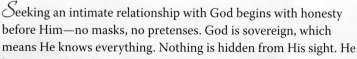

Seeking an intimate relationship with God begins with honesty
before Him—no masks, no pretenses. God is sovereign, which
means He knows everything. Nothing is hidden from His sight. He
knows our thoughts, attitudes, and actions.

Honesty brings relief, washes away guilt, and strengthens
our faith. When we attempt to cover up our sin, we've erected a
wall that separates us from God. Honesty is crucial in developing
openness and creating vulnerability. This paves the way for God
to get to the heart of sin in our lives. Honesty admits need. God
intervenes when we ask for help! No sin can ever separate us from
His love. Let's be honest before Him today so that our relationship
may be restored.

*Dear Lord, why do I pretend with You? Help me to be honest
and transparent before You so that our relationship is
real and I can receive forgiveness. Amen.*

DAY 263

Doer of the Word

*Do not merely listen to the word, and so
deceive yourselves. Do what it says.*

JAMES 1:22

—✦—

*I*t is easy to say one thing yet do another. Talk is easy. Following
through is the hard part. James is exhorting believers not only to
read God's Word but to obey it. In other words—to "walk the talk"
and not be a hypocrite. Be a doer of the Word.

The Pharisees were experts in the Law, yet their hearts were
far from God. We may know all about Jesus, yet if we do not obey
Him, we really don't have a relationship with Him. Jesus said, "Anyone who loves me will obey my teaching" (John 14:23). If we love
Jesus, we will obey His Word.

Be an effective, involved, attentive listener of God's Word.
Grasp the truth and apply it to your life. Be a doer of the Word so
that spiritual knowledge can move from your head to your heart.
Instruction plus involvement equals spiritual growth. Love and
serve others. This is where the rubber meets the road. We cannot
grow spiritually if we are not doers of the Word. It's that simple.

*Dear Lord, I do not want to deceive myself. May I obey
what I read in Your Word so that it truly impacts my
life and the lives of those around me. Amen.*

The Joy of the Holy Spirit

What we have received is not the spirit of the world,
but the Spirit who is from God, so that we may
understand what God has freely given us.

1 CORINTHIANS 2:12

Although every believer has the Holy Spirit, the Holy Spirit does not have every believer. We need to yield to the Holy Spirit's control. This is an everyday, moment by moment, conscious decision that we must make. As we defer to the Holy Spirit's leading, our lives take on new direction and meaning.

When the Holy Spirit is in control, we have purpose in life and a reason for our existence. We are no longer burdened by the guilt of sin. We sense forgiveness for past sins or failures. The Holy Spirit serves as our Comforter and Counselor. Spiritual truth is revealed to our heart. Wisdom is imparted when making decisions.

Peace results because the Holy Spirit leads us in the center of God's will. Inner joy is produced that knows no bounds. God's love flows in and through us. The natural result is a desire to share it with others. May it be so!

Dear Lord, life can either be unfulfilling or purposeful. With You in control, there are opportunities around every bend. May I have eyes to "see" and a heart willing to yield my life to You daily. Amen.

Day 265

The Bible—Our Textbook

*All Scripture is God-breathed and is useful for teaching,
rebuking, correcting and training in righteousness, so that the
servant of God may be thoroughly equipped for every good work.*
2 Timothy 3:16–17

The Bible is the inspired Word of God. It is the most important
book in existence. It serves as a guidebook and textbook for life. It
is ageless and timeless because it was authored by Creator God and
written by men inspired with His truth.

If we truly believed this, why wouldn't we read the Bible every
single day of our lives? Why wouldn't we first turn to the Bible for
the answers to life's questions instead of turning the channel to Dr.
Phil? Do we realize the treasure we've been given?

Reading and studying the Bible equips us for good works and
direction in life. When we get off track, it corrects and rebukes us.
There is no problem we'll encounter that the Bible doesn't address.
Money, sex, greed, gossip, love, parenting, marriage, family, relationships, and anger are biblical topics. *The Bible is good enough to
live by and good enough to die by.*

*Dear Lord, there are people in the world without access
to Your Word. May I not take my Bible for granted.
Help me devour Your Word and search it daily for
answers to the problems I face. Amen.*

Day 266

The Word of God

For the word of God is living and active. Sharper than any double-edged sword, it penetrates even to dividing soul and spirit, joints and marrow; it judges the thoughts and attitudes of the heart. Nothing in all creation is hidden from God's sight. Everything is uncovered and laid bare before the eyes of him to whom we must give account.

Hebrews 4:12–13

God loves a well-worn Bible. It is beautiful in His sight! The Bible should be the most well-read book in the house. Do you value your Bible more than your iPad, iPhone, or Facebook page?

The Bible is living and powerful. It cuts straight to truth and quickly exposes lies. It judges the thoughts and intentions of the heart. Could it be we shy away from opening our Bibles because we don't want to be convicted? Perhaps we have become comfortable with the sin that has crept into our lives.

Beware! Sin is like quick-spreading cancer. Why would someone refuse surgery to remove it? God's Word excises sin at the root. Although it is painful at the time, it brings healing and restoration. Open your Bible today so that positive change can begin.

Dear Lord, I know that nothing is hidden from Your sight. Penetrate my heart by Your Word so that my sin is exposed and I can receive Your forgiveness. Amen.

DAY 267

How to Praise God

I will extol the LORD at all times;
his praise will always be on my lips.
PSALM 34:1

What do you enjoy talking about? Sports, movies, people? Are compliments or complaining more likely to come out of your mouth? In this psalm, David proclaims that he enjoys talking about the Lord. David loves to praise and extol the Lord at all times. What a terrific mind-set!

Do we filter our lives through God's lenses? If we would, praise would continually be on our lips, too! God showers us with so many blessings we take for granted—food, clothing, shelter, not to mention jobs, cars, family, and friends. Even the air we breathe is a gift from Him!

There are so many ways to praise God. Tell others about Him and what He has done in your life. Read scripture and praise Him. Sing to the Lord. Music resonates with God's heart. Sing in your car, in your home, in church. We will sing in heaven for eternity! Use the spiritual gifts He has given you for His service. True faith bears fruit. Give of your financial resources to further His kingdom.

Ask the Lord to help you see Him in the circumstances of your life. Then, like David, His praise will always be on your lips!

Dear Lord, there are endless ways I can praise You.
You alone are worthy of my praise! Amen.

Day 268

The Holy Spirit—Our Teacher

*"But the Advocate, the Holy Spirit, whom the Father
will send in my name, will teach you all things and
will remind you of everything I have said to you."*
JOHN 14:26

Prior to His death and resurrection, Jesus comforted His disciples
by assuring them of heaven and the gift of the Holy Spirit. Although Jesus would not be physically with them forever, the Holy
Spirit would be. "I will not leave you as orphans; I will come to you,
Jesus promised" (John 14:18).

The Holy Spirit resides within believers to this day. He illumi-
nates the truths of scripture and is responsible for transforming us
into the likeness of Jesus Christ. He is our Counselor who never
leaves us, our faithful Teacher and Guide.

The Holy Spirit has four teaching methods: revelation, illumination, reminders, and guidance. The Bible is His *revelation* of truth.
The Holy Spirit helps us mine deep truths through *illumination*—
the "aha moments"! When we memorize scripture, the Holy Spirit
brings to *remembrance* God's truth just when we need it. The Holy
Spirit *guides* us into the application of these truths. Let's allow the
Holy Spirit to teach us so that we will be transformed into the image
of Christ.

*Dear Lord, may I be open to being taught by You. I want to be
transformed from the inside out by the power of the
Holy Spirit. Amen.*

Day 269

A Clear Conscience

*"So I strive always to keep my conscience
clear before God and man."*
ACTS 24:16

The apostle Paul was called before Felix, the governor of Caesarea, to face trumped-up charges against him (see Acts 24:10–16). Paul refuted the false accusations yet admitted to worshipping God and following Jesus. Then he stated, "So I strive always to keep my conscience clear before God and man." What a great goal for us to emulate!

Having a clear conscience brings peace with God and man. If we are doing right before God, we can let go of trying to impress others. God's approval, not man's, becomes our goal.

In order to have a clear conscience, we must make God's truth our standard. If our conscience is programmed by the world, it fails to be trustworthy, because situational ethics is the norm. Living by the world's standards can cause us to make decisions that are diametrically opposed to God's will. God gave us a conscience to prevent us from sinning. In order to have a blameless conscience, it must be programmed with God's Word— the Truth. His Word is the plumb line by which everything else is measured.

*Dear Lord, I desire a clear conscience before You and man.
Help Your Word become such a part of me that I will be
able to discern Your will in every situation. Amen.*

Praising the Lamb of God

Then I heard every creature in heaven and on earth and under
the earth and on the sea, and all that is in them, saying:
"To him who sits on the throne and to the Lamb be praise
and honor and glory and power, for ever and ever!"
REVELATION 5:13

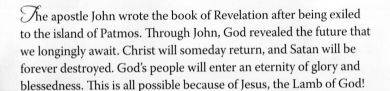

The apostle John wrote the book of Revelation after being exiled to the island of Patmos. Through John, God revealed the future that we longingly await. Christ will someday return, and Satan will be forever destroyed. God's people will enter an eternity of glory and blessedness. This is all possible because of Jesus, the Lamb of God!

Psalms and Revelation are perhaps the two most praise-filled books in the Bible. One of the most intense worship experiences is found in Revelation, 5. Take the time to read it. True worship is not based on emotion or feeling. We praise and adore God for who He is, what He has done, and what He is going to do. Make sure your worship is focused on Christ and free from selfish motives. Praise brings attention to God, not ourselves. Let your heart sing praises to the Lord today!

Dear Lord, You are truly worthy to be worshipped
and praised. May my life be filled with worship
and adoration because of who You are! Amen.

Day 271

True Worship

*I will extol the LORD at all times; his praise will always be on my
lips. I will glory in the LORD; let the afflicted hear and rejoice.
Glorify the LORD with me; let us exalt his name together.*

PSALM 34:1–3

In order to worship God properly, three things must be present.
First, we must know and love God. How can we worship a God
whom we do not know? We come to know Him through His Word,
the Bible. We enter into a personal love relationship with God
through His Son, Jesus.

But it is not enough to know and love Him. Jesus said, "Anyone who loves me will obey my teaching" (John 14:23). Our love
should compel us to follow Jesus in obedience. We must submit to
His will. The apostle Paul charges us in Romans 12:1: "Offer your
bodies as a living sacrifice, holy and pleasing to God—this is your
true and proper worship."

We must also have a pure heart—acknowledging that we are
nothing apart from Him. Our pride must be set aside. Humility
causes us to daily seek and defer to His will. The more spiritually
mature, the more dependent upon Him we become. Then praise
will freely flow from our lips!

*Dear Lord, may I truly worship You in spirit and in truth.
I know and love You. Help me live in faithful
obedience with a pure heart. Amen.*

Day 272

When a Brother Stumbles

Brothers and sisters, if someone is caught in a sin,
you who live by the Spirit should restore that person gently.
But watch yourselves, or you also may be tempted.

Galatians 6:1

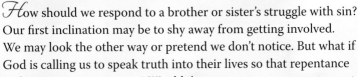

*H*ow should we respond to a brother or sister's struggle with sin? Our first inclination may be to shy away from getting involved. We may look the other way or pretend we don't notice. But what if God is calling us to speak truth into their lives so that repentance and restoration can occur? Wouldn't we want someone to step out of their comfort zone to bring us back to the Lord?

God uses the spiritually mature to *restore* those who have fallen into sin. The Holy Spirit must lead so that motives are restorative rather than judgmental or condemning. The person's sin should not be openly exposed. Gently confront, realizing that we are all human and not immune from temptation ourselves.

If the Lord is nudging you to intervene, pray for guidance. Look for open-door opportunities from the Lord to speak. Convey the overriding emotion of unconditional love, not judgment. May the words He gives fall on receptive hearts so that restoration can occur.

Dear Lord, when You call me to confront a brother or sister tangled
in sin, give me boldness yet gentleness. May I realize that I, too,
am sinful. Help me focus on their restoration in You. Amen.

DAY 273

Spirit-Filled Life

Be very careful, then, how you live—not as unwise but as wise,
making the most of every opportunity, because the days are evil.
Therefore do not be foolish, but understand what the Lord's will is.
Do not get drunk on wine, which leads to debauchery.
Instead, be filled with the Spirit.
EPHESIANS 5:15–18

❧

Which most characterizes your life: love, joy, peace, patience, kindness, goodness, faithfulness, gentleness, and self-control or anger, frustration, impatience, strife, envy, and jealousy? The first list is evidence of a life controlled by the Holy Spirit. In our own strength we are incapable of manifesting these attributes. Only the Lord can produce spiritual fruit as we are fully surrendered to Him.

In contrast, we can refuse to surrender to the Holy Spirit's control—even as Christians. We can take matters into our own hands instead of waiting for the Lord's timing. We can lash out at others who hurt us. We can adopt the world's philosophy rather than live by God's truth. Unfortunately, when we choose to live this way, we are miserable! Life is harder than it has to be because we are not living the Spirit-filled life God has designed for us. Let's choose to allow the Holy Spirit control!

Dear Lord, why, oh why, do I bang my head against the wall so many times? I surrender to Your control. I desire to be in the center of Your will. May the fruits of the Spirit characterize my life. Amen.

DAY 274

Our Counselor

*"And I will ask the Father, and he will give you another advocate
to help you and be with you forever—the Spirit of truth. The world
cannot accept him, because it neither sees him nor knows him.
But you know him, for he lives with you and will be in you.
I will not leave you as orphans; I will come to you."*

JOHN 14:16–18

———◈———

At the Last Supper, Jesus washed his disciples' feet and predicted His betrayal. The disciples were confused and scared. They
did not grasp that Jesus would be crucified, resurrected, and then
ascend into heaven. Although Jesus would be leaving them, He
promised to send a Counselor, the Holy Spirit, to be with them
forever. We are given the same promise! The Holy Spirit, the third
person of the Trinity, lives within us.

We possess the Holy Spirit as believers, but it is possible to
usurp His control in our lives. When we try to run our own lives,
we may be "heaven-bound," but we will fail to experience all that
God desires for us on earth. Let's defer to our Wonderful Counselor so that we can truly live the abundant life He desires for us!

*Dear Lord, I have You living in me in the person of the Holy Spirit.
May I lean on Your counsel and direction every day! Amen.*

DAY 275

Slaves to Righteousness

*You have been set free from sin and
have become slaves to righteousness.*
ROMANS 6:18

❧

*T*hankfully slavery in our country was abolished years ago. However, whether or not we care to admit it, on a personal level all of us are slaves to something. We are either slaves to sin or slaves to righteousness. There is no middle ground. We must choose either the world's path or God's path. Those who have not yet accepted Christ as their Savior are slaves to sin, which leads to death. But because of Jesus' finished work on the cross, we all have been given a choice!

A slave obeys his master. When we choose Jesus, He becomes our master. He desires that we follow Him. Disobedience causes our heart to become cold and numb toward His leading. We may even get the false impression that there won't be consequences for our sinful actions. But God will not let us go. He loves us too much to allow us to stray. He pursues us, disciplines us, and brings us back to Himself. Let's choose God's way for our lives. Being a slave to righteousness is not a burden but a blessing!

*Dear Lord, I would rather be a slave to righteousness
than a slave to sin. Teach me obedience so that I am
not led astray by the deceitfulness of sin. Amen.*

Success in God's Eye

Commit to the LORD whatever you do,
and he will establish your plans.
PROVERBS 16:3

*S*uccess from God's perspective is very different from the world's point of view. Worldly success focuses on the external: bank accounts, educational degrees, material possessions, and physical beauty. God looks at the heart; internal qualities that are invisible yet eternal.

After God removed Saul as king, He send the prophet Samuel to the house of Jesse to anoint Israel's next king. Samuel mistakenly thought Jesse's son Eliab was God's choice. "But the LORD said to Samuel, 'Do not consider his appearance or his height, for I have rejected him. The LORD does not look at the things people look at. People look at the outward appearance, but the LORD looks at the heart' " (1 Samuel 16:7). David the shepherd, Jesse's youngest son, would be God's choice.

God has a plan for our lives, and it includes success. He wants us to reach our fullest potential as we achieve the goals He has helped us set. Our focus must be on God, not on ourselves. Spiritual goals should be the priority. When we desire to please Him, our lives will bring success from God's perspective. David was a man after God's own heart. May God be able to say that of us as well!

Dear Lord, may Your goals be my goals. Transform my heart so that I will experience the success in this life that You desire for me. Amen.

Day 277

Steps to Success

In their hearts humans plan their course,
but the Lord establishes their steps.

Proverbs 16:9

*A*ny successful business knows the importance of setting goals. Mission and vision statements help ensure a stable course. Identifying core values is also key. Employees work with focus when goals are clearly established and communicated. Goal setting is an essential component to achieving personal success as well.

The following types of goals may be considered: physical, financial, professional, marital, and spiritual. Identify goals by writing them down. Set realistic expectations. Remember: godly goals can only be achieved with God's help. He is the One who carries us through and enables us to accomplish that which He purposes in our hearts.

Faith and prayer are crucial when setting goals. A consuming passion to reach your goal is paramount. God teaches us to desire good things, to hope for the impossible, and to dream of reaching goals that only He can help us achieve. Go ahead and plan your course, but allow the Lord to determine your steps. Be flexible if the Lord intervenes by taking you in a different direction. His ways are perfect. His path is best. So, write down your goals, but give the Lord permission to edit them as He so chooses.

Dear Lord, You place desires within my heart.
Fulfill Your purposes in my life. Amen.

Day 278

The Abiding Life

"Remain in me, as I also remain in you. No branch can bear fruit by itself; it must remain in the vine. Neither can you bear fruit unless you remain in me. I am the vine; you are the branches. If you remain in me and I in you, you will bear much fruit; apart from me you can do nothing."

John 15:4–5

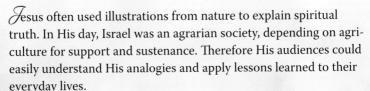

Jesus often used illustrations from nature to explain spiritual truth. In His day, Israel was an agrarian society, depending on agriculture for support and sustenance. Therefore His audiences could easily understand His analogies and apply lessons learned to their everyday lives.

Jesus is the Vine—the giver of spiritual life. We must remain attached to Him if we want to bear spiritual fruit. It is impossible to produce anything of spiritual value in our own strength.

If we abide in Him, He will abide in us. Jesus wants us to rest in Him, secure in the knowledge that His Spirit is living in us. His Spirit gives us power and strength to face any challenge, overcome any obstacle, or accomplish anything that He calls us to. Let us remain in Him so that we can bear spiritual fruit—fruit that will last.

Dear Lord, why do I think I can live this Christian life in my own strength? When I cease to remain connected to You through prayer, Your Word, and obedience, I can do nothing. Amen.

The Fruit of the Spirit

But the fruit of the Spirit is love, joy, peace, forbearance,
kindness, goodness, faithfulness, gentleness and self-control.
Against such things there is no law.
GALATIANS 5:22–23

Given a choice, most of us would pick love over hate, joy over sorrow, and peace over anxiety. Yet why do we seem to exhibit the polar opposites of the fruit of the Spirit much of the time? The truth of the matter is that the fruit of the Spirit cannot be willed by man. It cannot be conjured up. It is the by-product of Christ living in us.

The fruit of the Spirit is the manifestation of Christ's character. He exemplified all of the qualities listed in Galatians 5:22-23. That is why it is impossible to muster up these attributes in our own strength. The fruit of the Spirit can only be present when Christ is living in and through us.

Never substitute works and service for the Spirit-filled life. God's work done in our own strength produces frustration and burnout. However, when Christ flows in and through us, the fruit of the Spirit is clearly evident. Christ makes all the difference! Allow His life within you to produce spiritual fruit for all to see and be nourished by.

Dear Lord, I want to bear the fruit of the Spirit. Live in and through
me so that Your fruit can bless the lives of those around me. Amen.

Day 280

A Fruitful Life

*But the fruit of the Spirit is love, joy, peace, forbearance,
kindness, goodness, faithfulness, gentleness and self-control.
Against such things there is no law.*

Galatians 5:22–23

❦

The greatest contribution believers can make to the world is to live spiritually faithful lives. As believers walking in the Spirit, we do not respond to life based on our circumstances. We continue to manifest spiritual fruit regardless of what we are experiencing. We become living testimonies to the supernatural power God gives when we are resting in Him.

Unconditional love is freely given. Inner joy is felt amid sorrow. Abiding peace is present during adversity. Patience is displayed during times of waiting. Kindness is offered without reservation. Goodness is chosen in the worst situations. Faithfulness triumphs every time. Gentleness and self-control are displayed routinely. Isn't this an awesome way to live?

We must choose to abide with Christ—to allow the Holy Spirit to control our thoughts, speech, and actions. Fruitful believers are attuned to the Holy Spirit and responsive to His guidance. May our lives be overflowing with the fruit of the Spirit.

Dear Lord, regardless of my circumstances, I want to walk peacefully with You. You are my anchor in the storm. May I cling to You and be guided today by Your Holy Spirit so that I will bear fruit. Amen.

DAY 281

The Holy Spirit's Power

"But you will receive power when the Holy Spirit comes on you;
and you will be my witnesses in Jerusalem, and in all
Judea and Samaria, and to the ends of the earth."

ACTS 1:8

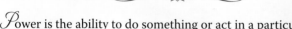

$\mathcal{P}$ower is the ability to do something or act in a particular way. Power infers overcoming and triumphing over obstacles that might be in the way. These could be outward or inward hindrances.

Before Jesus' ascension, He charged His followers to be His witnesses. What a tough assignment! Jesus had just been crucified. Now His followers would be persecuted for believing in Him. How could they witness without fear that death would also be their fate? Jesus promised His disciples power in the form of the Holy Spirit. This power would enable them to be His witnesses.

This same power is available to every believer who willingly surrenders moment by moment in submission and obedience. The Holy Spirit releases His power to us in three ways. The character of Christ is revealed in us through the fruit of the Spirit. His power works in and through us to carry out His redemptive work as we witness to others. And His power enables us to accomplish the work He calls us to do.

Dear Lord, I need Your power in my life. Give me the ability
to surrender moment by moment every day. Amen.

DAY 282

Anxiety

*Do not be anxious about anything, but in every situation,
by prayer and petition, with thanksgiving, present your requests to
God. And the peace of God, which transcends all understanding,
will guard your hearts and your minds in Christ Jesus.*

PHILIPPIANS 4:6–7

Given a choice, would you rather be anxious or peaceful? Obviously most of us would choose peace over anxiety. Yet why do so many things in this life leave us worried or anxious? Worry accomplishes nothing (see Matthew 6:25–34). Worry prevents us from living in the present effectively because our mind is focused on the past or future.

Worry and anxiety are quickly revealed by the lines on our face, tone of voice, negative attitudes, or lack of joy. We may even lose sleep. Our mind races to the what-ifs as we try to figure things out. In reality, anxiety exposes our lack of faith. Jesus deserves our total confidence. Instead of worrying—pray! Lay your anxieties at the foot of the cross, and leave them there. Walk away with peace, knowing that almighty God will take care of the burdens you've been carrying. Live peacefully in the present.

*Dear Lord, help me to worry less and pray more. Anxiety is sin—
plain and simple. I confess that I need to trust You more. Grow me
in this area. Impart peace as I present my requests to You. Amen.*

God's Forgiveness

*If we confess our sins, he is faithful and just and will forgive
us our sins and purify us from all unrighteousness.*

1 JOHN 1:9

People may withhold forgiveness from us, but God's forgiveness is always available. We must agree with God and admit when we've fallen short. Unfortunately, many times pride blinds us and we are incapable of acknowledging sin in our lives. We may view our sin as "no big deal." Or the opposite could be true: we may view our sin as so grievous that we doubt God could ever forgive us. Both of these erroneous mind-sets can keep us from seeking God's forgiveness.

The truth is—sin is sin. God does not rank sin as man does. Even the "smallest" sin required the death of a Savior. "For the wages of sin is death, but the gift of God is eternal life in Christ Jesus our Lord" (Romans 6:23). God never sees any sin as being unforgivable. Regardless of our unrighteous acts or sinful lifestyle, God will cleanse us from our sins. God's arms of forgiveness are open wide. Seek His forgiveness today. Return to the Shepherd of your soul.

*Dear Lord, I am in need of forgiveness. Thank You that there is
no sin too big or too small that Your love cannot cover. Amen.*

Gifts That Serve

Each of you should use whatever gift you have received to serve others, as faithful stewards of God's grace in its various forms.

1 PETER 4:10

Every believer has been given at least one spiritual gift. "We have different gifts, according to the grace given to each of us. If your gift is prophesying, then prophesy in accordance with your faith; if it is serving, then serve; if it is teaching, then teach; if it is to encourage, then give encouragement; if it is giving, then give generously; if it is to lead, do it diligently; if it is to show mercy, do it cheerfully" (Romans 12:6–8).

Our spiritual gift is meant to be shared by serving others. We are God's hands and feet in a needy world. As we use our gifts in the Lord's service, His grace overflows into the lives of others. Can you sing? Join the choir. Do you have the gift of hospitality? Invite people over. There is no good excuse for not serving God, for He supplies what we lack. Service is a natural by-product of the Spirit-filled life. You have been blessed with a gift. Don't keep it to yourself. Bless others by using it!

Dear Lord, help me see beyond myself. Show me how to use what You have given me to serve others. May the Holy Spirit empower me to be Your hands and feet today. Amen.

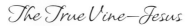

DAY 285

The True Vine—Jesus

*"I am the true vine, and my Father is the gardener. He cuts off
every branch in me that bears no fruit, while every branch that
does bear fruit he prunes so that it will be even more fruitful."*

JOHN 15:1–2

Gardeners understand certain basic pruning principles. Pruning
is necessary and requires time and expertise. Dead branches must
be cut out. Healthy branches are pruned to stimulate new growth
and help shape the tree. Suckers, those branches that will never
yield fruit, are cut out to force nutrients to the fruitful branches.

Jesus often used gardening principles to illustrate important
spiritual truth. Jesus is our true, spiritual Vine. Our heavenly Father is the Gardener. There are three types of branches in relationship to the True Vine, Jesus.

Barren branches are fruitless. Jesus said that God will take
away every branch in Him that does not bear fruit. Fruitful
branches are productive members of the body of Christ. They
worship, serve, and honor the Lord. God prunes them through discipline. This enables them to produce more abundant fruit. Dead
branches are lifeless wood and have not been born again.

What type of branch are you? Let's desire to be fruitful, knowing that although pruning is painful, it yields an abundant harvest.
May it be so!

*Dear Lord, I want to produce much spiritual fruit. Help me
not to become discouraged when I experience "pruning." May I
remember that the end result will be more fruitfulness. Amen.*

DAY 286

Pruning the Branches

"This is to my Father's glory, that you bear much fruit,
showing yourselves to be my disciples."
JOHN 15:8

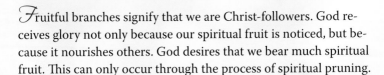

Fruitful branches signify that we are Christ-followers. God receives glory not only because our spiritual fruit is noticed, but because it nourishes others. God desires that we bear much spiritual fruit. This can only occur through the process of spiritual pruning.

Spiritual pruning stimulates spiritual growth. God cuts out areas of our lives that are spiritually harmful—unhealthy habits or relationships, for example. In fruitful areas, He prunes so that even more spiritual fruit will be produced. Although pruning is painful at the time, the rewards are worth it.

God prunes us because He knows what we don't, sees what we can't, and realizes potential we never conceived we had. God prunes us by using His Word to convict us of sin. He then encourages us to defer to the Holy Spirit for righteous conduct. The Lord also prunes us by using other people or circumstances in our lives. In all of this, His tender pruning is done out of love. Hand your heavenly Father the pruning shears so that you will be conformed to the image of His Son.

Dear Lord, I want to be spiritually fruitful, but I do
not enjoy the pruning process! Nevertheless, I will trust You
because You know what is truly best. Amen.

Maintaining the Spirit-Filled Life

So I say, walk by the Spirit, and you will not gratify the desires of the flesh. . . . But if you are led by the Spirit, you are not under law.
GALATIANS 5:16, 18

In our own strength we may try to live good, moral Christian lives. We attempt to keep the Ten Commandments and the list of "do's and don'ts." However, living the Christian life under the law produces failure every time. The apostle Paul encountered this exact dilemma. "I do not understand what I do. For what I want to do I do not do, but what I hate I do" (Romans 7:15).

There is a better way. Since we live under grace and not under law, sin does not have mastery over us. Sin is the biggest inhibitor to maintaining the Spirit-filled life. Although we will never live a sinless life, we can receive forgiveness and move forward by confessing our sin. Instead of living in our own strength and willpower, allow the Holy Spirit to help you live the Christian life. You will embark on each day with the grace and power to face any situation.

Dear Lord, I cannot successfully live the Christian life without Your Spirit living in and through me. This is the only way to live an abundant, victorious life regardless of my circumstances. Amen.

The Battlefield of the Mind

Since, then, you have been raised with Christ, set your hearts
on things above, where Christ is, seated at the right hand of God.
Set your minds on things above, not on earthly things.

COLOSSIANS 3:1–2

❈

The mind is the battlefield of sin. "Each person is tempted when they are dragged away by their own evil desire and enticed. Then, after desire has conceived, it gives birth to sin; and sin, when it is full-grown, gives birth to death" (James 1:14–15). Evil desires are birthed in the mind, enticing us to sin. Therefore we must purpose to focus our minds on spiritual truth rather than on earthly temptations. The battle can be won or lost with what we allow our minds to dwell on.

Unfortunately Satan knows our weaknesses. He may have gotten a stronghold by attacking those weaknesses so often. Pray and ask the Lord to reveal your vulnerabilities. Then ask Him to help you dismiss any thoughts in those weak areas the minute they pop into your mind. Take heart! God has equipped us with every weapon needed to defeat the forces of darkness.

Dear Lord, I know the enemy has gotten a foothold in some
areas of weakness in my life. Help me resist and stand firm.
Quickly divert my thoughts to things above—Your truth. Amen.

DAY 289

Forgiveness

Praise the LORD, my soul, and forget not all his benefits—
who forgives all your sins and heals all your diseases,
who redeems your life from the pit and crowns you with
love and compassion, who satisfies your desires with good
things so that your youth is renewed like the eagle's.

PSALM 103:2–5

God promises to forgive *all* our sins—not just the unintentional, small ones—but even the deliberate, defiant sins. Let's recall some heroes of the faith who received God's forgiveness so we may be encouraged.

God forgave Saul for persecuting Christians, and he became the apostle Paul. God forgave Moses for murdering an Egyptian, and he led the Israelites to the Promised Land. God forgave David of adultery and murder, and David was called "a man after God's own heart."

If God always forgives us when we repent and ask for forgiveness, why do we often have so much difficulty forgiving ourselves? When God forgives us, we are justified in His sight. He desires our justification, not our condemnation. "Therefore, there is now no condemnation for those who are in Christ Jesus" (Romans 8:1). All sin is ultimately against God. So if God has forgiven our trespasses against Him, we need to believe it and forgive ourselves!

Dear Lord, help me walk in Your forgiveness every day. May I keep
short accounts with You. Help me to forgive myself. Amen.

The Plans He Has

"For I know the plans I have for you," declares the LORD,
"plans to prosper you and not to harm you,
plans to give you hope and a future."

JEREMIAH 29:11

❈

The Lord has a marvelous plan for our lives! It begins with a relationship with Him through Jesus Christ. God blesses our lives when we desire to become all that He has planned for us. We tend to think of prosperity and success from a worldly point of view— material possessions, great jobs, perfect children, and so forth. But the Lord is referring to eternal prosperity—the intangibles that this world cannot begin to offer. The apostle Paul said it best in 2 Corinthians 4:8–9: "We are hard pressed on every side, but not crushed; perplexed, but not in despair; persecuted, but not abandoned; struck down, but not destroyed."

When encountering difficulties, it may be hard to believe that God has good plans for you. The future may look dismal. All hope may be lost. You may just be hanging on by a thread. That is the very time you need to remember the truth! God cannot lie. He will be faithful in your life. God has already gone before you and prepared the way. Believe it. Let's strive to become what God has planned, knowing that there is blessing in the center of His will.

Dear Lord, You have great plans for my life.
You will prosper and bless me spiritually. . .
and that far outweighs any earthly rewards. Amen.

DAY 291

Obedience Is Better

But Samuel replied: "Does the LORD delight in burnt offerings and sacrifices as much as in obeying the LORD? To obey is better than sacrifice, and to heed is better than the fat of rams."

1 SAMUEL 15:22

Through the prophet Samuel, the Lord told King Saul to attack the Amalekites and completely destroy everything that belonged to them. Instead, Saul destroyed the despised and weak but spared everything good. Nothing is hidden from God's sight. Saul could not fool God nor the prophet Samuel. Following this incident, God rejected Saul as king. Saul's half obedience was viewed as complete disobedience by the Lord.

How many times might we do most of what God asks of us and think we're being obedient? With God it's either complete obedience or disobedience. God knows our hearts. Nothing is hidden from His sight.

God chooses leaders and places them in positions of authority. Perhaps you are a leader. Take heed: if you want to lead successfully, you must first learn to follow God completely. Halfhearted obedience will result in complete failure. Obey the voice of the Lord *wholeheartedly*. Do not lead those following in your footsteps astray. Walk obediently with Him.

Dear Lord, may I take my leadership position as seriously as You do. I want to obey You wholeheartedly so that I can lead others in the right direction. Amen.

Be Strong and Courageous

"Have I not commanded you? Be strong and courageous.
Do not be afraid; do not be discouraged, for the LORD
your God will be with you wherever you go."

JOSHUA 1:9

❦

After the death of Moses, God commissioned Joshua to lead the Israelites into the Promised Land. Moses would not be going with them. Joshua was undoubtedly terrified at the ominous task before him. However, God reassured him by reminding Joshua that He would be with him. God's presence alone would be enough.

It is human nature to become frightened or discouraged. There are mountains we must face in life that we *know* we cannot climb! We encounter troubling times that are like tidal waves threatening to swallow us whole. God's words to Joshua are being spoken to you. God is with you!

Regardless of what God has chosen for us to do, we do not bear the burden alone. The Lord is also with us wherever we go! Do not allow doubts or thoughts of failure to discourage you. Claim your position as a child of God. Recall God's past promises and His faithfulness. God never gives up on us. He will provide the strength we need to complete our assignment.

Dear Lord, I can be strong and courageous because You are with
me. You will remain faithful and see me through. Amen.

DAY 293

Pressing On

Brothers and sisters, I do not consider myself yet to have taken hold of it. But one thing I do: Forgetting what is behind and straining toward what is ahead, I press on toward the goal to win the prize for which God has called me heavenward in Christ Jesus.

PHILIPPIANS 3:13-14

Olympic athletes are inspirational to watch. Years of training culminate in one single performance, event, or race. It is all on the line. To win the gold, their minds must be razor focused. Their eyes must be on the finish line rather than on fellow competitors. They must put forth their total effort.

How are we responding to this race called life? "Do you not know that in a race all the runners run, but only one gets the prize? Run in such a way as to get the prize. Everyone who competes in the games goes into strict training. They do it to get a crown that will not last, but we do it to get a crown that will last forever" (1 Corinthians 9:24–25).

What goals have you set for your life? Are you confident that God would put His seal of approval on those plans? Pray and ask God to help you set life goals that reflect His desires for you. Then do not look back, but keep your eyes on that goal and persevere toward it. He will provide the insight you need for the future. He will direct your path and show you the way to go. Then, like Paul, we, too, will press on to win the prize God has for us.

Dear Lord, I need Your wisdom and direction to set goals that are in keeping with Your will. Help me press on with focus and determination. Amen.

Day 294

Successful Plans

Commit to the LORD whatever you do,
and he will establish your plans.

PROVERBS 16:3

⁂

Setting goals and having plans gives purpose and direction to life. Excitement and energy can be felt as we focus on achieving those goals. Having a purpose enables us to use creative energy and talents toward that common goal. How can we enjoy the fulfillment of a successful plan?

Do not make your plans apart from God. Seek His counsel. Pray and ask God to give you His vision for your life. Ask Him to give you a heart that is receptive to His plans because they may be quite different from your own. " 'For my thoughts are not your thoughts, neither are your ways my ways,' declares the LORD. 'As the heavens are higher than the earth, so are my ways higher than your ways and my thoughts than your thoughts' " (Isaiah 55:8–9).

God desires to use you to touch others with His love. Examine your goals. Are they selfish, or do they positively impact others? God will make your path straight when you commit your plans to Him and desire His will above your own. His plans are successful plans.

Dear Lord, make known Your plans for me. May I desire to be in the center of Your will for my life. May my plans be Your plans. Amen.

Practical Tips to Reach Your Goals

*"All those gathered here will know that it is not by sword
or spear that the LORD saves; for the battle is the LORD's,
and he will give all of you into our hands."*

1 SAMUEL 17:47

*M*ost of us are familiar with the story of David's triumph over
Goliath (see 1 Samuel 17:24–47). David issued the statement above
to the Philistines before defeating Goliath. David was confident
in the Lord's ability to win the battle. We may have "giants" in our
own lives that we need to stand against. We can learn much from
David on reaching goals. We must have the following:

1. Clear picture of the goal.
2. Consuming desire to reach the goal.
3. Confidence based on God's faithfulness.
4. Course of action.
5. Calendar of events.
6. Cooperation of others.
7. Consistency.
8. Control of emotions.
9. Courage to act.
10. Conscious dependence on God.

*Dear Lord, help me remember that the battle is Yours.
I am triumphant when I boldly go into battle in Your strength—
nothing more, nothing less. Amen.*

Day 296

True Repentance

*"For the Son of Man came to
seek and to save the lost."*

Luke 19:10

Zacchaeus was a short, wealthy tax collector who shimmied up a sycamore tree to catch a glimpse of Jesus passing by. I'm sure he was shocked when Jesus stopped at the foot of that tree! Jesus called him by name and told him to come down. Jesus then announced that he would be staying at Zacchaeus's house that day (see Luke 19:1–10). Zacchaeus immediately knew in his heart that Jesus was who He claimed to be. Repentance quickly followed.

True repentance results in dramatic transformation. We cannot be complacent about sin and be truly repentant. Repentance isn't simply saying you're sorry for something you did. You need to take corrective steps so that you don't repeat that sin. True repentance means that you agree with God about your sin and that you desire, as God does, to do away with it.

Jesus sees straight to the heart. He sought out Zacchaeus that day because He knew he was spiritually hungry. Jesus knows your struggles. He is calling you by name. Will you come down from your distant vantage point and invite Jesus in?

*Dear Lord, sometimes I'm just sorry I got caught. Help me
view sin as You do so that true repentance can come
from my heart and I can be transformed. Amen.*

DAY 297

The Abiding Life

"If you keep my commands, you will remain in my love, just as I have kept my Father's commands and remain in his love."

JOHN 15:10

*J*esus and the Father are one. When Jesus lived on earth, he had an inseparable connection with His heavenly Father. This "oneness" was maintained through prayer and obedience on Jesus' part. Jesus perfectly submitted to His Father's will in every situation—even dying on the cross.

In the Garden of Gethsemane on the night He was betrayed, Jesus prayed, "My Father, if it is possible, may this cup be taken from me. Yet not as I will, but as you will" (Matthew 26:39). Jesus did not want to die. Yet willingly He went in obedience to His heavenly Father.

Jesus is our perfect role model. Perhaps God is leading you on a path you would not have chosen. Obedience produces blessing. Believers must consciously submit to becoming a branch that maintains a vibrant connection to its Vine (Jesus). We must accept the authority of God's Word and maintain constant contact with Him through prayer. The abiding life is a life of obedience. We remain forever in God's love.

Dear Lord, when I am not connected to You, I have truly ceased to live. Help me obey Your Word and converse with You throughout my day through prayer. Amen.

Commit Your Way

Commit your way to the Lord; trust in him and he will do this:
He will make your righteousness reward shine like the dawn,
your vindication like the noonday sun.

Psalm 37:5–6

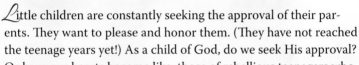

Little children are constantly seeking the approval of their parents. They want to please and honor them. (They have not reached the teenage years yet!) As a child of God, do we seek His approval? Or have our hearts become like those of rebellious teenagers who are more concerned about peer pressure than about pleasing their parents?

Just as children seek the approval of their parents, we should seek God's approval. What does the Lord require of us? "To act justly and to love mercy and to walk humbly with your God" (Micah 6:8). We can only "commit [our] way to the Lord" if we are humble before Him. Success is not something we do. It is something God grants us when we trust and obey Him. If a man dies without knowing Christ as his Savior, he dies a spiritual pauper. Let's desire to live successful spiritual lives by humbly committing our ways to the Lord. He will be faithful to do the rest!

Dear Lord, may I desire success as You define it. Success in Your
eyes is the ultimate. May I seek Your approval alone. Amen.

DAY 299

Success and Money

"But God said to him, 'You fool! This very night your life will be demanded from you. Then who will get what you have prepared for yourself?' This is how it will be with whoever stores up things for themselves but is not rich toward God."

LUKE 12:20–21

The world equates money with success. So, to appear successful we drive fancy cars, live in ostentatious homes, and wear designer clothes. Sadly, many times this outward display is just a smoke screen. How does God view success and money? Are they synonymous with each other?

God sees money as a tool. Lives are blessed when we act as a conduit that allows God's financial resources to flow through us. God has not blessed us financially for our own consumption. Remember: God owns it all. We are called to be His stewards. He intends for us to share with others.

Money in and of itself is not evil. However, when we hoard it or love it above God Himself, we can easily develop a godless attitude. Conversely, God blesses us when we cheerfully give. When we are faithful in little things, God will trust us with even greater things. Times of austerity can serve as a check for our priorities.

Dear Lord, You have bestowed on me material blessings. May I not hold on to money too tightly, but be rich toward You and others. Amen.

DAY 300

Success Blockers

*Therefore, since we are surrounded by such a great cloud
of witnesses, let us throw off everything that hinders and
the sin that so easily entangles. And let us run with
perseverance the race marked out for us.*

HEBREWS 12:1

As we run this race called life, we are to run with perseverance.
Do not grow weary or lose heart. Never give up. That's easy to say
when the road is smooth and straight. But what happens when
there are obstacles in our path? Many hindrances can impede our
forward progress: fear, doubt, procrastination, greed, guilt, sloth-
fulness, and trials, to name a few. These are all success blockers.
How do we cope? How can we have the strength to persevere?

Our eyes must be set on victory. Our eyes must be fixed on
Jesus at the finish line. Spiritual success is a reality, but we must
first believe that it is God's desire for us. Our vision of success can
only be as great as our faith in Him. Allow the Lord to infuse you
with His strength to run this race.

Always remember that you are surrounded by a great cloud of
witnesses. Imagine that those who have gone before you are cheer-
ing you on. Be aware that others may be watching and receiving
encouragement from you as you persevere. So let us run toward
the Lord with gusto!

*Dear Lord, sometimes I am my own worst enemy.
I sabotage my own progress. Help me stay focused
on You in order to stay the course. Amen.*

The Golden Rule

*"So in everything, do to others what you would have them
do to you, for this sums up the Law and the Prophets."*
MATTHEW 7:12

*G*od gave Moses the Ten Commandments on Mount Sinai. The first four commandments have to do with our relationship with God. The last six focus on our relationship with one another. We are told to honor our parents, not to commit murder or adultery, not to steal, lie, or covet. Jesus issues a new commandment that He says sums up the Old Testament law, "Do to others what you would have them do to you."

We are all familiar with the Golden Rule. Although it may be easy to recite, in reality it is hard to implement. We naturally expect others to treat us well. Yet do we take the first step by extending respect, forgiveness, or love to them? When the Golden Rule is followed, good things happen. Relationships are born. Marriages are strengthened. Racial prejudices are laid aside. Forgiveness is extended.

Treat others as you would want to be treated. The rule is simple yet profound. Jesus was right. Parents would be honored. Murder, adultery, stealing, lying, and coveting would cease. Take the opportunity to extend kindness to someone today. You will be blessed in return!

*Dear Lord, I am selfish. I know how I want to be treated,
but many times I don't see others in the same light.
Open my eyes so that I can live out Your commands. Amen.*

Day 302

Faith vs. Reason

*"Call to me and I will answer you and tell you
great and unsearchable things you do not know."*

Jeremiah 33:3

Intellectual prowess can actually be a stumbling block to faith.
Having to understand everything about God can prevent someone
from coming to know Him in the first place. There is only one way
to truly know God: through faith and not human reasoning. First
Corinthians 1:25 states, "For the foolishness of God is wiser than
human wisdom."

God is infinite. Man's finite intellect cannot comprehend spiritual
truth—it makes no sense to him. Only God can reveal spiritual truth.
We need the Holy Spirit to comprehend the things of God. When we
believe in Jesus by simple faith, the Holy Spirit comes to reside within
us. Then and only then can we understand spiritual truth.

When we take that leap of faith and place our trust in Christ
as our Lord and Savior, it's as if scales fall from our eyes. Once we
were spiritually blind—now we can see. We were once spiritually
dead—now we have been born anew. His Spirit resides within us,
teaching us spiritual truth. Let's take that leap of faith so that God
can reveal unsearchable truths to our heart.

*Dear Lord, I want to know You more and learn from You.
Teach me Your truth and wisdom. Amen.*

DAY 303

Sin

"He himself bore our sins" in his body on the cross, so that we might die to sins and live for righteousness; "by his wounds you have been healed." For "you were like sheep going astray," but now you have returned to the Shepherd and Overseer of your souls.

1 PETER 2:24–25

Sheep and shepherd analogies are found throughout the Bible. Sheep desperately need shepherds. Without them sheep easily become lost and fall prey to wild animals. Jesus likened us to sheep for good reason. We frighten easily, have a mob mentality, and are prone to wander off.

Just as sheep succumb to wild animals when they wander off, we succumb to sin when we leave our Good Shepherd's side. Temptation presents itself when we are scared and frightened. When we follow the crowd, we are often led astray.

Sin robs us of our innocence. Sin pollutes our lives with a spiritual darkness so deep and intense that only one thing can save us—the sacrificial death of Jesus Christ. No sinner is so far removed that he cannot come home to God. Sin has many consequences. However, it can never keep us from experiencing God's grace and mercy. Return to the overseer of your soul.

Dear Lord, sin blocks my relationship with You. I wander and get lost often. Bring me back to Your loving embrace. Amen.

Day 304

Jesus Has Overcome!

"I have told you these things, so that in me you may have peace. In this world you will have trouble. But take heart! I have overcome the world."

JOHN 16:33

*S*in is simply missing the mark of God's perfect will. If God is indeed perfect, why would we ever want to fall short of His will for our lives? Yet all of us sin—sometimes accidentally, other times on purpose. Sin may seem enticing at first. However, the farther we continue down that road, the darker it becomes until it reaches a dead end and we are completely lost.

When facing sin, we must believe that we need a Savior. We need God's strength and protection. Sin is rebellion against God because it entices us to act independently of Him. Sin blinds us to God's truth and leaves us feeling ashamed, fearful, and alone. Sin enslaves us spiritually, emotionally, and physically. Not only does sin impair our relationship with God, but it also puts a wedge in our relationship with others.

The enemy has one mission: to destroy man's relationship with God. But take heart! Jesus has already defeated our enemy. We have a Savior. We will not be destroyed! Turn your eyes upon Him and receive His peace today.

Dear Lord, thank You for overcoming sin and death. Please give me the same victory over sin—may it not rule in my life. Amen.

Day 305

Complete Surrender

For it is God who works in you to will and
to act in order to fulfill his good purpose.
PHILIPPIANS 2:13

God has a special purpose for each of our lives. And it is good! How do we achieve the purpose for which we were created? Trust God's Word. Believe that His ways are best. Completely surrender to His will. When we do these things, He will direct our steps.

" 'For I know the plans I have for you,' declares the LORD, 'plans to prosper you and not to harm you, plans to give you hope and a future' " (Jeremiah 29:11). When we are going through a difficult time in life, it's easy to become discouraged and lose hope. But that is precisely when we need to be reminded of this truth! Hold God to His promise. He will be faithful!

God is constantly working in our lives, even when circumstances threaten to change our outlook. God beckons us to follow Him whether we are traversing steep mountains or navigating through dark valleys. When we are on His path for our lives, we always end up in a good place! Let's surrender completely and allow the Lord to have His way in us.

Dear Lord, work in and through me so that I am on
Your path. I know that's the best place to be. Amen.

Holiness

*"Consecrate yourselves and be holy, because I am
the LORD your God. Keep my decrees and follow them.
I am the LORD, who makes you holy."*

LEVITICUS 20:7–8

Holiness is the state of being dedicated to or set apart for God's purposes. The Lord is the One who makes us holy. It is not something we manufacture from within ourselves. As believers, we have been born again—given spiritual life from God. This means that we have the power of the Holy Spirit living within us. The Holy Spirit enables us to live holy lives.

Children inherit character traits, physical attributes, and personalities from their parents. Our unique DNA carries God's designed blueprints. Children reflect their parents. Similarly, since we have His Spirit living within us, we should reflect our heavenly Father.

Holiness is a reflection of God's character. As children of God mature, they should look more and more like Jesus. Does your life in any way resemble the life of Jesus? Do you reflect his love, compassion, patience, and humility? Let's allow the Holy Spirit to change us more and more into the image of Christ. Do not be discouraged. This transformation does not occur overnight, but over a lifetime!

*Dear Lord, You are the One who makes me holy.
Help me cooperate with what You are doing in my
life so that I may accurately reflect You. Amen.*

God's Answer to the Problem of Sin

Since we have now been justified by his blood, how much more shall we be saved from God's wrath through him!

ROMANS 5:9

"Wait until your Father gets home!" may be a common threat from mothers everywhere. Fear and trepidation sets in as the child anticipates punishment for the crime committed. When we sin, aren't we glad that we do not have to fear the wrath of our heavenly Father? Although there are consequences for our sin, loving discipline, not wrath, is what awaits us.

God's provision for human sin is the blood that Jesus Christ shed on Calvary's cross. All who look to the cross and trust Jesus as their Savior will escape the wrath of God. What a tremendous promise! God's wrath was poured out on Jesus, sparing us the punishment for sin. "For God did not appoint us to suffer wrath but to receive salvation through our Lord Jesus Christ" (1 Thessalonians 5:9).

Not only has Jesus redeemed us for all eternity, but He has also given us the power to live victorious lives on earth. The Holy Spirit lives within each believer, empowering us to overcome temptation and the power of sin in our lives. Let's appropriate that power today!

Dear Lord, sometimes I forget all that You have done for me. Because I never have to fear Your wrath, I am free to live for You! Amen.

Day 308

Our Father's Love

*As a father has compassion on his children, so the LORD
has compassion on those who fear him; for he knows how
we are formed, he remembers that we are dust.*

PSALM 103:13–14

God has revealed Himself to us as our Father. The name Father suggests protection, love, provision, and discipline. Unlike our earthly father, God is the perfect heavenly Father. This means He loves us unconditionally. His love is not based on our performance. He provides for our needs but may withhold our "wants" because He knows what is best for us. God understands our human frailties but still requires obedience from us. Even God's discipline is birthed out of love.

No child of God will ever be rejected, abandoned, or orphaned. God continually lavishes His love on us because God is love. He loved us first, before we ever loved Him. God's love is constant. He never withdraws or withholds His love from us. Even if we are angry with Him or confused by life's circumstances, He still loves us unconditionally. God has compassion on us. He is our heavenly Father and is worthy of our adoration and praise!

*Dear Lord, although I cannot fully comprehend Your love
for me, I receive it today and give You praise! Thank You
for being my perfect heavenly Father. I love You! Amen.*

DAY 309

The Names of God

God said to Moses, "I AM WHO I AM. This is what you
are to say to the Israelites: 'I AM has sent me to you.' "
EXODUS 3:14

God called to Moses from a burning bush, revealing who He was by demonstrating His power. God had set the bush on fire, but the bush did not burn up. Who but the Creator God could have done that? It certainly got Moses' attention!

When God gave Moses the assignment of bringing the Israelites out of Egypt, Moses balked. God assured Moses that He would be with him. Moses asked God His name so he could tell the Israelites who was sending him. God responded by saying, "I AM."

I AM WHO I AM reveals God's character. He is the One who is, the One who has always been, and the One who shall always be. God has many names throughout the Bible. Each name reveals who He is. Some names of God are Alpha and Omega, Deliverer, Eternal God (El Olam), God (Elohim), God Almighty (El Shaddai), God Most High (El Elyon), God who sees, Lord (Adonai), LORD (Yahweh/Jehovah), LORD Almighty (Yahweh Sabaoth), Refuge, Rock, Shepherd, Stronghold, King of kings, and Lord of lords! Hallelujah!

Dear Lord, help me grasp who You truly are so that I
can know You more and worship You. Amen.

Day 310

The Lord Is My Shepherd

The LORD is my shepherd, I lack nothing. He makes me lie down in green pastures, he leads me beside quiet waters, he refreshes my soul. He guides me along the right paths for his name's sake. Even though I walk through the darkest valley, I will fear no evil, for you are with me; your rod and your staff, they comfort me. You prepare a table before me in the presence of my enemies. You anoint my head with oil; my cup overflows. Surely your goodness and love will follow me all the days of my life, and I will dwell in the house of the LORD forever.

PSALM 23

David experienced God as his Shepherd throughout his life—from shepherding sheep to hiding from Saul to reigning as king. He turned to God for the restoration of his soul. God guided him on the paths of righteousness. Even in his darkest hour, David was never afraid because God was his Shepherd.

Follow David's example. Allow the Good Shepherd to lead and guide you. Let Him restore your soul and comfort you. Let His presence chase away any fears. Follow the Good Shepherd and experience the love and goodness He has for you.

Dear Lord, You are my Good Shepherd. May I trust You to lead, guide, and provide for me. Help me follow You always. I am secure in You. Amen.

DAY 311

The Lord Is the Everlasting God

Do you not know? Have you not heard? The LORD is the everlasting God, the Creator of the ends of the earth. He will not grow tired or weary, and his understanding no one can fathom.

ISAIAH 40:28

$\mathcal{S}$teve Green wrote a song entitled "People Need the Lord." The refrain says, "People need the Lord, people need the Lord. At the end of broken dreams, He's the open door. People need the Lord, people need the Lord. When will we realize, people need the Lord?"

Imperfect, powerless people like us need a God who does not wear out, run down, or give up! The God of Israel is eternal and everlasting. The God who comforted His people in Old Testament times is the same God today. He promises to uphold and strengthen us when we are weary.

Jesus said, "Come to me, all you who are weary and burdened, and I will give you rest. Take my yoke upon you and learn from me, for I am gentle and humble in heart, and you will find rest for your souls. For my yoke is easy and my burden is light" (Matthew 11:28–30). Are you weary or worn out? Come to Jesus. He is always willing and able to handle your burdens. He longs to give you rest.

Dear Lord, I am so thankful that You never grow tired or weary like I do! Please carry my burdens and give me the rest I yearn for! Amen.

Day 312

The Conflict

You then, my son, be strong in the grace that is in Christ Jesus.
And the things you have heard me say in the presence of many
witnesses entrust to reliable people who will also be
qualified to teach others. Join with me in suffering,
like a good soldier of Christ Jesus.
2 Timothy 2:1–3

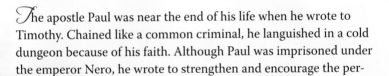

The apostle Paul was near the end of his life when he wrote to Timothy. Chained like a common criminal, he languished in a cold dungeon because of his faith. Although Paul was imprisoned under the emperor Nero, he wrote to strengthen and encourage the persecuted church.

We may not be imprisoned like Paul or face persecution like the church in his day, but most of us have endured trials. Have we ever thought about our Christian testimony during times of personal testing? Paul endured hardship like a good soldier of Christ Jesus. That is God's will for us as well.

At times God allows us to be buffeted in order to test and stretch us. We must remember that God has limited the enemy's power. God has promised never to leave us or forsake us. As we endure hardship, we can also receive God's grace and strength. We then become powerful witnesses to the God we profess. Trust in God's promises and await His deliverance!

Dear Lord, in my times of hardship, please give me
Your grace and strength so that I may endure
victoriously! I await Your deliverance! Amen.

DAY 313

The Challenge

That is why I am suffering as I am. Yet this is no cause for shame, because I know whom I have believed, and am convinced that he is able to guard what I have entrusted to him until that day.

2 TIMOTHY 1:12

The apostle Paul was suffering for the Gospel. Yet he would not back down. His imprisonment was a testimony to the truth of God's Word. Even in prison, facing possible death, Paul was convinced that he could confidently put his life in the Lord's hands.

Jesus suffered. His followers will suffer. Peter warns us in 1 Peter 4:12–14, "Dear friends, do not be surprised at the fiery ordeal that has come on you to test you, as though something strange were happening to you. But rejoice inasmuch as you participate in the sufferings of Christ, so that you may be overjoyed when his glory is revealed. If you are insulted because of the name of Christ, you are blessed, for the Spirit of glory and of God rests on you."

Suffering is an essential part of growing in Christ. Each time we endure hardship or temptation, God simply peels away another veil. As we rely on the Holy Spirit to give us power and grace, we gain His wisdom.

Dear Lord, help me stay strong in You in the midst of suffering so that my life is a testimony to Your truth. Like Paul, I want to put my life confidently in Your hands. Amen.

DAY 314

Guard the Gospel

Guard the good deposit that was entrusted to you—
guard it with the help of the Holy Spirit who lives in us.
2 TIMOTHY 1:14

The most valuable treasure in our homes is the Bible. The Bible has been entrusted to us, and we have been instructed to guard it. How do we view the Gospel? Do we take it for granted? Does it impact the way we live our lives? Or are we indifferent?

The Gospel is not meant to be kept to ourselves. Are we intent on passing it on to the next generation? Do we talk about what the Lord is doing in our lives with our children, grandchildren, and friends? "How, then, can they call on the one they have not believed in? And how can they believe in the one of whom they have not heard? And how can they hear without someone preaching to them?" (Romans 10:14).

All believers should know what they believe and why. We must never be ashamed of the treasure that has been entrusted to us. "I am not ashamed of the gospel, because it is the power of God that brings salvation to everyone who believes: first to the Jew, then to the Gentile" (Romans 1:16). The Bible contains the Gospel, the good news of eternal life. Cherish and value the treasure we've been given. Share the Good News with others!

Dear Lord, You have given me the greatest treasure—
eternal life in You. May that reality impact me today.
May I share the Gospel message with others. Amen.

God Most High

*Whoever dwells in the shelter of the Most
High will rest in the shadow of the Almighty.*

PSALM 91:1

God Most High—El Elyon. This name for God underscores His absolute supremacy. He is above all and over all. He is Creator of heaven and earth. "God Most High" was first used by Melchizedek after Abram rescued his nephew Lot from the four kings from the east (see Genesis 14:19–24). Moses referred to the "Most High" in his song to the whole assembly of Israel as he neared death and passed the mantle to Joshua. When Mary questioned the angel about the virgin birth, the angel responded by saying, "The Holy Spirit will come on you, and the power of the Most High will over-shadow you" (Luke 1:35).

Is the Lord "God Most High" to you? Does He have preeminence in your life, or are other "gods" trying to usurp His rightful place? God is Most High, whether or not we acknowledge that fact. He is above all and over all! Let us dwell in the shelter of the Most High so we can rest in the shadow of the Almighty. There's no better place to be!

Dear Lord, You are truly God Most High, El Elyon. May I acknowledge that fact and worship You as God Most High. Amen.

DAY 316

The Character of a Good Soldier

No one serving as a soldier gets entangled in civilian affairs,
but rather tries to please his commanding officer.

2 TIMOTHY 2:4

*I*n Paul's letter to Timothy, he makes an analogy between a soldier and a follower of Jesus Christ. There are many similarities. Soldiers have focus, discipline, and purpose. They undergo rigorous training in order to be prepared for battle. Soldiers dutifully obey their commanding officer instead of being distracted by civilian matters.

As Christians, we can have focus by fixing our eyes on Jesus. The world should not entrap or entangle us, causing us to negate our first priority—an active, abiding relationship with Jesus Christ. Of course this does not mean that we cannot seek jobs or have worldly interests. But if our relationship with Christ tops our heart's list, then everything else will be placed in proper perspective!

Our commanding officer is Jesus Christ. Our desire should be to please Him. Colossians 3:23 reminds us of the following: "Whatever you do, work at it with all your heart, as working for the Lord, not for human masters." May our hearts desire that we become good soldiers for Jesus Christ!

Dear Lord, I want to be a good soldier for You. Help me keep my eyes on You and desire to please You above anything else. Amen.

DAY 317

The Tongue

Don't have anything to do with foolish and stupid arguments,
because you know they produce quarrels.

2 TIMOTHY 2:23

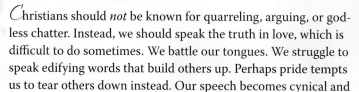

*C*hristians should *not* be known for quarreling, arguing, or god-less chatter. Instead, we should speak the truth in love, which is difficult to do sometimes. We battle our tongues. We struggle to speak edifying words that build others up. Perhaps pride tempts us to tear others down instead. Our speech becomes cynical and negative. Arguments and quarrels ensue.

Perhaps we have tried to curtail unwholesome talk by "biting our tongues." This may be a temporary fix, but the root of our problem is our hearts. Jesus said, "For the mouth speaks what the heart is full of" (Matthew 12:34). Ouch! What is your speech revealing about your heart? If you harbor jealousy or bitterness, it will eventually spill out of your mouth. If your heart is full of love and mercy, that will overflow instead.

Ask the Lord to change your heart. This will not happen overnight. Yet as you allow God to change you from the inside out, your speech will reflect that transformation. Your words will begin to edify and pour forth love into the lives of those around you.

Dear Lord, "May these words of my mouth and this meditation
of my heart be pleasing in your sight, LORD, my Rock
and my Redeemer" [Psalm 19:14]. Amen.

Struck Down but Not Destroyed

*Put on the full armor of God, so that you can take your
stand against the devil's schemes. For our struggle is not
against flesh and blood, but against the rulers, against the
authorities, against the powers of this dark world and
against the spiritual forces of evil in the heavenly realms.*

EPHESIANS 6:11–12

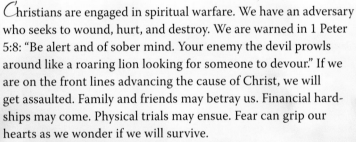

Christians are engaged in spiritual warfare. We have an adversary
who seeks to wound, hurt, and destroy. We are warned in 1 Peter
5:8: "Be alert and of sober mind. Your enemy the devil prowls
around like a roaring lion looking for someone to devour." If we
are on the front lines advancing the cause of Christ, we will
get assaulted. Family and friends may betray us. Financial hardships may come. Physical trials may ensue. Fear can grip our
hearts as we wonder if we will survive.

God's Word assures us that we will not be destroyed. Our
enemy can never mortally wound us because Jesus has given us
eternal life. Christ conquered death once and for all when He was
resurrected. He has given us the same victory. Knowing that the
war has been won gives us strength to get back up and persevere.
We can "fight the good fight" (see 2 Timothy 4:6–8). Jesus is with
us in battle. He goes before us. He walks beside us. He is our rear
guard. We will never be destroyed. Let's remember this awesome
promise when the battle is raging!

*Dear Lord, although I am in a spiritual battle, You have
won the victory! May I experience Your presence
in tangible ways today. Amen.*

Spiritual Worship

*Therefore, I urge you, brothers and sisters, in view of God's mercy,
to offer your bodies as a living sacrifice, holy and pleasing to God—
this is your true and proper worship. Do not conform to the pattern
of this world, but be transformed by the renewing of your mind.
Then you will be able to test and approve what God's will is—
his good, pleasing and perfect will.*

ROMANS 12:1–2

*W*orship begins by entering into His presence and humbly acknowledging that Jesus is Lord. Prayer ushers us into His presence. Our focal point is Jesus rather than the world. We offer ourselves—our bodies—to be used by Him. As we purpose to go God's way and not the world's way, a wonderful transformation takes place. Our hearts begin to change. Our minds are renewed by the Holy Spirit. Things of the world begin to fade—things of the Lord come into focus.

Our greatest act of worship is to entrust ourselves to our Creator. *Love* is an action word. Our love for God is demonstrated by allowing Him to have His way in our lives. Allow Him to direct where and how you are to serve. Submit to His leading, regardless of where He takes you. True spiritual worship means being "all in"—"fully committed."

*Dear Lord, I want to be all Yours. Transform me so that I don't
have the desire to conform to the world's priorities. Amen.*

DAY 320

Rain, Rain, Go Away!

In all this you greatly rejoice, though now for a little while you may have had to suffer grief in all kinds of trials. These have come so that the proven genuineness of your faith—of greater worth than gold, which perishes even though refined by fire—may result in praise, glory and honor when Jesus Christ is revealed.

1 PETER 1:6–7

Trials are much like rain. They can suddenly come from nowhere and disrupt our plans. But just as rain softens hard ground, bringing nourishment to plants, trials have a way of softening our hearts so that God's truth can penetrate. Trials humble us and cause us to acknowledge that we are not in control—He is!

When our lives are devoid of trials, it's easy to become self-reliant. Our heart can become hard and calloused. God in His wisdom allows trials to enter our lives to be used for our good. We need to learn to rely on Him instead of on ourselves. Trials give us an opportunity to exercise our faith. Through perseverance, spiritual maturity is developed. So let's allow the Lord to grow our faith through our trials as we trust Him.

Dear Lord, I want to believe that even the trials in my life have a good purpose. Help me through this trial. Grow my faith. Amen.

Day 321

Undivided Attention

Fixing our eyes on Jesus, the pioneer and perfecter of faith.
For the joy set before him he endured the cross, scorning its shame,
and sat down at the right hand of the throne of God.

HEBREWS 12:2

This generation prides itself on multitasking. But the truth is we are distracted by trying to focus on so many things at once. This phenomenon can carry over to our relationship with the Lord. We may be checking text messages while reading our Bibles, or making out our grocery lists during the Sunday sermon. News flash—the Lord desires our full attention! Only then can we hear Him speak to our hearts.

The circumstances of life can cause our thoughts to race ahead to the future. We can become so distracted that we fail to live in the present. The Lord wants us to focus on Him as we walk through each day, moment by moment. When the Lord maintains our undivided attention, we can resist the distractions of this world and follow Him. Then our priorities will line up with His priorities, and He will be able to lead us on the path we should go. So put away your phone and give God your full attention!

Dear Lord, I want to give You my undivided attention,
but I admit I struggle with this. Please help me. Amen.

DAY 322

Spinning Out of Control

In the same way, the Spirit helps us in our weakness. We do not know what we ought to pray for, but the Spirit himself intercedes for us through wordless groans. And he who searches our hearts knows the mind of the Spirit, because the Spirit intercedes for God's people in accordance with the will of God.

ROMANS 8:26–27

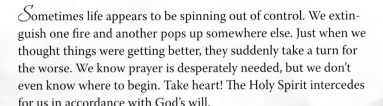

Sometimes life appears to be spinning out of control. We extinguish one fire and another pops up somewhere else. Just when we thought things were getting better, they suddenly take a turn for the worse. We know prayer is desperately needed, but we don't even know where to begin. Take heart! The Holy Spirit intercedes for us in accordance with God's will.

When your life seems to be spinning out of control, remember the One who created all things and holds everything together. For encouragement find out the predicted time of the sunrise. Then wake up early and sit and wait. God will bring the sun over the horizon at precisely the time predicted! God is faithful in His creation. He will be faithful to you!

God is never confused, perplexed, or panicked. He has a plan and will unveil His purpose at the proper time. He will be with you through life's uncertainties, reassuring you of His presence. Cling to the Lord. Trust Him to uphold you. He will!

Dear Lord, thank You for interceding for me when I don't even know what to pray! You are there. You are always there! Amen.

Day 323

Set the Captives Free!

The Spirit of the Sovereign LORD is on me, because the LORD has anointed me to proclaim good news to the poor. He has sent me to bind up the brokenhearted, to proclaim freedom for the captives and release from darkness for the prisoners.

ISAIAH 61:1

Early in His ministry, Jesus went to Nazareth and entered the synagogue on the Sabbath. He stood up and read this very passage from Isaiah. After reading it, He said, "Today this scripture is fulfilled in your hearing" (Luke 4:21). What powerful words!

Although Satan schemes to take us captive, Jesus came to set us free! Many subtle traps are set to ensnare us—drugs, alcohol, food, or sex. We may be enticed with greed, pride, envy, or ambition. Behind these ploys are lies disguised as truth. Once we embrace the lies, we become blind to truth and vulnerable to becoming a prisoner. We are in an utterly helpless state, not possessing the power on our own to gain freedom.

Our path to freedom begins by admitting that we need to be rescued. Our only hope is Jesus Christ. He came to set us free—to redeem us from the pit—to save us! Cry out to God for help. He will hear, come, and set us free. Christ is our victory!

Dear Lord, once again I need You to rescue and save me.
My hope is in You! Amen.

Day 324

Letting Go

*"Be still, and know that I am God; I will be exalted
among the nations, I will be exalted in the earth."*
PSALM 46:10

———

Letting go is a struggle for most of us. Yet many times in life we are called to "let go." We may be dropping off a child at college. Perhaps we are settling a parent into an assisted living facility. Or maybe we're having to sell our home and move. Letting go is an act of faith that requires us to "be still"—to cease striving and to allow God full control.

Fear may prevent us from completely letting go. We want to protect and guide. Fearing the loss of control, we are compelled to hold on tightly. However, God is God—we are not. He is the one in control, not us. When experiencing anxiety and fear about letting go, realize that God is sovereign. He can be trusted. His ways are higher and better than our own. Demonstrate your trust in God by opening your hand and releasing whatever you've been holding on to. Be still, and know that He is indeed God!

Dear Lord, I hold on tightly to my children, my husband, my friends. . .so many things. May I release them into Your care—which is far better! Give me wisdom today. Take away my fears. Amen.

Puzzle Pieces

Now you are the body of Christ, and each one of you is a part of it. And God has placed in the church first of all apostles, second prophets, third teachers, then miracles, then gifts of healing, of helping, of guidance, and of different kinds of tongues.

1 CORINTHIANS 12:27–28

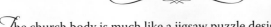

The church body is much like a jigsaw puzzle designed by God. The Church is made up of many unique members. Each has at least one spiritual gift. Members are intended to bond together as these gifts are exercised. When everyone participates and the pieces come together, a picture of Jesus emerges. The Church can then reflect Christ to a lost world.

However, unlike puzzle pieces, we have free will. Although God shaped us to fit perfectly into the Church body, we must respond. We may be content to stay in our comfort zone or remain uninvolved because we fear getting close to others. Perhaps we erroneously believe we have not been given a spiritual gift. Do not allow your puzzle piece to remain in the box. Allow God to place you where He has designed you to fit. Then the picture will be perfect and reflect Christ's image.

Dear Lord, You have given me at least one spiritual gift. Give me the courage and desire to use that gift for Your glory within my church body. I want others to see You. Amen.

DAY 326

A Father's Love

And I pray that you, being rooted and established in love,
may have power, together with all the Lord's holy people,
to grasp how wide and long and high and deep is the love
of Christ, and to know this love that surpasses knowledge—
that you may be filled to the measure of all the fullness of God.
EPHESIANS 3:17–19

---

*G*od's love for us is unconditional. It has *nothing* to do with our
performance or living up to His expectations. His love has *everything*
to do with who He is. God is love. Our Creator loves us regardless
of our faults and failures. He could not love us any more or any less
than He always does! That truth brings freedom. No longer are we
compelled to strive for perfection in order to earn His love.

In Psalm 17:8, David states that our heavenly Father considers us the "apple of [his] eye." What does that mean? It is literally
translated to mean "little man of his eye," referring to the pupil.
The pupil, the delicate part of the eye essential for vision, must
be protected at all cost. God considers us precious, valuable, and
loved. He will protect us at all cost! What greater love can you receive? Grasp the unconditional love God has for you so that it can
be extended to others.

Dear Lord, Your love is truly greater than I can ever grasp.
Give me a glimpse today as I rest in Your everlasting
arms and bask in Your love. Amen.

Rejected

*He was despised and rejected by mankind, a man of suffering,
and familiar with pain. Like one from whom people hide their
faces he was despised, and we held him in low esteem.*

ISAIAH 53:3

Rejection leaves us with a gaping, emotional wound. Heartache fills our chest. Bitterness permeates our soul. As a downward emotional spiral begins, we feel helpless as we draw closer to a dark, bottomless pit. Our only positive recourse is to cry out to the Lord. He understands rejection like no other. Jesus can empathize with our pain. Although He came to give eternal life to any who would believe, the majority rejected Him. As He hung on the cross, Jesus even felt forsaken by His heavenly Father and uttered, "My God, my God, why have you forsaken me?"

Once we acknowledge our hurt, we must extend forgiveness. Jesus is our perfect example. Hanging on the cross, He said, "Father, forgive them, for they do not know what they are doing." Jesus forgave His enemies. He can give us the ability to forgive those who wound us. When we forgive others, the healing process can begin in our own hearts. Lord, may it be so!

Dear Lord, my rejection pales in comparison to what You experienced on Calvary. By Your wounds, I have been healed. Not only can You empathize, but You bring emotional healing. Amen.

Roller Coasters

"Come to me, all you who are weary and burdened, and I will give you rest. Take my yoke upon you and learn from me, for I am gentle and humble in heart, and you will find rest for your souls. For my yoke is easy and my burden is light."

Matthew 11:28–30

Many circumstances in life can quickly catapult us on a scary, emotional roller coaster—a job termination, a medical emergency, a financial setback, or a prodigal child. Our emotions are turned upside down. One minute we're up, the next we're down—we don't know if we're coming or going. Sleepless nights become the norm. Anxious thoughts are constant companions.

This life can certainly be difficult and burdensome at times. Yet even in the most difficult trials, the Lord desires to give us rest and peace. He wants us to get off the roller coaster and stand on solid ground emotionally. He wants to be our Rock, our Strength, our Strong Tower.

Are you weary and burdened? Come and learn from Him. Allow Him to give you the rest you are craving. Peace from the Lord is possible even amid the roller coasters of life.

Dear Lord, I find myself on an emotional roller coaster too often. Help me choose to get off and come to You instead. I need Your rest and peace. Amen.

Day 329

Mountains in Life

"So do not fear, for I am with you; do not be dismayed,
for I am your God. I will strengthen you and help you;
I will uphold you with my righteous right hand."

ISAIAH 41:10

There are mountains in life that the Lord calls us to traverse. From a distance the feat may seem impossible. Fear may grip us as we even contemplate the journey. Yet as we take one step at a time and persevere, the difficulties do not seem as overwhelming as they did from a distance.

God reminds us that we do not have to fear. Why? Because He is with us. He is the One who helps us climb the mountains in life. God has the game plan. Our responsibility is to make the effort to take baby steps of faith. Perseverance and endurance are also required.

Although fear and trepidation may haunt us, the Lord gives energy, strength, and encouragement along the way. When we make it to the mountaintop, He rewards us by saying, "Well done!" Let's not shrink back when facing mountains in life but scale those mountains with the strength that He provides! His presence is enough.

Dear Lord, You are always with me. You uphold me when
I cannot stand. Your presence alone can enable me
to climb any mountain in this life. Amen.

The Scent of a Christian

But thanks be to God, who always leads us as captives in Christ's triumphal procession and uses us to spread the aroma of the knowledge of him everywhere. For we are to God the pleasing aroma of Christ among those who are being saved and those who are perishing.

2 CORINTHIANS 2:14–15

The scent of a Christian is distinct and recognizable. It is the aroma of Christ. As Christians we have Christ in us. Therefore His aroma should permeate our bodies as well as the atmosphere around us. This aroma should smell pleasant and appealing to those we come in contact with. It should compel them to draw closer to investigate. Our fragrance should attract others to Christ.

Christ's aroma is given off in many ways. His fragrance is emitted when we act in a Christlike manner. It may come through a warm smile or gentle embrace. It may be conveyed through tears or prayers. An act of kindness may cause the aroma to be noticed. The scent should permeate our homes as well. As guests enter, they may detect a difference in your home—that difference is Christ. His presence may be evident as visitors notice a Bible on a nightstand or a verse above the kitchen sink. Christ wants to draw others to Himself by allowing His fragrance to spread everywhere we go. He desires that others see Him in us. Do you have the scent of a Christian?

Dear Lord, I want the aroma of Christ to be present in me. May You increase in my life so that others are drawn to Your pleasing aroma! Amen.

DAY 331

Every Spiritual Blessing

Praise be to the God and Father of our Lord Jesus Christ,
who has blessed us in the heavenly realms with
every spiritual blessing in Christ.

EPHESIANS 1:3

———⚬≋⚬———

*L*ife can sometimes leave us feeling discouraged, dejected, or disillusioned. Even though the Lord has abundantly blessed us, at times it's easy to forget that truth. Perhaps we're struggling financially, maritally, or healthwise. How can we respond with praise when our earthly life appears to be in conflict with spiritual truth?

Regardless of our circumstances, God has blessed us with every spiritual blessing in Christ. Although we never lack anything in the heavenly realm, many times our focus remains worldly. Jobs, family, houses, finances, health—these all pull at our heartstrings. When experiencing difficulty in one of these areas, it's hard to offer God praise. What is the solution?

Focus your thoughts heavenward, and count the spiritual blessings at your disposal. The Lord's indwelling presence guides our minds and comforts our hearts. His resurrection power enables us to persevere triumphantly. His sustaining peace imparts encouragement for today and hope for tomorrow. When we meditate on eternal blessings, our momentary struggles are put into proper perspective. Earthly trials are temporary. Spiritual blessings are eternal!

Dear Lord, help me keep my focus in the heavenly realms.
I have everything I need because of You! Amen.

DAY 332

Humility

*"For all those who exalt themselves will be humbled,
and those who humble themselves will be exalted."*

LUKE 14:11

Humility is not an attribute we easily embrace. As humans we are naturally prideful. We yearn to be on top of the world. Recognition and applause are what we seek. We enjoy being number one.

Yet sometimes we find ourselves humbled, forsaken, or rejected—like a barren tree stripped of its leaves. Do not become discouraged! God has not forsaken you. Just as the sun can shine more easily through the branches of a barren tree, so can God's glory be revealed through us when we are humble. Many times when we are puffed up, that's all people will notice. Our humility allows others to see the Lord more clearly because the focus is on Him instead of us. When we decrease, He can increase.

So do not view humility with disdain. "Humble yourselves, therefore, under God's mighty hand, that he may lift you up in due time" (1 Peter 5:6). Allow the Lord to shine through you so that His glory may be known. Trust that He will lift you up in due time.

*Dear Lord, humility is not fun, yet Jesus is my perfect example.
May I follow in His footsteps so that Your glory can
be revealed in and through me today. Amen.*

DAY 333

Receive God's Embrace

See what great love the Father has lavished on us, that we should be called children of God! And that is what we are! The reason the world does not know us is that it did not know him.

1 JOHN 3:1

God lavished His love on us by sending His Son, Jesus, to earth. Jesus' sacrificial death on our behalf paved the way for adoption into God's family by faith. We become children of God by receiving the gift of Jesus. No longer are we alienated from a holy God. We have become family!

"You see, at just the right time, when we were still powerless, Christ died for the ungodly. Very rarely will anyone die for a righteous person, though for a good person someone might possibly dare to die. But God demonstrates his own love for us in this: While we were still sinners, Christ died for us" (Romans 5:6–8).

Ponder God's great love for you. Try to visualize Jesus hanging on the cross with outstretched arms. He came to embrace the world with God's love. He came to embrace you! The unconditional love of our Creator is the greatest gift we could ever receive. Allow His love to be lavished on you! Receive the embrace of your heavenly Father today!

Dear Lord, with outstretched arms on the cross, You embraced me. "Greater love has no one than this: to lay down one's life for one's friends" (John 15:13). Thank You for this indescribable gift! Amen.

DAY 334

You Have Not

What causes fights and quarrels among you? Don't they come from your desires that battle within you? You desire but do not have, so you kill. You covet but you cannot get what you want, so you quarrel and fight. You do not have because you do not ask God.

JAMES 4:1–2

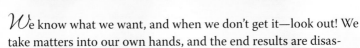

We know what we want, and when we don't get it—look out! We take matters into our own hands, and the end results are disastrous. We have not because we ask not. James 4:3 says, "When you ask, you do not receive, because you ask with wrong motives, that you may spend what you get on your pleasures."

God has a better way. Trust Him to meet your needs. When you "want" something, ask the Lord. Should I take this job? Is this the right home for us? Ask with open palms, submitting to God's perfect will. Be willing to accept His answers of "no" or "wait."

God knows what is best. Present your needs and requests to the Lord. Examine your motives. God will respond by supplying what you truly need. His grace will enable you to submit to His wisdom.

Dear Lord, may I present my requests to You and submit to Your sovereignty in my life. May my motives be pleasing to You. Amen.

DAY 335

Seek First

*"But seek first his kingdom and his righteousness,
and all these things will be given to you as well."*
MATTHEW 6:33

There are many things in life that vie for our attention: jobs, spouses, children, homes, hobbies. At times we may feel like a juggler in a three-ring circus! All of these things are good, but what should we concentrate on? Where should we devote our energy? Jesus simplifies things in the verse above. If we focus on seeking God's kingdom and righteousness, everything else will fall into place.

Seek the Lord within the context of your job and home. Enjoy your hobbies with Him. When we allow the Lord to become part of every facet of our lives, He will put those areas into proper perspective.

When making difficult choices, seek God's wisdom for discernment. Then trust Him in obedience. This may require that we follow our heads rather than our hearts. Exercise faith instead of succumbing to fear. When we trust and obey Him, the Lord will take care of the rest. He will reward our faith and confirm that His way is indeed best. Seek His kingdom first, and everything else will be taken care of as well.

*Dear Lord, there is truly one thing I need to focus on—You!
When I do that, You help me navigate through life. Amen.*

DAY 336

In Word or Deed

And whatever you do, whether in word or deed, do it all
in the name of the Lord Jesus, giving thanks
to God the Father through him.

COLOSSIANS 3:17

———◆———

*T*here is no such thing as a Sunday Christian. Bearing the name of Christ is a 24/7 proposition! Regardless of where we are or what we are doing, our lives reflect the One we profess. Being united with Christ means our secular and spiritual lives are united as well. We should not live one way during the week and then act differently on Sundays. People are watching. Hypocrisy is offensive.

Although Christians are far from perfect, we are called to be Christ's ambassadors. So whatever you say or do, represent Jesus well. No American would purposely fly the American flag upside down. Someone not knowing better would erroneously conclude that the flag was flying correctly. In the same way, be careful how you represent Christ to a world that may not know Him. It is imperative that you represent Jesus correctly.

Let His light in you shine brightly through you. Then others will see Jesus and desire to know Him. Do not hide your light under a bushel!

Dear Lord, what a privilege it is to be Your ambassador!
Remind me daily of my mission so that I
may represent You well. Amen.

Day 337

Fleeting Beauty

Charm is deceptive, and beauty is fleeting;
but a woman who fears the LORD is to be praised.
PROVERBS 31:30

*O*ur society shuns aging. Commercials try to convince us that we need to look younger. Countless antiaging beauty products have flooded the markets. Botox and collagen injections are commonplace. Nevertheless the truth remains—beauty is fleeting! Our physical bodies were not created to live forever.

Instead of being distraught, be encouraged! The Lord reminds us that the spiritual aspect of the aging process is far more important than our physical bodies. Our physical life is for a season. Our spiritual life is forever! "Your beauty should not come from outward adornment, such as elaborate hairstyles and the wearing of gold jewelry or fine clothes. Rather, it should be that of your inner self, the unfading beauty of a gentle and quiet spirit, which is of great worth in God's sight" (1 Peter 3:3–4).

Choose to age gracefully by concentrating on the spiritual aspect of who you are. Live in awe and respect for the Lord. Realize that your relationship with Him is the most important thing in this life. You will be able to laugh at your wrinkles because your inner beauty will shine forth by the transforming power of the Holy Spirit. You will truly become more beautiful with each passing day!

Dear Lord, help me focus on You more than my aging body!
May I embrace spiritual priorities instead of
chasing antiaging fads. Amen.

DAY 338

Jesus Wept

Jesus wept.
JOHN 11:35

❧

*A*lthough this is the shortest verse in the Bible, it speaks volumes. Jesus had emotions and was not embarrassed to express them. He cried when his good friend Lazarus died. In the Garden of Gethsemane, his soul was overwhelmed with sorrow. His anger was unleashed as He drove the money changers out of the temple. Jesus cared intensely. He was passionate about life. Jesus was sent to earth to redeem fallen man. How could He not care? How could things not matter? How could He not weep?

We were created in His image. We were created to feel—to have emotions. If tears come easily to you, do not be embarrassed. Tears are an expression of your soul. They can minister mightily to someone else. So embrace them.

Emotions are an expression of the heart. Yet we need a soft heart, not a hard one, if we want to reflect godly emotions. Ask the Lord to give you a heart that is passionate about the things He is passionate about. Then your emotions will be held in check and can be used to further His kingdom. Don't be afraid to reveal your heart to others. Follow Jesus' example.

*Dear Lord, show me how to express my emotions
appropriately like You did. My heart belongs to You.
Soften it today to reflect Your heart. Amen.*

Day 339

Anxious Thoughts

Search me, God, and know my heart; test me and
know my anxious thoughts. See if there is any offensive
way in me, and lead me in the way everlasting.
Psalm 139:23–24

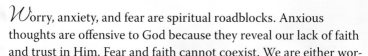

Worry, anxiety, and fear are spiritual roadblocks. Anxious thoughts are offensive to God because they reveal our lack of faith and trust in Him. Fear and faith cannot coexist. We are either worrying and anxious or trusting and peaceful.

Our minds are constantly racing with questions and scenarios about the future. Many times our past haunts us. We fear future consequences for past failures. Or current circumstances tempt us to try to figure out future outcomes. We obsess about the what-ifs. Jesus commands us, "Do not worry about tomorrow, for tomorrow will worry about itself. Each day has enough trouble of its own" (Matthew 6:34).

Come before the Lord. Invite Him to search your heart. Allow His light to expose any anxious thoughts lurking in the shadows. Acknowledge and confess your anxiety. Then trust Him with those concerns. Leave your anxiety in His hands. Ask that His will be done, knowing and believing that His will is best. Then receive His peace by faith.

Dear Lord, anxiety rules my heart much of the time.
I want to trust You more. I need Your peace.
Lead me in the way everlasting. Amen.

Day 340

Unfading Beauty

Your beauty should not come from outward adornment, such as elaborate hairstyles and the wearing of gold jewelry or fine clothes. Rather, it should be that of your inner self, the unfading beauty of a gentle and quiet spirit, which is of great worth in God's sight.

1 PETER 3:3–4

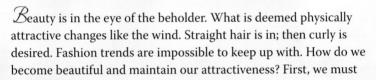

*B*eauty is in the eye of the beholder. What is deemed physically attractive changes like the wind. Straight hair is in; then curly is desired. Fashion trends are impossible to keep up with. How do we become beautiful and maintain our attractiveness? First, we must realize that physical beauty is fleeting.

True beauty doesn't fade, because it resides within our hearts. It has nothing to do with hair, jewelry, or fine clothes. A beautiful heart is eternally radiant. It is precious to God.

What does a beautiful heart look like? It is molded and shaped after God's own heart. It loves others unconditionally. Compassion and grace freely flow from it. Forgiveness is ever present. It is gentle and kind, putting the interest of others first. Do you desire lasting charm and beauty that never fades? Give attention to your heart. Adorn it with God's attributes. Dress it in eternal style. Unfading beauty is a heart that radiates God's love.

Dear Lord, change my heart to reflect a gentle and quiet spirit—one that trusts You in all things. Then I will possess unfading beauty that radiates Your love. Amen.

Day 341

Through the Valley

Even though I walk through the darkest valley, I will fear no evil,
for you are with me; your rod and your staff, they comfort me.
PSALM 23:4

⸺※⸺

*J*ust as God created both mountains and valleys, He permits
peaks and valleys in our own lives as well. We would much rather
reside on the mountaintop, yet we know that those experiences do
not last forever. When entering the valley, remember that if we are
walking with the Lord, we are always in His territory. He is with us!
Nothing can separate us from His love or His presence.

In fact, many times His closeness is experienced more when
we're walking through the valleys. Why is that? Perhaps our vulnerability and humbleness cause us to acknowledge our need and
admit our weakness.

Jesus is our Living Water. In the valleys, we can drink from the
stream of Living Water and be sustained. So don't despair when
you're in the valleys of life. Remember this truth: God is with you!
Come to Him and drink. He will give you the strength and sustenance you need. God will see you through!

Dear Lord, I would much rather be on the mountaintop than
drudging through the valley. Open my eyes to see Your closeness,
Your strength, and Your sustenance that are available to me. Amen.

DAY 342

My Cup Overflows

You prepare a table before me in the presence of my enemies.
You anoint my head with oil; my cup overflows.

PSALM 23:5

What is your outlook on life? Some people inherently focus on the negatives in life regardless of what is happening. Others seem optimistic even while facing hardship and pain. Would you say that your glass is half empty or half full? Why do we tend to measure our lives by a small glass to determine if we are experiencing blessing or hardship? God's perspective is so much larger!

When we look at our lives from God's eternal vantage point, it's like comparing our small glass of water with His ocean that's always filled to the brim. There is no comparison! His blessings are in abundance—too numerous to count.

God's blessings may seem obscured when we are enduring hardships and trials, but rest assured they are still there. Ask the Lord to help you see the rainbows in the storms of life—indications of His presence. Instead of looking at your little glass, consider His vast ocean. Focus on God's blessings and you will realize that your cup is indeed overflowing!

Dear Lord, You certainly cause my cup to overflow.
May I focus on Your blessings instead of what I think
my life is lacking. I want Your perspective today. Amen.

DAY 343

The Joy of the Lord

Nehemiah said, "Go and enjoy choice food and sweet drinks,
and send some to those who have nothing prepared. This day is holy
to our Lord. Do not grieve, for the joy of the LORD is your strength."
NEHEMIAH 8:10

It has been said that a parent can only be as happy as their unhappiest child. Perhaps this is true since happiness has to do with circumstances. If our child is not doing well, empathy causes us to take on their negative emotions. But is it God's will that another person should dictate our enjoyment of life? There must be a better way.

Believe it or not, inner joy can be experienced regardless of our circumstances. We may be battling cancer, going through a divorce, or enduring the travails of a prodigal child. Certainly our circumstances are painful and troubling.

Yet joy is available to every believer when we choose to focus on Him. Joy is a gift from the Lord—a fruit of His Spirit. The joy of the Lord is our strength! So don't allow external circumstances to dictate your emotional state of well-being. Choose to focus on the Lord and experience inner joy in the midst of your current situation.

Dear Lord, I seek joy that can only be found in You.
Happiness is fleeting, but Your joy is constant.
Help me keep my eyes on You today. Amen.

DAY 344

The Vine and Branches

"I am the vine; you are the branches. If you remain in me and I in you, you will bear much fruit; apart from me you can do nothing."
JOHN 15:5

The vine gives life. Branches submit to the authority of the vine. Nature understands God's design far better than we do at times. Consider a deciduous tree in winter. Every branch has shed its leaves. It is completely barren. One branch can't decide to keep its leaves through the winter. No branch can bud before spring. The entire tree submits to the life-giving trunk! God is in charge.

What about us? Do we submit to our Creator God or do we attempt to call the shots and go our own way? We may purposely choose to go one way when we know God has said to go another. Or perhaps we intentionally neglect to pray about a certain decision so we can claim ignorance. God cannot be fooled.

Learn from God's design found in nature. We must "abide" or "remain" attached to the life-giving Vine, Jesus. Simply put: we must submit to His will or we can do *nothing* of spiritual significance. Abide.

Dear Lord, I am Your creation. You have given me free will. May I choose to submit to You and remain in You. Amen.

DAY 345

Everything or Nothing

I can do all this through him who gives me strength.
PHILIPPIANS 4:13

*T*here are two extremes from a spiritual perspective—everything or nothing. Which would you prefer to do? Apart from Christ we can do *nothing* of spiritual significance. We must abide in Him. Our wills must be yielded to His. We must follow His lead, be obedient to His path, and defer to His wisdom. Otherwise our efforts are in vain and nothing of lasting value will be left.

Yet when we do rely on the Lord and allow Him to call the shots, we can do *everything*! This does not mean we can do everything *we* want to do, but everything He is calling us to do. Great discernment must be taken to know the difference. Spend much time in prayer. Ask God to speak clearly to reveal His will. Then step out in faith, knowing that He will equip you to fulfill His purposes for you.

The secret is found in being in tune with God's will and obediently following His lead. The Lord infuses us with His strength, enabling us to carry out His will. His will can be discerned by spending time in His Word and prayer.

Dear Lord, I want to do everything You desire me to do.
Make Your will clear, and give me Your strength today. Amen.

Day 346

Pour Out Your Heart

*Trust in him at all times, you people; pour out
your hearts to him, for God is our refuge.*

Psalm 62:8

*H*ave you ever been accused of talking too much? Are you needy and desperate for someone to attentively listen to your ramblings? There is good news! You can come to God anytime day or night. It doesn't matter where you are. You can talk to Him as long as you want and never fear getting cut off. You can even repeat yourself if necessary!

The Lord never gets tired of hearing from you. He never becomes impatient with your verbosity. He never urges you to "cut to the chase" or give him the "CliffsNotes version." The Lord desires that you pour out your heart to Him. He encourages you to "come to Him."

What a friend we have in Jesus! To "pour out our hearts" means to empty them. Keep going until you've given Him *all* your cares and worries. Do not stop short. Do not hold back. Lay everything at His feet. God is our refuge. Our soul is refreshed when we pour out our hearts to Him.

*Dear Lord, thank You that I can go to You anytime, anyplace,
and pour out my heart to You. You are my Friend indeed! Amen.*

Be Inspired!

As iron sharpens iron, so one person sharpens another.
PROVERBS 27:17

❦

The Olympic Games are inspirational to watch. Athletes combine perseverance, determination, and hard work with God-given ability. Competition brings out their best efforts. The results are awe inspiring. Athletes spur one another on. Even though competitors might be from different countries, they share mutual respect and admiration for one another.

We may not be world-class athletes, but our Christian walks should inspire others. Our lives should reflect Christ and His power that is at work within us. Inspirational living is contagious! "And let us consider how we may spur one another on toward love and good deeds" (Hebrews 10:24). Your generosity can encourage others to be generous. Extending forgiveness can soften another's heart. Faithful Bible study attendance can be an example that someone wants to emulate.

Realize that your life can impart hope, motivation, and encouragement to others. Athletic competition isn't just about winning. It's about "raising the bar" in order to achieve greater performance. We need each other in order to reach our spiritual potential. Let's inspire one another so that greater things can be accomplished for the Lord's kingdom. Be inspired!

Dear Lord, help me surround myself with believers who inspire and sharpen me spiritually. I need to "raise the bar" in my spiritual life so that I do not become complacent. It's all for Your glory. Amen.

Day 348

Receiving Glory

*"Then your Father, who sees what
is done in secret, will reward you."*

Matthew 6:4

Jesus admonished those who gave, prayed, or fasted in order to be seen by others. The Pharisees were notorious for seeking recognition for their righteous acts. Jesus called them hypocrites. Although they pretended to follow God, their hearts were far from Him. They loved the praise of men.

What are the motives behind our actions? We may be unaware of our true motives until our good deeds go unnoticed or we do not receive the recognition we had hoped for. Then our hearts stand exposed and convicted.

If we secretly do "righteous acts" to be seen and admired by men, then we are using God to bring glory to ourselves. God can see our hearts. Our desire should be to do the right thing in order to bring glory to God alone. We all like to be appreciated for our efforts. Yet when we seek to please the Lord first, our service will not go unnoticed. Live your life before an audience of One. God sees what you do, and He will indeed reward you!

*Dear Lord, I must confess that my motives are not always
what they should be. May I live my life to please You alone.
May I decrease so that You can increase. Amen.*

Meeting Our Needs

And my God will meet all your needs according
to the riches of his glory in Christ Jesus.
PHILIPPIANS 4:19

———❦———

How can you experience answered prayer? Pray according to God's will. But how do you know what God's will is? Be willing to let go of your "wants," and be content with having your "needs" met by Him. This is God's will for you.

"But godliness with contentment is great gain. For we brought nothing into the world, and we can take nothing out of it. But if we have food and clothing, we will be content with that. Those who want to get rich fall into temptation and a trap and into many foolish and harmful desires that plunge people into ruin and destruction" (1 Timothy 6:6–9).

Many times it is difficult to discern the difference between "wants" and "needs." Pray and allow God to show you. Leave the results in His hands. Be willing to gracefully accept a "no" answer and thank Him for knowing best. Perhaps the timing is not right. Or maybe you truly did not "need" whatever you were praying for. Submit to the spiritual reality that if you "need" it, God will provide it.

Dear Lord, You alone know what I truly "need." Thank You for
meeting all my needs. Help me trust You more in this area. Amen.

Day 350

Thankful Hearts

Every good and perfect gift is from above,
coming down from the Father of the heavenly lights,
who does not change like shifting shadows.

JAMES 1:17

God is a giver of good gifts. Do we take the time to acknowledge and enjoy the gifts He bestows on us every day? Perhaps we are like a child on Christmas morning who rifles through one gift after another. The hurried frenzy makes it impossible to appreciate the gifts or thank the giver.

Savor the blessings in life. Pause. Give thanks. God loves for His children to acknowledge and enjoy the gifts He so freely gives. Don't wish your life away, yearning for some future event that you think will enable you to enjoy life; like retirement, for example. Count your blessings, and enjoy life today! That future event may never come. Or if it does come, it may prove to have been an allusion.

Give thanks for the ability to see the sunrise, hear the birds sing, or take a walk. Praise God for providing a roof over your head and food on the table. His gifts are limitless. May we not take His blessings for granted. May our hearts overflow with thankfulness!

Dear Lord, I have so much to be thankful for!
Help me slow down enough to give You thanks.
May I enjoy Your daily blessings to the fullest. Amen.

Day 351

Circuitous Paths

Show me your ways, Lord, teach me your paths.
Guide me in your truth and teach me, for you are
God my Savior, and my hope is in you all day long.

PSALM 25:4–5

Following the Lord does not always mean walking in a straight line from point A to point B. Sometimes the Lord takes us on a winding, meandering path. Why? Wouldn't it be quicker to go in a straight line? Yet if we could clearly see the road before us, perhaps we would be tempted to run ahead of the Lord. He desires that we walk *with Him* on this journey through life.

It took the Israelites forty years to enter the Promised Land from Egypt. God provided the cloud by day and fire by night. When the cloud lifted, the Israelites would break camp and set out. When the cloud settled, they would stop. God's presence guided them as they wandered in the wilderness.

When life has twists and turns, we must follow the Lord closely to know what path to take. We must listen intently and obey completely. We must seek His will. There are many teachable moments along this circuitous path. Savor the time. Enjoy the journey. Learn to listen. Allow the Lord to show you His ways, teach you His paths, and guide you in His truth. The journey will be well worth it!

Dear Lord, I want to enjoy life's journey with You.
Teach me Your ways on the circuitous paths of life. Amen.

Day 352

Contentment

But godliness with contentment is great gain.
1 Timothy 6:6

<hr />

Are you content in your marriage, your job, your home? Is your heart at rest with what you have, or are you always yearning for more? Unfortunately our heart is fickle. We seek the latest and greatest. We desire the newest phone, largest flat-screen TV, updated computer, and latest fashions. It takes all of our time just keeping up with what we should be chasing after! It leaves us feeling exhausted and overwhelmed!

Lasting satisfaction is elusive. We may obtain our hearts' desires, but before long our hearts are searching once again. Wouldn't it be great if our hearts could find true rest and contentment? What if the perpetual searching could cease? Be encouraged! It is possible.

God's Word clearly teaches that lasting contentment is found in the Lord alone. When our heart seeks Him first, we are never disappointed. When we find contentment in the Lord, we experience contentment in other areas of life. We are no longer searching. We can enjoy and appreciate what we have been given. If we have the Lord, we have everything we need! What a gift! Lord, may it be so!

Dear Lord, may I find my contentment in You alone.
Help me own this truth so that I am not constantly
chasing after the wind. Amen.

DAY 353

Light

"You are the light of the world.
A town built on a hill cannot be hidden."

MATTHEW 5:14

𝒜 simple journey from Egypt to the Promised Land became an ordeal for the Israelites as they wandered in the wilderness for forty years! Why did it take so long? What was God trying to teach them along the way? God wanted His chosen people to be a light to other nations, pointing them to the one true God. But first they had to learn to trust Him, follow Him, and worship Him. This was a long process because of their rebellion.

The same is true for us today. God wants us to radiate His light in a world full of darkness. Just as God was preparing the Israelites prior to entering the Promised Land, He may be preparing you now for some future ministry. Do not become discouraged if you feel you are simply wandering in the wilderness. God has important lessons He wants to teach you.

Do not become like the stiff-necked Israelites. Have a teachable spirit. Trust God completely. Follow Him closely. Worship Him reverently. You can then be used as a light, pointing others to the Lord. Let's be quick learners so we do not have to wander in the wilderness for forty years!

Dear Lord, what a privilege to be Your light! May I shine
brightly and point others to Your saving grace. Amen.

God's Work

Being confident of this, that he who began a good work in you
will carry it on to completion until the day of Christ Jesus.
PHILIPPIANS 1:6

---

*I*ndividually and corporately, God's plans cannot be thwarted. "For the LORD Almighty has purposed, and who can thwart him? His hand is stretched out, and who can turn it back?" (Isaiah 14:27). His purposes will prevail.

God will be faithful to finish the work He began in your life when you came to know Him as Lord and Savior. Your spiritual journey will take a lifetime, but God will walk beside you each step of the way. Do not become discouraged when forward progress appears slow. God is still at work.

The same is true when God gives you a kingdom vision, when He calls you to participate in furthering the Gospel message. When you hear His call, do not hesitate. Step out in faith. Believe that He will provide. Many times we may have to wait for His fulfillment. His timing is not ours. However, God *is* faithful. Believe. Pray. God *will* carry His work on to completion until the day of Christ Jesus! Amen.

Dear Lord, You are always working behind the scenes.
You are faithful and will accomplish Your purposes in
my life so that others will come to know You also. Amen.

DAY 355

Do You Love Me?

When they had finished eating, Jesus said to Simon Peter,
"Simon son of John, do you truly love me more than these?"
JOHN 21:15

---

*B*efore Jesus' crucifixion, Peter had denied Jesus three times. After Jesus' resurrection, Jesus asked Peter three times if he loved Him. Jesus' first question was worded, "Do you truly love me more than these?" What was Jesus referring to? Did Peter love Jesus more than he loved the other disciples? Did Peter love Jesus more than the other disciples did? Did Peter love Jesus more than anything else? Jesus was calling Peter to "feed His sheep"—to spiritually feed those in his flock. Jesus knew that Peter could not spiritually feed others unless he was completely "sold out" to Him.

Jesus is asking us the same question: "Do you truly love me more than these?" Does our heart belong to the Lord first? Do we love Him above family, friends, career, or material possessions? Are we willing to lay down our life for Him? Jesus said in Matthew 16:25, "For whoever wants to save their life will lose it, but whoever loses their life for me will find it." These are sobering questions to ask ourselves. Like Peter, we can be effective for Christ if we love Him first.

Dear Lord, You know my heart. I want to love You more
than anything, yet I know I fall short. Show me my idols.
Help me willingly set them aside so I can love You with
my whole heart and be used by You. Amen.

Day 356

Encouragement

*And let us consider how we may spur one another on toward
love and good deeds, not giving up meeting together, as some
are in the habit of doing, but encouraging one another—
and all the more as you see the Day approaching.*
Hebrews 10:24–25

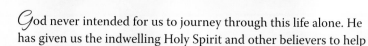

God never intended for us to journey through this life alone. He
has given us the indwelling Holy Spirit and other believers to help
us. The body of Christ encourages us when life gets difficult.

The story is told of a young married couple who woke up one
rainy Sunday morning. The wife was tempted to roll over and
skip church because she had seen her mother do the same. The
husband responded just the opposite. His parents always went to
church when it rained because they couldn't play golf. Laughingly,
the couple made the decision that they would attend church "rain
or shine"!

We all need encouragement from time to time. We need to
be reminded of God's truth. We need others to walk beside us in
our pain. Make the decision to attend church "rain or shine." Your
life will be blessed. God knows just what we need. You will never
regret attending church.

*Dear Lord, I admit I skip church too often. May I realize the
spiritual benefits of attending regularly. May I not be fooled into
thinking I can navigate through life without Christian friends. Amen.*

DAY 357

Reminders

So I will always remind you of these things, even though you know
them and are firmly established in the truth you now have.

2 PETER 1:12

❧

*H*ow do you remember things? Do you tie a string around your
finger, put a sticky note on the refrigerator, or set an alarm on your
phone? We all need reminders from time to time.

The apostle Peter knew the importance of reminders. Peter
exhorted his readers to grow in Christian virtues so they would
remain strong in the faith even after his death. Regardless of how
long we have been a Christian, our faith can falter. Life has a way
of throwing us curve balls and knocking us to our knees. Although
we may know truth in our head, when we are assailed by the
storms of life, our emotions may take over. Truth may be temporarily forgotten.

Do you have Christian friends or family members that remind
you of truth when you are being buffeted by the winds of life? Do
you look for opportunities to speak truth into the lives of those
around you? We all need reminders! Open God's Word so that you
will know truth. Then you will be able to speak truth when others
are floundering. Truth gives life.

Dear Lord, thank You for surrounding me with Christians
who are not afraid to remind me of Your truth.
May I be that kind of friend to someone today. Amen.

DAY 358

Prayer Is Powerful

*Therefore confess your sins to each other and pray for
each other so that you may be healed. The prayer of
a righteous person is powerful and effective.*

JAMES 5:16

*J*esus prayed. We are commanded to pray. God is omniscient—all knowing, omnipresent—all present, and omnipotent—all powerful. Yet, somehow our prayers are heard and answered by Him. They make a difference. Although this is a mystery to us, it is truth just the same.

There are examples throughout the Bible where prayer seemed to influence God. Remember Abraham's prayer that saved Lot when Sodom and Gomorrah were destroyed? Job prayed for his friends, and God said he would accept his prayer and not deal with them according to their folly (see Job 42:8).

Do you believe that prayer is powerful and effective? If so, then you should have an active prayer life. Take God at His Word. Believe that He wants you to pray. Trust that He answers prayer. Don't just tell someone, "I'll be praying for you." Pray for them! Right then and there—on the phone or in person. Share your concerns and struggles so others can pray for you. Be vulnerable so that God can intervene. Prayer is powerful and effective. Believe it. Pray today.

*Dear Lord, I believe Your Word is true. Even if I don't understand
how prayer works, I believe that You do work through my prayers.
Help me to be a faithful prayer warrior! Amen.*

Day 359

For God So Loved

For God so loved the world that he gave his one and only Son,
that whoever believes in him shall not perish but have eternal life.
JOHN 3:16

God is love. He demonstrated His love when He humbled Himself and came to earth as baby Jesus. He was born so He could die and pay the debt of sin once and for all. He willingly laid down His life so that we could have eternal life. God has given you this gift. Have you accepted it?

We must personally receive Jesus by faith to receive eternal life. Ephesians 2:8–9 states, "For it is by grace you have been saved, through faith—and this is not from yourselves, it is the gift of God—not by works, so that no one can boast." Make no mistake about it: We cannot earn our salvation. We must believe and receive it by faith. Have you done that? If so, rejoice this Christmas for His indescribable gift! If not, make this an unforgettable Christmas! Accept Baby Jesus as your personal Lord and Savior. He was born for You! Why not receive Him today. Jesus is the best gift you will ever receive!

Dear Lord, what greater gift could You have given than
the gift of Yourself? Thank You. May others understand
this truth and come to know You personally. Amen.

Day 360

Utilize Your Time

Be wise in the way you act toward outsiders;
make the most of every opportunity.
Colossians 4:5

No one likes to think about their own mortality. However, we each have a limited number of days to live on this earth. Don't allow that reality to depress you. Instead, purpose to make the most of the time you have. Pay attention. Savor each moment. Look for opportunities. We cannot go back and do life over. We have one chance to live today. Once tomorrow is ushered in, today is in the past.

Today is a gift we have been given. Be alert! The Lord gives you opportunities for personal spiritual growth. Take them. It is obvious that the great evangelist Billy Graham has spent countless hours alone with God and His Word over a lifetime. What would happen if your relationship with God were top priority in your life? How might your life be changed for the better?

Not only does God want you to spend personal time with Him, He also opens doors for you to speak truth into the lives of those around you. Be aware. Don't miss the great things the Lord has planned for you today. Keep your eyes open. See Him work. Be a willing participant. Utilize your time for the Lord's purposes. You may be just the blessing someone else needs today!

Dear Lord, many days I am just going through the motions
and miss opportunities to be about Your business. Keep me
aware so that I can make the most of each day. Amen.

Day 361

The Pitfalls of Prosperity

*Those who want to get rich fall into temptation and a trap and
into many foolish and harmful desires that plunge people into
ruin and destruction. For the love of money is a root of all kinds
of evil. Some people, eager for money, have wandered from
the faith and pierced themselves with many griefs.*

1 Timothy 6:9–10

What would you do with a million dollars? You would be financially set for a lifetime, right? Wrong. Sadly, statistics show that
many people who win the lottery are broke within years and their
lives are in shambles. Contrary to popular belief, money cannot
buy happiness, perhaps temporary pleasures at best.

The apostle Paul warned Timothy of the pitfalls of material
prosperity. He did not say that money is evil, but that the *love of
money* is the issue. When the accumulation of money becomes our
goal, we take our eyes off the Lord. Money then becomes our idol
and usurps God's rightful place of preeminence in our lives.

Instead of chasing after money, chase after the Lord. Regardless of your financial net worth, ask the Lord for wisdom in man-
aging your resources. Be willing to sacrifice. Stay within the budget
the Lord helps you set. Allow the Lord to control your money
rather than having your money control you. Love God more than
money. You will save yourself from many griefs!

*Dear Lord, I want You to have control over my finances.
Help me to always seek You first. Amen.*

DAY 362

Keep Knocking

*"Ask and it will be given to you; seek and you will find;
knock and the door will be opened to you. For everyone
who asks receives; the one who seeks finds; and to the
one who knocks, the door will be opened."*
MATTHEW 7:7–8

God is our heavenly Father. He longs for us to present our requests to Him. Jesus said, "Which of you, if his son asks for bread, will give him a stone? Or if he asks for a fish, will give him a snake? If you, then, though you are evil, know how to give good gifts to your children, how much more will your Father in heaven give good gifts to those who ask him!" (Matthew 7:9–11).

In the Greek, "ask, seek and knock" are written as Greek present imperatives indicating constant asking, seeking, and knocking. The words also suggest an increased urgency as time passes without receiving what was asked for. What spiritual lessons can be gleaned from this verse?

God encourages persistent prayer. He wants us to present our requests to Him. Time may pass. It may appear that nothing is happening. Trust that God is still at work. Continue to seek His will. Do not become discouraged and give up. Keep knocking. God is faithful. He will open the right door at the right time. Trust Him and keep knocking!

Dear Lord, help me not give up when my prayers do not get answered immediately. Give me perseverance in prayer. Help me to keep knocking and graciously accept your "no" answers. Amen.

DAY 363

A Time for Everything

*I*n our fast-paced, instant gratification society, we want every-thing *now*! Why wait? Solomon's wisdom reminds us that there is a time and place for everything. Many times we must wait for God's perfect timing. God is never late. He is rarely early. God is always right on time! May these verses in Ecclesiastes serve as a reminder of God's faithfulness.

> *There is a time for everything, and a*
> *season for every activity under the heavens:*
> *A time to be born and a time to die,*
> *A time to plant and a time to uproot,*
> *A time to kill and a time to heal,*
> *A time to tear down and a time to build,*
> *A time to weep and a time to laugh,*
> *A time to mourn and a time to dance,*
> *A time to scatter stones and a time to gather them,*
> *A time to embrace and a time to refrain from embracing,*
> *A time to search and a time to give up,*
> *A time to keep and a time to throw away,*
> *A time to tear and a time to mend,*
> *A time to be silent and a time to speak,*
> *A time to love and a time to hate,*
> *A time for war and a time for peace.*
> ECCLESIASTES 3:1–8

Dear Lord, give me wisdom every day to know
what time it is. Help me to let go when it's time to move on.
My time belongs to You. Amen.

DAY 364

Fight the Good Fight

I have fought the good fight, I have finished the race, I have kept the faith. Now there is in store for me the crown of righteousness, which the Lord, the righteous Judge, will award to me on that day—and not only to me, but also to all who have longed for his appearing.

2 TIMOTHY 4:7–8

The apostle Paul knew his life was drawing to a close when he penned this letter to Timothy. Paul had been Timothy's mentor in ministry. He wanted to encourage Timothy to live a life of faith, wholeheartedly committed to the Lord. Although during his lifetime Paul had been shipwrecked, beaten, and imprisoned because of Christ, it had all been worth it. Paul was now looking forward to receiving His eternal reward from the Lord Himself!

What about us? Can we say that we are fighting the good fight for the cause of Christ, despite the sacrifices and obstacles? Are we running the race well with our eyes fixed on Jesus, the author and perfecter of our faith? Have we kept the faith, even during our darkest hours? Let's not grow faint or weary. Someday we, too, will receive our heavenly reward from Jesus.

Dear Lord, help me stay in the fight, run the race, and keep the faith. I look forward to receiving a heavenly crown from You someday that I can immediately place at Your feet. Amen.

Day 365

Well Done

"His master replied, 'Well done, good and faithful servant!
You have been faithful with a few things; I will put you in charge
of many things. Come and share your master's happiness!' "

Matthew 25:21

This scripture serves as the epitaph on my mother's tombstone. Hers was a life well lived for the Lord. Even the last year of her life, while battling cancer, she used her time for His service. Each day she read and meditated on a passage of scripture. She faithfully recorded what the Lord had taught her in a daily journal, never knowing that those pearls of wisdom would be read by anyone else. This is how she was personally preparing to meet her Lord. She persevered, even on days she did not feel like it. Her sacrifice made this devotional book possible.

The parable of the talents is a lesson for us all (see Matthew 25:14–30). Talents could represent abilities, gifts, money, time, families, jobs, etc. These talents are for our use, but we do not own them—they ultimately belong to God. God has given us free will to decide how to appropriate what He has loaned us. We can use His resources wisely and build something of eternal value, or we can squander our opportunities.

May my mother inspire all of us! Until we meet Jesus face-to-face, may our lives be used for eternal purposes. May the Lord be able to say of us, "Well done, good and faithful servant."

Dear Lord, I want to live my life to please You. May I be a
good and faithful servant until we meet face-to-face. Amen.

Scripture Index

OLD TESTAMENT

NEW TESTAMENT

About the Author

Julie's passion is encouraging the application of Biblical truth. She and her husband Scott reside in Atlanta and have two grown children and three grandchildren. Julie has co-authored six devotional books and is currently working part-time as a surgical nurse. In the past she has been a Teaching Director and Area Director for Community Bible Study. Julie also enjoys golf and gardening whenever she can find some spare time.